The Acquisition of Knowledge and Skills for Taskwork and Teamwork to Control Complex Technical Systems

Annette Kluge

The Acquisition of Knowledge and Skills for Taskwork and Teamwork to Control Complex Technical Systems

A Cognitive and Macroergonomics Perspective

Springer

Annette Kluge
Business and Organizational Psychology
University Duisburg-Essen
Duisburg, Germany

ISBN 978-94-007-5048-7 ISBN 978-94-007-5049-4 (eBook)
DOI 10.1007/978-94-007-5049-4
Springer Dordrecht Heidelberg New York London

Library of Congress Control Number: 2014938716

Printed on acid-free paper

Springer is part of Springer Science+Business Media (www.springer.com)

Acknowledgements

This book is dedicated to my wonderful team who managed my chair of Business and Organisational Psychology at the University of Duisburg-Essen while I was writing this book during my research semester in winter 2012/2013. Thank you all!

Ananda von der Heyde
Barbara Frank
Björn Badura
Florian Watzlawik
Gerrit Elsbecker
Joseph Greve
Julia Miebach
Nikolaj Borisov
Nina Gross
Palle Presting
Sebastian Brandhorst
Vera Hagemann
& Susanne Heinemann

My cordial thanks to Dirk Sterczala and Jochen Kruip, Center for Simulator Training, GfS/KSG Essen, as well as Detelf Vielahn, BP Gelsenkirchen, and Gabriele vom Ende, HKM, Duisburg, for supporting this book with photos, stories and further illustrative material. Many thanks also to Erich Brodmann, OMV, who years ago took many hours to explain his perspective on simulator and virtual reality training to me. My gratitude also goes to the simulator trainers in the German-speaking countries who invited me to participate in their annual meetings to learn about simulator training and its organisational constraints and challenges.

Special thanks to Björn Badura for the illustration which he fine-tuned and for creating the character of the operator in the illustrations which aim at supporting the understanding of the operator's tasks, and also to Barbara Frank for her endless patience in formatting the manuscript according to the layout guidelines. My cordial thanks also to Vera Hagemann who kept the team together so wonderfully.

Many thanks also to Conny Tosch who provided valuable feedback on a first "preliminary final" version of this book.

Finally, I want to thank Sarah Mannion for her great support in translating my thoughts into readable English.

Contents

Chapter 1
Why This Book Has Been Written: Purpose and Structure of the Book

This book came about from my motivation to bring together research on the acquisition of knowledge and skills for performing complex tasks for controlling complex technical systems, research on the challenges of ergonomics in activities with high automation, and research on training design. My own roots lie in classical industrial and organisational psychology with a main emphasis on personnel and vocational training, personnel selection and human resources. In the year 2000, my empirical research into complex systems (summarised e.g. in Kluge and Schüler 2007; Kluge 2008) led me to a refinery in Southern Germany, where I was able to look at a refinery simulator. In the years that followed, I had the opportunity get to know the small group of committed refinery simulator trainers in the German-speaking area and to interview them in depth (Kluge 2007; Kluge et al. 2008/ZfA).

Inspired by these contacts and conversations, my research into the skill acquisition for complex technical activities developed away from abstract complex systems and artificial microworlds (Kluge 2007, 2008) and towards concrete application situations in so-called High Reliability Organisations (HROs, Weick and Sutcliffe 2003). HROs operate complex hazardous technologies and manage to remain accident-free "while simultaneously retaining their capacity to meet highly unpredictable and demanding production goals" (Shrivastava et al. 2009, p. 1362). HROs operate on a very high level of trust, because technical failures and slip-ups can have severe consequences for human beings and the environment if they are not identified and resolved immediately (Kluge et al. 2009; Hagemann et al. 2012). Chemical plants, refineries, and nuclear power plants (NPP) belong to the category of HROs. They are assumed to be of great size, both physically and conceptually, and face the presence of risk and a high level of hazard, based on interconnected real-time dynamics (Crossman 1974; Moray 1997).

HROs are assumed to be highly *complex*, tightly *coupled* systems (Table 1.1), which are vulnerable to catastrophic failure (Perrow 1984; Wickens et al. 2004, p. 493). Complexity, as outlined in detail in Chap. 2, is characterised by the number of interconnected subsystems (interconnectivity), further divided by Perrow (1984) into loose and tight coupling, invisible, sometimes unexpected interactions (Wickens et al. 2004), and dynamic effects (Funke 2010; Kluge 2008). Coupling

A. Kluge, *The Acquisition of Knowledge and Skills for Taskwork and Teamwork to Control Complex Technical Systems*, DOI 10.1007/978-94-007-5049-4_1,

Table 1.1 Examples of industries in the clusters of combinations of complexity and coupling by Perrow (1984) and Shrivastava et al. (2009)

	Low/loose coupling	High/tight coupling
Low complexity	Traditional manufacturing, assembly line production, single-goal agencies (post office)	Marine transport, rail transport, continuous processing
High complexity	Universities, government agencies, R&D firms, mining	Nuclear power plants, refineries, chemical plants, airplanes, space missions

as defined by Perrow (1984) is defined by the degree of missing slack and tight connection between subsystems so that a disruption in one part of the system strongly affects other parts.

Coupling specifies the qualities of interconnectivity with regard to time and degrees of freedom. While loose coupling allows certain parts of the system to express themselves according to their own interest and/or logic, tight coupling restricts this. Loosely coupled systems tend to have flexible performance standards, while tightly coupled systems include more time-dependent processes: They cannot wait or stand by until they are attended to (Perrow 1984).

Insufficient training and experience also affects the perceived complexity of a system (Hollnagel and Woods 2005) by aggravating intransparency (see also Kluge 2004) in which incomplete understanding leads to an incorrect situation assessment and to problems in choosing or selecting an action. An operator must be able to identify or recognise what happens as well as to interpret it in a context, since not knowing what happens affects the ability to predict future events (Hollnagel and Woods 2005). Therefore, persons working in HROs who are of special interest in this book are *control room operators*, whose failures in performance might lead to high financial and safety costs (Woods et al. 1987). One might argue that there are (more important) groups of workers in the world who are more worthy of having a whole book devoted to them. However, I am convinced that from the training design for activities of process control, much can be transferred to other vocations and tasks which contain partial aspects of this specific activity and which can, in principle, be generalised.

The tasks of a *control room operator* are to monitor and control a complex technical system (as will be described later). Monitoring and controlling a complex technical system is not a challenge for human motor capabilities (Wickens and Hollands 2000). Rather, it challenges *human factors* aspects, such as attention allocation (Wickens and McCarley 2008), perception, situation assessment (Vicente et al. 2004), situation awareness (Endsley 1995), decision making and execution, memory (Ericsson and Kintsch 1995), and mental workload (Tsang and Vidulich 2006; Vidulich 2003).

The topic of *human factors* encompasses the "study of those variables that influence the efficiency with which the human performer can interact with the inanimate components of a system to accomplish the system goals" (Proctor and van Zandt 2008, p. 9). Karwowski (2006, p. 4) cites the definition of the

International Ergonomics Association as "ergonomics (human factors) *as the scientific discipline concerned with the understanding of the interaction among humans and other elements of a system and the profession that applies theory, principles, data, and methods to design in order to optimize human well-being and overall system performance*". He further distinguishes between

- **physical** ergonomics, which addresses human anatomical, anthropometric, physiological and biomechanical aspects of work,
- **cognitive** ergonomics, which focuses on mental processes such as perception, memory, information processing, and motor responses, as they affect interactions among humans and other elements of the systems, and
- **organisational** ergonomics or macroergonomics, which addresses the organisation of socio-technical systems, such as the structure, policies and processes (Karwowski 2006, p. 4). It focuses both on organisational and human-machine interface issues (Proctor and van Zandt 2008) in order to seek an integration of humans with advances in manufacturing technology (Nagamachi 2002).

The book's **perspective** is **one of cognitive and organisational ergonomics**. Both can be viewed under the label of "cognition in organizations" (Hodgkinson and Healy 2008). Hodgkinson and Healy (2008) advocate that the complexities of the modern workplace require an increased cooperation across and between organisational and human factors tradition.

The book describes the knowledge and skills required for complex tasks for controlling complex technical systems from a cognitive ergonomics point of view. It then turns to organisational ergonomics, as it proposes training strategies and training regimes for successfully acquiring this knowledge and these skills in "Staged Process Control Readiness Training" (SPCRT). It describes training views on how to impart, develop, and change members' knowledge structures not only to perform immediate day-to-day routine tasks but also to expand their repertoire for managing uncertainties in a wider transfer environment (Hodgkinson and Healy 2008). Training, as well as highly skilled and competent workers, is an essential prerequisite for HROs to function on a high level of reliability, because HROs, as complex and highly coupled systems, require centralisation in order to carefully coordinate resources and concurrently require decentralisation to cope with the unexpected (Perrow 1984; Wickens et al. 2004). Even though Perrow (1984) is not confident that organisations can successfully employ centralisation and decentralisation at the same time, there is consensus regarding the demand for highly skilled and qualified personnel. Decentralised decision making requires continuous learning and training (Weick et al. 1999; Shrivastava et al. 2009), but a comprehensive review of research results and a theoretical overview model of training development and design is still lacking.

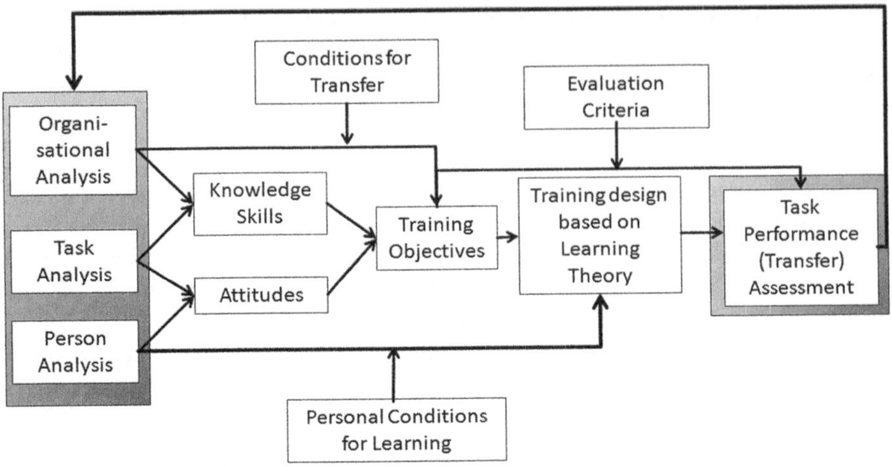

Fig. 1.1 A general schema of a systematic approach to training (Based on Goldstein and Ford 2002)

1.1 The Book's Structure

The structure of the book as regards content is oriented to the "Systematic Approach to Training" model of Goldstein (1993), Goldstein and Ford (2002), Salas et al. (2006) and Coultas et al. (2012), as displayed in Fig. 1.1.

The organisational analysis in the context of this book is important for understanding the jobs and performance conditions under investigation. These jobs have to be performed in organisations in which incorrect actions can have severe consequences for humankind and the environment, as was apparent, for instance, in accidents in the last few years, for example in the refinery in Texas City in 2005 (Fig. 1.2), in the explosion of the Deepwater Horizon in 2010, or in the battle to control the damage following the tsunami disaster in Fukushima in 2011.

To read and learn more about the interplay of organisational factors contributing to theses accidents, such as training issues, process safety, management and leadership issues, accident investigation reports are available, for example, from the Chemical Safety Board in the US (www.csb.gov) or from the IAEA webpage (http://www-pub.iaea.org).

Analyses of blackouts in the electricity power system and investigations of large-scale outages in the North American interconnected electric system in the US and Canada have demonstrated the need to enhance the operators' ability to understand the state of the system and to anticipate possible problems (Greitzer et al. 2009). The scope and complexity of power grid operations continue to grow: "*Widespread electrical outages, such as the one that occurred on August 14, 2003, are rare, but they can happen if multiple reliability safeguards break down. Providing reliable electricity is an enormously complex technical challenge, even on the most routine of days. It involves real-time assessment, control and coordination of electricity production at thousands of generators, moving electricity*

Fig. 1.2 Texas City, 2005: On March 23rd 2005, 15 people were killed and over 170 injured as the result of a fire and explosion on the isomerization plant (ISOM) at the refinery owned and operated by BP Products North America in Texas City, Texas, USA. http://www.bp.com/liveassets/bp_internet/us/bp_us_english/STAGING/local_assets/downloads/t/final_report.pdf (retrieved September 10th 2012)

across an interconnected network of transmission lines, and ultimately delivering the electricity to millions of customers by means of a distribution network" (Greitzer et al. 2009, p. 37). Greitzer et al. (2009) propose that to meet the demands and expectations of this industry, effective training and maintenance of a high level of mastery are required of the system operators and plant personnel.

Organisational and task analysis and the description of the (complex) skills to be performed in the (complex) organisational environment are important steps for deriving the knowledge and skills which are necessary to perform the job of a control room operator in the HRO context. For the purpose of this book, it is important to consider the distinction between routine and non-routine/normal and non-routine/abnormal situations (Kluge et al. 2013) as *conditions for transfer* (referring to the systematic approach to training, Fig. 1.1), because these determine under which conditions, for example under high stress or during night shifts, the trained tasks have to be performed, and to what level they need to be proceduralised, for example when the start-up of a plant only occurs once every five years. Although a great deal could also be said about the technical process and the forms and philosophy of automation which are employed in the process industries, I will limit myself in each case to the consequences of automation, which is relevant for knowledge and skill acquisition.

With regard to needs assessment, this book is not focused on a *person analysis* and the detection of person-related variables required *for the job*. Instead, I only address the group of persons to be trained insofar as this is important in order to design the training under consideration of prior job experiences, e.g. as a field operator, i.e. the *learning biographies*. The group of persons about whom we speak here has (at least in Germany) completed vocational training, e.g. as chemical workers or electronics technicians for industrial plants if they are in a refinery, or as graduates with a Bachelor or Master degree in engineering if they are undergoing initial training as shift personnel in charge of control rooms in NPPs. In many cases, they have already worked in the plant for several years before they switch to the control room as operators, i.e. they already have a long employment history. Frequently, it is also a particular accolade for employees who have proved themselves in production for several years to be permitted to switch to the control room.

From the needs assessment and the derivation of the training objectives, implications emerge for the training design and evaluation criteria. Training design includes the instructional techniques, their sequence (what in which order?), the technical equipment (e.g. full-scope or generic simulator) and the environment (e.g. classroom, immersive environments) in which they are applied. The decision of how to best combine and integrate instructional techniques, sequence, technical equipment and environment is based on learning theories and models addressing the acquisition of knowledge and skill for performing complex tasks (defined in Chap. 2).

When deriving evaluation criteria, the book is less concerned with the theory of evaluation per se. Generally speaking, evaluation means the systematic, scientific, empirical, hypothesis-oriented investigation of effectiveness and efficiency of an intervention, with the aim of using the evaluation results to (re)design and apply the findings in the socio-technical context of training decisions (Goldstein 1993, p. 147; Mittag and Hager 2000, p. 103). The book will address the aspects of how to assess training effectiveness in terms of measuring training results by providing ideas on how to measure learning improvements from a Human Factors perspective as well as successful transfer to the predefined routine, non-routine/normal and non-routine/abnormal situations that can occur. The usefulness will only be described briefly based on verbal statements of various refinery trainers in order to provide an impression of what efficiency of training means in HROs.

In summary, the book aims to

- facilitate the understanding of the task and target job in the context of the organisation (needs assessment) by describing complex technical systems (the process industries), complex tasks and to specify conditions of transfer, meaning conditions under which the later trained knowledge and skills need to be applied in the working context,
- derive the knowledge and skills required to fulfil the task in order to define training objectives,
- develop propositions for how to best acquire the knowledge and skills (defining the learning environment, based on learning theories) and the conditions of transfer by providing theoretical propositions for their acquisition based on the state-of-the-art research on knowledge and skill acquisition for complex taskwork and teamwork tasks, and
- propose the concept of the "Staged Process Control Readiness Training" (SPCRT) as the instructional techniques and within a comprehensive framework on how to best support skill and knowledge acquisition in High Reliability Organisations which can be transferred to routine, non-routine/normal and non-routine/abnormal situations.

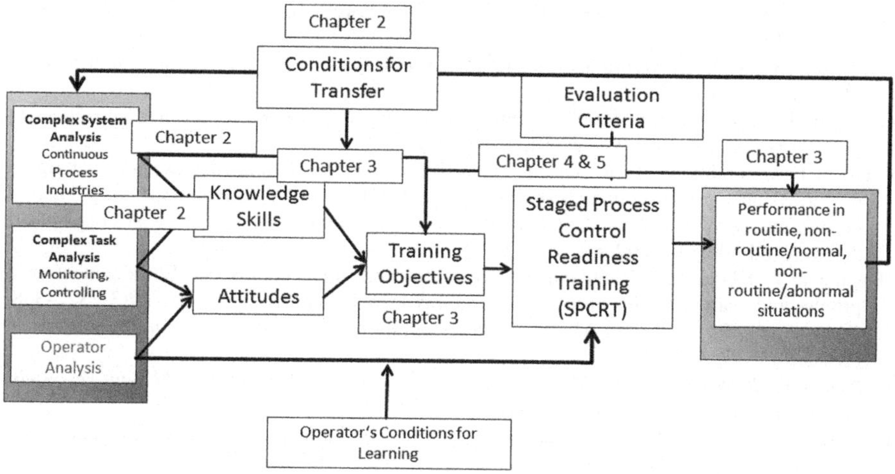

Fig. 1.3 Systematic approach to training applied to knowledge and skill acquisition for controlling complex technical systems

The structure of the book should therefore facilitate the design of training programs to achieve training objectives based on a generic but solid requirement analysis of process control tasks and familiar jobs. In summary, the structure is oriented to Fig. 1.3, in which the steps of the procedure for training design are categorised into chapters.

This book refers to various theoretical foundations from cognitive psychology, the psychology of learning and skill acquisition, and from industrial and organisational psychology. Knowledge of the foundations is presupposed. The primary concern in this book should be with the application of theories and models in this context of complex tasks to control complex technical systems.

I wish all readers as much enjoyment reading and working with this book as I had writing it. In doing so, I am fulfilling my wish for a book that I would have liked to have had when I was beginning my training research in process industries 13 years ago. Now, it is an interim result of my research and that of my team.

References

Coultas, C. W., Grossman, R., & Salas, E. (2012). Design, delivery, evaluation and transfer of training systems. In G. Salvendy (Ed.), *Handbook of human factors and ergonomics* (pp. 490–533). Hoboken: Wiley.

Crossman, E. R. F. W. (1974). Automation and skill. In E. Edwards & F. P. Lees (Eds.), *The human operator in process control* (pp. 1–25). London: Taylor & Francis.

Endsley, M. R. (1995). Toward a theory of situation awareness in dynamic systems. *Human Factors, 37*, 32–64.

Ericsson, K. A., & Kintsch, W. (1995). Long-term working memory. *Psychological Review, 102*, 211–245.

Funke, J. (2010). Complex problem solving: A case for complex cognition? *Cognitive Processing, 11*, 133–142.

Goldstein, I. L. (1993). *Training in organisations. Needs assessment, development and evaluation*. Monterey: Brooks/Cole.

Goldstein, I. L., & Ford, J. K. (2002). *Training in organisations. Needs assessment, development, and evaluation* (4th ed.). Wadsworth: Cengage Learning.

Greitzer, F. L., Podmore, R., Robinson, M., & Ey, P. (2009). Naturalistic decision making for power system operators. In *Proceedings of the NDM9, the 9th international conference on naturalistic decision making*, London, UK. Also available online: http://www.bcs.org/upload/pdf/ewic_ndm09_s1paper2.pdf

Hagemann, V., Kluge, A., & Ritzmann, S. (2012). Flexibility under complexity: Work contexts, task profiles and team processes of high responsibility teams. *Employee Relations, 34*(3), 322–338.

Hodgkinson, G. P., & Healy, M. P. (2008). Cognition in organizations. *Annual Review of Psychology, 59*, 387–417.

Hollnagel, E., & Woods, D. D. (2005). *Joint cognitive systems. Foundations of cognitive systems engineering*. Boca Raton: Taylor & Francis.

Karwowski, W. (2006). The discipline of ergonomics and human factors. In G. Salvendy (Ed.), *Handbook of human factors and ergonomics* (pp. 3–31). Hoboken: Wiley.

Kluge, A. (2004). *Wissenserwerb für das Steuern komplexer Systeme*. Lengerich: Pabst.

Kluge, A. (2007). Experiential learning methods, simulation complexity and their effects on different target groups. *Journal of Educational Computing Research, 36*(3), 323–349.

Kluge, A. (2008). What you train is what you get? Task requirements and training methods in complex problem solving. *Computers in Human Behavior, 24*, 284–308.

Kluge, A., & Schüler, K. (2007). Experience management by means of simulator trainings in high reliability organizations – Re-enacting critical incidents and learning from experience – Examples form nuclear power plants and oil refineries. In N. Gronau (Ed.), *4th conference on professional knowledge management – Experiences and vision* (pp. 77–84). Berlin: Gito.

Kluge, A., Schüler, K., & Burkolter, D. (2008). Simulatortrainings für Prozesskontrolltätigkeiten am Beispiel von Raffinerien: Psychologische Trainingsprinzipien in der Praxis. *Zeitschrift für Arbeitswissenschaft, 62*, 97–109.

Kluge, A., Sauer, J., Schüler, K., & Burkolter, D. (2009). Designing training for process control simulators: A review of empirical findings and current practices. *Theoretical Issues in Ergonomics Science, 10*, 489–509.

Kluge, A., Frank, B., Burkolter, D., & Greve, J. (2013). *Die Wirkung von Refresher Interventionen auf den Fertigkeitserhalt in der Prozesskontrolle* [The impact of refresher interventions on skill retention in process control]. Beitrag auf dem Frühjahrskongress der GfA, in Krefeld, 282.-1.3.2013 (pp.153–156). Dortmund: GfA-Press.

Mittag, W., & Hager, W. (2000). Ein Rahmenkonzept zur Evaluation psychologischer Interventionsmaßnahmen. In W. Hager, J.-L. Patry, & H. Brezing (Hrsg.) *Handbuch Evaluation psychologischer Interventionsmaßnahmen. Standards und Kriterien* (pp. 102–128). Bern: Huber.

Moray, N. (1997). Human factors in process control. In G. Salvendy (Ed.), *Handbook of human factors and ergonomics* (pp. 1944–1971). New York: Wiley.

Nagamachi, M. (2002). Relationship among job design, macroergonomics, and productivity. In H. W. Hendrick & B. M. Kleiner (Eds.), *Macroergonomics: Theory, methods, and applications* (pp. 111–131). Mahwah: Lawrence Erlbaum.

Perrow, C. (1984). *Normal accidents: Living with high risk technology*. New York: Basic Books. (Reprint 1999, by Princeton University Press, Princeton)

Proctor, R. W., & van Zandt, T. (2008). *Human factors in simple and complex systems* (2nd ed.). Boca Raton: CRC press.

Salas, E., Wilson, K. A., Priest, H. A., & Guthrie, J. W. (2006). Design, delivery, and evaluation of training. In G. Salvendy (Ed.), *Handbook of human factors and ergonomics* (pp. 472–512). Hoboken: Wiley.

Shrivastava, S., Sonpar, K., & Pazzaglia, F. (2009). Normal accident theory versus high reliability theory: A resolution and call for an open systems view of accidents. *Human Relations, 62*, 1357–1390.

Tsang, P. S., & Vidulich, M. A. (2006). Mental workload and situation awareness. In G. Salvendy (Ed.), *Handbook of human factors and ergonomics* (pp. 243–268). Hoboken: Wiley.

Vicente, K. J., Mumaw, R. J., & Roth, E. M. (2004). Operator monitoring in a complex dynamic work environment: A qualitative cognitive model based on field observations. *Theoretical Issues in Ergonomics Science, 5*, 359–384.

Vidulich, M. A. (2003). Mental workload and situation awareness. Essential concepts in aviation psychology. In P. S. Tsang & M. A. Vidulich (Eds.), *Principles and practice of aviation psychology* (pp. 115–147). Mahwah: Lawrence Erlbaum.

Weick, K. E., Sutcliffe, K., & Obstfeld, D. (1999). Organizing for high reliability. *Research in Organizational Behavior, 21*, 81–123.

Weick, K. E., & Sutcliffe, K. M. (2003). *Managing the unexpected: Assuring high performance in an age of complexity*. San Francisco: Jossey-Bass.

Wickens, C. D., & McCarley, J. S. (2008). *Applied attention theory*. Boca Raton: CRC Press.

Wickens, C. D., Lee, J. D., Liu, Y., & Gordon Becker, S. E. (2004). *An introduction to human factors engineering* (2nd ed.). Upper Saddle River: Pearson Education.

Woods, D. D., O'Brien, J. F., & Hanes, L. F. (1987). Human factors challenges in process control: The case of nuclear power plants. In G. Salvendy (Ed.), *Handbook of human factors* (pp. 1725–1770). New York: Wiley.

References

Chapter 2
Controlling Complex Technical Systems: The Control Room Operator's Tasks in Process Industries

2.1 Setting the Scene

If you enter a control room, the quietness is something you will notice first. The work in control rooms during routine operations is silent. After you shut the door, the sounds of producing steel, food, or pharmaceutical products, refining oil, or producing energy are kept outside. The tranquillity of the atmosphere is intensified by the shaded atmosphere of the room, in which PC screens flicker in black, blue and green, showing filigree displays of pipes, valves and numbers. Workers alone, in pairs or in teams watch the displays arranged on one, two, three or more screens in a focused manner, talk to each other in soft tones, pointing to a certain part of the displayed plant, moving the computer mouse to a detail, perhaps altering a value. In most control rooms I have visited, the outside world, the outside weather, the technical construction of the production process, the converted materials, the physical, chemical or biological process steps as well as the workers operating the plant are viewed through the lens of the PC screens (Fig. 2.1).

On the surface, the job of a control room operator in routine situations does not appear to be very spectacular. Compared to jobs which have been examined over the last century by industrial psychologists and human factors and ergonomics specialists, which emphasise physical ergonomics (anthropometric, biomechanical, physiological factors, factors related to posture such as sitting and standing, manual handling of material), a control room is clean, silent and tidy, and the work in a control room does not require hard physical labour or coping with heat, cold, dangerous substances, assembly line pace-based time pressure or motor dexterity. Nevertheless, process control plants are assumed to notably challenge human factors research (Moray 1997).

A control room can be defined as a location designed for an operator to be in control of a process (Hollnagel and Woods 2005). In the case of process industries, the location is a physical room in a physical building (in contrast to a cockpit that is moving). *The meaning of control in this context is to minimise or eliminate unwanted process variablities*; the process is a continuous activity. The process

A. Kluge, *The Acquisition of Knowledge and Skills for Taskwork and Teamwork to Control Complex Technical Systems*, DOI 10.1007/978-94-007-5049-4_2,

Fig. 2.1 Control room at German NPP (Photo courtesy of GfS/KSG, Essen, Germany)

has its own dynamics and hence changes if left alone (Hollnagel and Woods 2005). The control room is a room with a view to the past, present and the future (Hollnagel and Woods 2005). The view to the past is necessary to understand the current situation, to build up expectation, and to anticipate what may lie ahead (Hollnagel and Woods 2005)

Vicente's (2007) and Vicente et al.'s (2004) description of a control room of a Canadian NPP is a rather representative example of a control room in general. The control room for the plant has four control units (each controlling its own reactor). The single operator runs a unit together with other personnel serving support roles. Each control unit occupies a demarcated workspace within a single, large room that is completely open and has no barriers to visibility. The operator of each unit can see the panels and alarms of all other units, allowing him/her to follow and monitor activities on other units and maintain an overall awareness of plant activity (Vicente 2007, p. 91). An example of a German NPP that illustrates Vicente's descriptions (2007) is displayed in Fig. 2.2.

Not only in an NPP control room but also in control rooms in refineries, the units include control panels, an operator desk with one or more telephones, a printer, and bookshelves upon which to place procedure documents and other operation documents. Alarms are presented on computer screens, which light up and provide an audio signal (buzzer) if an alarm condition occurs. In many control rooms, an operator monitors 3–4 screens placed on his desk, on which physical schematics, trend displays, and bar chart displays etc. are presented. In some systems, screens show 1,000 detailed displays and 20 system-oriented overview displays (Veland and Eikas 2007).

What do control room operators control? As introduced above, control room operators control material and energy flows, which are made to interact with and

Fig. 2.2 NPP control room in Germany (Photo by GfS/KSG, Essen, Germany), because the room is windowless, the control room teams have hung up a poster with the outside view (in the back). Files with standard operating procedures on the shelves

transform each other. By means of physical or chemical transformation, the "process control industry" incorporates the continuous and batch processing of materials and energy in their operations (Moray 1997). "Examples include the generation of electricity in conventional fuel and nuclear power plants, the separation of petroleum by fractional distillation in refineries into gas, gasoline, oil, and residue, hot strip rolling in steel production, chemical pulping in the production of paper; pasteurization of milk, and high pressure synthesis of ammonia" (Woods et al. 1987, p. 1726). A comprehensible overview of the process industries is provided by Austin (1984) and further below (Sect. 2.2.2).

2.2 Defining the Term "Complex" in a Complex Technical System

Continuous process systems are physically large, covering many hectares (e.g. Fig. 2.3) and are named as complex technical systems. As will be outlined further below in more detail, the process industries range from continuous facilities in the petrochemical industry to large-batch manufacturing in steel production and glass manufacturing, to small-batch manufacturing in the food and pharmaceutical industry (van Donk and Fransoo 2006).

A system can be defined as a collection of components that act together to achieve a goal that could not be achieved by any single component or part alone (Proctor and van Zandt 2008, p. 569; Walker et al. 2010).

Fig. 2.3 Coker plant in the Gelsenkirchen Horst refinery at night, http://www.deutschebp.de/liveassets/bp_internet/germany/STAGING/home_assets/images/raffinerie_verarbeitung/raffinerie_nacht.jpg (retrieved April 8th 2013)

The "technical" aspects include the technological component (Emery 1959), e.g. material, machines that convert inputs (e.g. raw material) into outputs (e.g. heat, gas, products) as well as territory which are "belonging" to the organisation (Emery 1959).

According to Perrow (1984), systems are divided into four levels of increasing aggregation:

- parts (e.g. a valve, the smallest component of a system),
- units (e.g. a steam generator, functionally related collection of parts),
- subsystems (an array of units, such as a steam generator and the water return system including condensate polisher and motors, pumps, and piping – the secondary cooling system) and
- systems (including many subsystems, e.g. the complex NPP or refinery, Perrow 1984, p. 65).

In particular, the process of a continuous process system (e.g. a chemical plant or refinery) is additionally geographically widely distributed (e.g. in contrast to a cockpit), with subsystems and components spread over great distances in three dimensions involving hundreds of variables (Moray 1997). *But what specifically constitutes a "complex" system?* The complexity of a system is defined as "the number of elements and relations of a system" (Fischer et al. 2012, p. 22; Funke 1985). The number of elements and relations within a technical system can be more precisely characterised in terms of element interactivity/interconnectivity, dynamic effects, non-transparency, multiple goals (Brehmer and Dörner 1993; Funke 1985; Kluge et al. 2008; Sterman 1994), and social complexity (Dörner 1989/2003; Table 2.2).

The process to be controlled typically consists of a large number of interrelated and cross-coupled variables (Moray 1997; Vicente 2007; Wickens and Hollands 2000), meaning that various aspects of a situation are not independent and therefore cannot be independently influenced, a characteristic called **interconnectivity** (Kluge et al. 2008). Interconnectivity also stresses the importance of recognising unfamiliar and unintended feedback loops (Perrow 1984), control parameters with potential interactions and undesired and desired "parallel effects" (Blech and Funke 2005). Parallel effects are caused by ramified cause-and-effect chains, initiated by altering only one single input variable at the beginning of the chain (Kluge et al. 2008). Perrow (1984) calls this phenomenon a complex interaction in which one component can interact with one or more components outside of the normal production sequence, either by design or not by design. Complex interactions as they affect the operators are those "unfamiliar sequences of unplanned and unexpected sequences and either not visible or not immediately comprehensible" (Perrow 1984, p. 78).

In addition to parallel effects, variables can change dynamically in terms of their own state, which is called **dynamic effects** (Kluge et al. 2008; Sterman 1994; Walker et al. 2010). These dynamic effects play a role, for example, in heat generation, for instance in terms of the residual heat in an NPP, or whenever one speaks of an "uncontrolled reaction". Somewhat less dramatic effects are found, for example, in the form of weather influences, when the technical plant parts heat up strongly with strong heat in the summer. Additionally, the dynamic effects are caused by the continuous process, in which materials continuously flow through the plant, for example in board mills, chemicals, oil, electricity, food production, or glass production (Crossman 1974). In some continuous process systems, such as electricity generating plants and petrochemical plants, dynamics and time delays are extreme, as it may take many hours or even days to start up (Moray 1997).

The technical process which is responsibly monitored and controlled by the operator is controlled by technical monitoring devices, precisely because of the tremendous complexity of the process, hazardous environments in which they take place and toxic materials which are employed (Wickens and Hollands 2000). Due to the automation, the complex technical systems to be controlled are characterised by **non-transparency** for the operator, which means that neither structure nor dynamics are fully disclosed to the operator's senses (Funke 2010). The control room operator's task is therefore also called centralised remote control (Crossman 1974). The operations being controlled are inaccessible to the operator and are handled in an artificial setting such as the control room. Due to the hazards associated with, for example, high levels of radiation and the potential consequences of even small accidents, the personnel in NPP are rather remote from the physical process (Figs. 2.4, 2.5, and 2.6.), whereas in steel production, for example, parts of the plants are still directly accessible to human senses in that they are observable and audible. An NPP control room (as in Fig. 2.1.) is isolated from the physical process that is being controlled (Gaddy and Wachtel 1992). Control is exercised by switches and buttons and telephones are used to communicate with the field operators in the plant (Moray 1997), while current technical developments also allow for the usage of head-mounted displays for communication and knowledge

Fig. 2.4 Photo of a control room in a steel plant (with window) control room at HKM (Hüttenwerke Krupp Mannesmann) (Photo courtesy of HKM Duisburg)

sharing (Grauel et al. 2012) between control room operators and maintenance personnel in the plant for collaborative troubleshooting.

In contrast, the control rooms for controlling continuous casting in the steel industry are much closer to the production process, which is extremely hot, noisy and dangerous for the workers, and which is not under moment-to-moment manual control. Along the length of the process, there are a series of local control stations for different tasks along the line (Moray 1997) and operators can directly see the casting process and the molten steel. There is a subordinate control room considerably above the floor of the plant enabling the controller to directly inspect/oversee the entire plant through its window (Figs. 2.4 and 2.5). In Fig. 2.6, the window does not allow the process to be monitored, but does allow the outside weather conditions to be monitored in order to be able to proactively consider weather impacts on the process.

The more the control room is isolated from the plant to be monitored and controlled, the more the operator has to rely on the information presented by the screens and displays. Non-transparency, as in the case when operators are isolated from the operations being controlled, is also due to the keyhole effect (Woods et al. 1990; Woods 1984). The operator might get lost in the large number of (up to thousands) of displays which he/she is able to call up, rendering him/her unable to maintain a broad overview, and becoming disoriented, fixated or lost in the display structure (Kim and Seong 2009; Woods et al. 1990).

Fig. 2.5 Example photo of a control room in a steel plant (HKM) with window, casting operation HKM (Photo courtesy of HKM Duisburg)

Fig. 2.6 Control room at BP Gelsenkirchen/Ruhr Oel GmbH (Photo courtesy of BP Gelsenkirchen/Ruhr Oel GmbH)

Accordingly, non-transparency is expressed through the fact that the chemical, physical or biomechanical processes which are controlled cannot be easily visualised. This means that, as described above, the control room operator (a) perceives only a limited number of the parts of the plant, and (b) these are mediated by a Human Machine Interface (HMI) that informs the operator about the states of the plant. Only part of the relevant information is made available to an operator, who is controlling the 'outer-loop' variables, for example sets a set point of a desired temperature of blast furnace, whereas automated feedback loops control the 'inner loop', for example provides the amount of energy to the furnace required to reach the desired temperature (Wickens and Hollands 2000). The operator monitors the result produced by the automated process, adjusts the set point as required and may "trim" the control characteristics for optimum efficacy (Crossman 1974).

Additionally, the automated process might also be non-transparent in itself. Although some process control plants include rather simple operations such as baking or pasteurisation, with more transparent processes, other industrial systems are the most complex (interconnected, dynamic) ever built, in which physics and chemistry are only imperfectly understood and in which unforeseen events can therefore occur under special conditions of abnormal operations, with the risk of potentially catastrophic releases of toxic material and energy (Moray 1997, p. 1945; Perrow 1984).

With regard to non-transparency in terms of the physical visibility of the process, the process in an NPP is the least visible, followed by petrochemical refineries and steel production, which is assumed to be more visible compared to the other two (Moray 1987).

The **combination of dynamic effects and non-transparency** is also apparent in that the process variables that are controlled and regulated are reacting slowly and have long time constraints (Wickens and Hollands 2000), leading to delayed feedback with regard to the actions taken by the operator. The *control action taken may not produce a visible system response* for seconds or minutes. In contrast, dynamic effects and non-transparency can be become immediately apparent in cases in which a warning indicates the existence of a system failure. The *warning can quickly lead to an exponentially growing number of hundreds of subsequent warnings* which – although they transparently indicate a problem – taken together will lead to non-transparency in the current moment. As outlined by Wickens and Hollands (2000), from the operator's point of view, one warning alone is often not interpretable: "This unfortunate state of affairs" (Wickens and Hollands 2000, p. 530) occurs due to the vast interconnectedness that one primal failure will drive conditions at other parts of the plant out of their normal operating range so rapidly that within seconds or minutes, scores of warning lights and buzzers create a buzzing-flashing condition. A severe failure in an NPP can potentially cause 500 annunciators to change status in the first minute and more than 800 within the first 2 min (Wickens and Hollands 2000).

Additionally, the human operator must simultaneously pursue **multiple and even contradictory objectives**, so-called conflicting goals, such as achieving production and safety goals in parallel (Kluge et al. 2008; Reason 2008; Verschuur et al. 1996; Wickens and Hollands 2000). A human operator in a control room is confronted with a number of different goal facets to be weighted and coordinated (Funke 2010). As Crossman (1974) formulates, what the operator is trying to achieve is what the management wants him/her to achieve and represents the characteristics of multiple goals. The operator

- has to keep the process running as closely as possible to a given condition (regulation or stabilisation),
- has to adjust the process to give the best results according to criteria such as yield, quality, minimum use of power, least lost time (optimisation),
- has to avoid breakdowns as far as possible,
- has to regain normal running as soon as possible, and minimise loss of material or risk of serious damage if a breakdown has occurred (Crossman 1974, p. 7).

With regard to conflicting goals, Hansez and Chmiel (2010) address the general problem that production and safety are often not valued equally in practice, for example "the visibility of production over safety, imbalances in the resources allocated to each, and the rewards available, such as praises or bonuses for achieving production targets" (Hansez and Chmiel 2010, p. 268). Especially when the pressure for production is on, there is potential for safety to be compromised. Particularly in cases of non-routine/normal and abnormal situations (see below), the operator is faced with the choice of what do to, taking three not always compatible goals into consideration (Wickens and Hollands 2000):

1. Actions have to ensure system safety,
2. Actions should not jeopardise system economy and efficacy,
3. Actions should be taken that localise and correct the fault.

Goals might be incompatible because, for example, taking a plant off line to ensure safety will lead to a potential sacrifice of economy, mainly because of a costly loss of production while the plant is offline and a costly start-up of the plant after a shutdown to localise the failure correctly and in a timely manner.

This shows that the growing technological potential is seized upon and exploited to meet performance goals or efficiency pressures (Hollnagel and Woods 2005), for example reduced production costs and improved product quality. But, once the technology potential is exploited, this generally leads to an increase in system complexity, subsequently leading to increased task complexity (Hollnagel and Woods 2005; Perrow 1984). Increased system complexity together with an increased task complexity results in more opportunities for malfunctions and more cases in which actions have unexpected and adverse consequences (Hollnagel and Woods 2005). Additionally, the striving for higher efficiency brings the system closer to the limits of safe performance, which leads to a higher risk. In turn, higher risks are countered by applying various kinds of automated safety and warning systems, which in turn again lead to an even greater risk (Hollnagel and Woods 2005).

Finally, in many HROs, small crews are responsible for overall system operations, in terms of controlling multiple systems and decision making concerning system functioning (Carvallo et al. 2005; Reinartz 1993; Reinartz and Reinartz 1992; Vicente et al. 2004). In continuous process systems too, these systems are controlled by multiple agents such as the control room operators, plant floor

Fig. 2.7 Field operators discussing issues with the control room crew (Photo courtesy of BP Gelsenkirchen/Ruhr Oel GmbH)

Fig. 2.8 BP employee in the Emsland crude oil refinery on his tour during the nightshift, http://www.deutschebp.de/liveassets/bp_internet/germany/STAGING/home_assets/images/presse/raffinerie_verarbeitung/23_imagebroschuere.jpg (retrieved April 8th 2013)

workers, maintenance workers, foremen, supervisors, managers (Moray 1997; Roth and Woods 1988; Woods et al. 1990) and workers from external companies and suppliers. For example in NPP, "Control room crews have the ultimate responsibility for daily operation, never perform work alone in the control room, and coordinate the immediate response to emergency situations" (Gaddy and Wachtel 1992, p. 383). NPP control room crews (each unit has five to six crews) are

Table. 2.1 Plant operations team roles (Based on Bullemer et al. 1997)

Team role	Description
Console operator	Is responsible for controlling the process via the DCS, monitors and controls plant, responsible for coordinating the actions of field operators, keeping abreast of the maintenance activities in the field. He/she is the focal point of communication between various distributed operations personnel throughout the complex task because he/she has the central view and control via the DCS.
Field operator	Responsible for his/her own plant area, often also qualified for other areas (to rotate between areas and monitor other areas), supports maintenance activities in the field, serves as human sensor, who checks or validates the correctness of the sensors, to ensure the view of the process is accurate. They identify potential problems with the process equipment, initiate preventive maintenance, take periodic product samples, prepare and warm up equipment, are responsible for directing maintenance personnel to the appropriate worksite. In a disturbance, they are the first "on the scene" and provide a critical diagnosis and mitigating response role in disturbance situations management by assessing the situation (e.g. confirming/refuting DCS data) or by taking actions (e.g. fire fighting); he/she can also support the console operator with assistance.
Shift leader	Is responsible for overseeing the field and console operator in the detailed monitoring of the process and ensuring the execution of the relevant preventive maintenance (daily routine duties), is a senior operations staff member, also in charge of the field, e.g. noting equipment problems and verifying sensor readings, responsible for filling out shift log book, during non-routine/normal and abnormal situations, shift leader supports console operator and calls for backups.
Operations superintendent	Responsible for productive and safe operations of the complex (complex is typically run by multiple shift teams); responsibilities: Monitoring and reporting of budget and costs, safety reporting and documentation, environmental compliance, incident reporting, training, production reporting to upper plant management, tracking and meeting higher-level plant objectives.
Shift coordinator	Plays the role of operation teams coordinator and management interface between operations superintendent and operations staff.
Site planner	Responsible for tracking possible market opportunities (e.g. high demands, high price, scheduled shipments, weather conditions) that may arise along with planning maintenance and turnarounds.
Process engineer	Responsible for generating daily production orders for each process unit (developed by site planner), troubleshoots process unit problems.
Control engineer	Maintains control tuning, objectives and develops improved control, often troubleshoots process and control-related problems after operations have been stabilised by operators.
Maintenance coordinator	Responsible for coordination of maintenance activities for plant units, coordinates periodic preventive maintenance and requests put in by operations team, orders material, determines whether contractors need to be hired
Maintenance technician	Responsible for maintaining and repairing all process equipment.

DCS distributed control system

comprised of two licensed senior reactor operators, one of whom is the supervisor, and two licensed reactor operators who share the duties of monitoring and controlling the plant (Gaddy and Wachtel 1992, p. 383). Additionally, a shift technical advisor with an engineering background is available but is not directly involved in the team (Gaddy and Wachtel 1992, p. 383).

Control rooms are therefore called multi-agent systems (Woods et al. 1990). Consequently, added to the features of technical complexity described so far is the complexity of relationships, which is called social complexity (Dörner 1989/2003) or **crew coordination complexity**, which results from the interconnectedness between multiple agents through coordination requirements. The dynamic control aspect of the continuous process is coupled with the need to coordinate multiple highly interactive processes imposing high coordination demands (Hagemann et al. 2012; Roth and Woods 1988; Waller et al. 2004).

A high level of communication between the multiple agents is required to coordinate activities and to avoid working at cross purposes (Roth and Woods 1988, p. 54; Stachowski et al. 2009, see Fig. 2.7). The human operators who are responsible for separate but strongly coupled units of the plant also need to be aware of their own actions with regard to the consequences they will bring about in another operator's units. Breakdowns in coordination across these units of responsibility may contribute to unnecessary trouble, near shutdowns or complete shutdowns (Roth and Woods 1988, p. 59).

If one looks, for example, at refineries, the console operator, who is controlling the process via the distributed control system (DCS), works as a team member in a plant operation team (Bullemer et al. 1997). The plant operation team in refineries and petrochemical plants consists of several plant roles as listed in Table 2.1. A prototypical operations shift team consists of a shift leader, a console operator, and two to five field operators (Bullemer et al. 1997). During the weekdays, many maintenance projects are going on, and the engineers, craftsmen, and management personnel are all available to interact with the shift team.

2.2.1 A Definition of a Complex Technical System

To sum up, the characteristics of a complex technical system are listed in Table 2.2. A complex technical system is characterised by the interconnectedness of a large number of variables and system parts, in which variables can change dynamically in terms of their own state, and in which structure and dynamics of the system are only partly disclosed to the operator (non-transparency), who is confronted with multiple goals that need to weighted and coordinated (conflicting goals), and who has to coordinate his/her activities with other interconnected agents (crew coordination complexity).

Table 2.2 Overview of constituent characteristics of complexity in complex technical systems

Characteristic	Definition and example
Element interactivity/ Interconnectedness	Various aspects of a situation are not independent and therefore cannot be independently influenced, e.g. the interplay of several subunits
Dynamics	Variables can change dynamically in terms of their own state, e.g. high outside temperatures heat the plant up in a deflagration, residual heat of fuel rods
Non-transparency	Structure and dynamics of the system are not fully disclosed to the operator, e.g. because the operator is isolated from the physical/chemical process and/or the process cannot be easily visualised e.g. a single warning can quickly lead to an exponentially growing number of hundreds of subsequent warnings, which taken together will lead to non-transparency, e.g. process variables that are controlled and regulated are reacting slowly and have long time constraints, meaning that the control action taken may not produce a visible system response for seconds or minutes
Multiple/conflicting goals	The operator is confronted with a number of different goal facets to be weighted and coordinated e.g. achieving production and safety goals in parallel
Crew coordination complexity	Interconnectedness between multiple agents (control room operators, field operators, plant floor workers, maintenance workers, foremen, shift supervisors, managers, in the case of an accident also firemen, first responder team, government, journalists) imposes high coordination demands

What does this mean for skill and knowledge acquisition?

The constituents of a complex technical system are relevant for deriving knowledge requirements as training objectives. These knowledge requirements take the form of mental models. Control room operators need a mental model representing the interconnectedness and dynamics of parts, units, and sub-processes (process mental model), the equipment to manage the process, for example automation and its displays, and the extent of non-transparency which this implies, in which the conflicting goals of the organisation are also integrated as well as the coordination requirements within the control room crew and supporting and supervisory roles (i.e. Bainbridge 1983; Craik 1943; Johnson-Laird 1983; Kluwe 1997; Kragt and Landweert 1974; Moray 1996; Vicente et al. 2004; Wilson and Rutherford 1989). Mental models help to inertly visualise performance strategies and their consequences in relation to the organisational goals and explain goal-directed decision making and behaviour. Using their mental models, operators are able to move up and down to different levels of abstraction (Rasmussen 1990; Wickens and Hollands 2000): In the case of a failure of a part or subsystem, the operator thinks at a very concrete level in terms of variables such as steam or water flows, valve settings or heat measurement. At other times, he/she must conceptualise at more abstract levels, for example related to thermodynamics of energy conversion, which requires thinking about the appropriate balance between mass and energy. Finally, the mental model must enable thinking on an even more abstract level, defined in terms of concepts like plant safety, human risk and company profits (Wickens and Hollands 2000). These thoughts will be taken up in Chap. 3 and taken a step further for the derivation of knowledge and skill requirements.

After having described the physical workplace as well as the plants which are usually controlled in process control, in the following, we look at what a control room operator does.

2.2.2 *The Operator's Task in Handling Complex Technical Systems: Process Control*

As Woods et al. (1987) describe, one of the earliest processes under human control was the making of and tending to fire: "Those responsible for a fire had to add chunks of wood of an acceptable size and condition, at the correct time and in the proper amount, to maintain the fire so that heating and cooking could take place" (Woods et al. 1987, p. 1725). Control of this process was considered to be an art, relying on the operator's skills to sense process conditions directly and to perform appropriate control actions in order to adapt to the requirements. Over time, and affected by industrialisation, processes became larger and products and processes had to meet predefined standards, leading to the introduction of regulators or feedback controllers and a decrease in the direct sensing and experiencing of process states. The human operator has progressed from direct sensing and control of the process (the fires) to the situation in control rooms today, which is characterised by indirect knowledge of the process through instruments fed by sensors and computed measurements and computer control of most elements of the process (Woods et al. 1987).

In Table 2.3., the operator's tasks in process control based on the work of Kragt and Landweert (1974), Woods et al. (1987), Moray (1997, p. 1948), Wickens and Hollands (2000), and Vicente (2007) as well as on our own interviews in continuous process industries (Kluge et al. 2008) are listed and grouped according to the categorisation introduced by Ormerod et al. (1998) for task analysis.

I personally often find it very helpful if one contrasts the activity which one specifically wants to look at with another activity in order to clarify the differences, for example the comparison between the tasks of a control room operator and the tasks upon which industrial and organisational psychology has concentrated over the decades, namely mass production. In **comparison to work in mass production**, control room operators do not work according to a definite work cycle, there is usually no need for physical exertion and no emphasis on speed, meaning that it is inappropriate to apply financial incentive schemes based on piecework measurement because of the continuous flow of production (Crossman 1974). Although the operator's tasks are less physically effortful, occasionally, the mental effort

Table 2.3 The operator's tasks grouped according to sub-goal template method categories

Monitoring
During normal operation, the process must be monitored.
Decision
Disturbances must be detected and their consequences must be predicted.
Any such disturbances must be counteracted.
If faults occur, they must be detected.
Diagnose process problems: the causes of faults must be diagnosed.
Appropriate countermeasures to control the effects of the faults must be selected.
Communication
Read: operating procedures must be consulted as needed.
Receive information/read: databases of information about possible options may need to be consulted.
Record: a record must be kept of significant events.
Give information: significant events must be communicated to other members of the crew and where appropriate to management and maintenance, so that operations may be coordinated and required maintenance operations are undertaken at appropriate times.
Action
Scheduled testing of routine equipment to ensure that backup and safety systems are in an acceptable state.
Changes may be made to the system either during normal or abnormal operations in the light of observations of the system state in order to prevent or compensate for drifts and faults.
Changes may be made manually or by changing the program of automated controllers.
Perform emergency shutdown or other control actions to avoid dangerous accidents, or cooperate with automated system for this purpose.
Combining action and communication
Special actions may be needed during the handover at the end at the shift, or during special conditions such as start-up or shutdown.
Combining monitoring and action
Appropriate strategies must be adopted to support both safety and productivity.
Introduce long-term changes and adjustments to the system so that it will tend to evolve toward a more efficient system.
Combining monitoring, action and communication
After detecting some disturbances or irregularities, operator asks (calls) maintenance worker (on the telephone) to go to a particular component of the plant for a special inspection and to give feedback.
Skill maintenance[a]
Undertake training and retraining to ensure the retention and improvement of skills.
Take a walk through the unit to maintain a "process feel" by directly observing plant components (if applicable, Fig. 2.8).

[a]Skill maintenance is not included by Ormerod et al. (1998) but is listed in several publications

increases during start-ups, shutdowns and breakdowns. Due to the greater distances between workplaces and the remote control, the operator is under less close supervision, for example by the supervisors, but has more direct contact with technical staff and managers, who ask for status information about the plant in order to integrate the activities of many people at many levels of the plant, from management to maintenance workers (Moray 1997). Shift work is common because of the high financial costs of the plant or of waste of material involved if the plant is shut down, for example during the night or at weekends. This also means more responsibility for the operators on night shifts when the engineering staff are less available on site (Crossman 1974).

Digression: Macroergonomics – Task-relevant differences in process industries

The list of tasks for which the operator is responsible includes monitoring and controlling, in terms of action taking. *But what does the operator actually control when "everything is automated"*? In this digression, I would like to describe the particularities of production in the process industry, which in turn provides important hints regarding knowledge and skill acquisition and the subsequent training development, because here, fine differences can be highly relevant to training.

The process industries range from continuous facilities in the petrochemical industry (Fig. 2.9) to large-batch manufacturing in steel production and glass manufacturing, to small-batch manufacturing in the food and pharmaceutical industry (van Donk and Fransoo 2006). Process industries share the characteristic that they handle non-discrete materials (Dennis and Meredith 2000b). "Process industries are businesses that add value to materials by mixing, separating, forming, or chemical reactions. Processes may be either **continuous** or **batch** (bold type added by author) and generally require rigid process control and high capital investment" (Wallace 1984, p. 28). Process industries often initiate their flows with only a few raw materials and subsequently process a variety of blending and resplitting operations, which means that many products are produced from a few kinds of raw material (Fransoo and Rutten 1994, p. 49).

The mixing, separating, forming and chemical reactions are operations that are usually performed on non-discrete products and materials. Commercial chemical processing involves chemical conversions and physical operations and operators also have to operate the process in such a way that the plant is also kept from corroding (Austin 1984), which is why maintenance and servicing plays a very important role in these processes.

These processes can only be performed efficiently using large installation as introduced above, which tend to be an immense investment. If large quantities are demanded, this justifies continuous production. If the demand is low, the investment into a large installation is not worthwhile, and batchwise production is used (Fransoo and Rutten 1994).

Harmful impurities in raw materials must be controlled and product purities monitored (Austin 1984). Material might be forms of gases, liquids, slurries, pulps, crystals, powders, pellets, films, and/or semi-solids which can only be tracked by weight and volume (Dennis and Meredith 2000a). Process industries often obtain their raw materials from mining or agriculture industries (Fransoo and Rutten 1994). These raw materials have natural variations in quality, for example crude oils from different oil fields have different sulphur contents and different proportions of naphtha, distillates, and fuel oils (Figs. 2.10 and 2.11). The production plans and operating schedules need to account for this variability (Dennis and Meredith 2000a). Second, material variability associated with natural raw materials

Fig. 2.9 BP operates the second largest refinery system in Germany (Pictured: cracker plant of the Ruhr oil refinery in Gelsenkirchen, http://www.deutschebp.de/liveassets/bp_internet/germany/STAGING/home_assets/images/presse/raffinerie_verarbeitung/bild_14696.jpg) (retrieved April 8th 2013)

Fig. 2.10 In the aromatics and olefin plant of the Ruhr oil refinery in Gelsenkirchen, e.g. plastic is produced, http://www.deutschebp.de/liveassets/bp_internet/germany/STAGING/home_assets/images/presse/raffinerie_verarbeitung/bild_14690.jpg (retrieved April 8th 2013)

Fig. 2.11 In the distillation plant in the refinery, crude oil is further processed, e.g. into petrol, http://www.deutschebp.de/liveassets/bp_internet/germany/STAGING/home_assets/images/raffinerie_verarbeitung/A8_Destillation_HighRes.jpg (retrieved April 8th 2013)

result in uncertainty about the yield and potency until the process has started, for example in the chemical industry. *Yield* is the fraction of raw material recovered as the main or desired product (e.g. in the synthesis of ammonia, the yield is above approx. 98 %), and *conversion* is the fraction changed into something else, for example by-products or other products (Austin 1984), for instance the conversion of ammonia is limited to about 14 % (per pass), which means that 86 % of the charge does not react and must be recirculated. Conversion is also used to indicate the amount changed by a single pass through a technical subsystem when multiple passes are used (Austin 1984).

The variability in the quality of raw materials might determine which products will be produced (Rice and Norback 1987). Variations in raw material quality, for example moisture content, acidity, colour, viscosity or concentration of active ingredient, can also lead to variations in recipes for producing, for example in

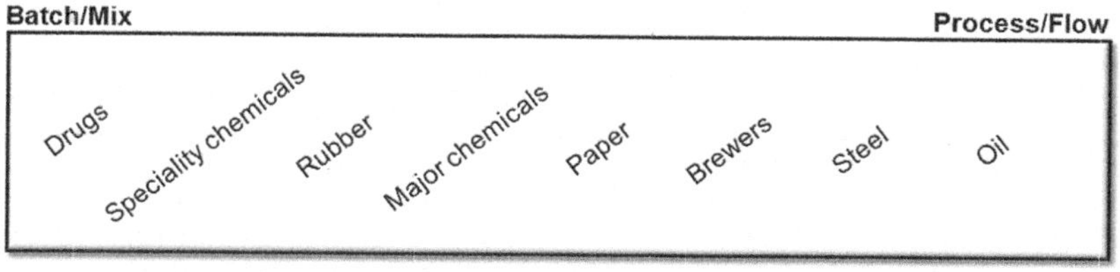

Fig. 2.12 Typology for process industries by Fransoo and Rutten (1994, p. 52)

terms of variations in ingredient proportions required to make quality specifications of the finished product, for instance in the oil or food industries (Fransoo and Rutten 1994, p. 49). Other variations can be caused by variations in quantity and availability or price, for example in the agricultural industry.

To make the difference between continuous and batch processing clear, I refer to the typology introduced by Fransoo and Rutten (1994) and their description of batch/mix and process/flow process industries (Fig. 2.12). Fransoo and Rutten (1994) define **batch/mix** as "*A process business which primarily schedules short production runs of products*" (Fransoo and Rutten 1994, p. 47; Connor 1986).

Process/flow is defined as "*A manufacturer who produces with minimal interruptions in any one production run or between production runs of products which exhibit process characteristics such as liquids, fibres, powders, gases*" (Franso and Rutten 1994, p. 47; Connor 1986).

Batch production can be described as intermittent (Dennis and Meredith 2000b; Woodward 1965), whereas process/flow is continuous or mass production. Batch/mix and process/flow operations can also be combined when the product becomes discrete at some point in the production process (Dennis and Meredith 2000b; Woodward 1965).

In process/flow businesses, the lead time is mainly determined by the cycle time, i.e. the time between two consecutive runs of the same product. The number of different products is limited and there is also a little variety between products. "Little variety, low product complexity and the small number of production steps cause all products to have the same routing" (Fransoo and Rutten 1994, p. 52). Investments in specialised single-purpose equipment are economically justifiable because the total market demand for a relatively small number of products is high. Installations and plants are used continuously around the clock, and material costs account for 60–70 % of the cost price since the production speed is very high (Fransoo and Rutten 1994, p. 52). Control systems for continuous processes aim at minimising fluctuations in process variables caused by different raw materials (e.g. flow rate, composition, temperature) and changes in equipment performance parameters (ASM Consortium 2012), which cannot be handled by the regulatory control system. When an equipment failure occurs, that part of the process often becomes non-functional, which leads to production or product quality loss, potentially resulting in a shutdown of a unit or a plant.

In batch/mix industries, the number of process steps is larger and the level of product complexity is higher (Rippin 1991). In the fine chemical production, sometimes ten different production steps are distinguished. Since the large variety

Table 2.4 Characteristics of process/flow versus batch mix industries (Fransoo and Rutten 1994, p. 53)

Process/flow business	Batch/mix businesses
High production speed, short throughput time	Long lead time, much work in process
Clear determination of capacity, one routine for all products, no volume flexibility	Capacity is not well defined (different configurations, complex routings)
Low product complexity	More complex products
Low added value	High added value
Strong impact of changeover times	Less impact of changeover times
Small number of product steps	Large number of production steps
Limited number of products	Large number of products

of products requires the use of the same, general type of equipment, routings are more diverse. Series of installations are rebuilt and reconnected to make a certain type of process possible (retrofitting), lead times are longer and the work in progress is higher (Fransoo and Rutten 1994). Typically, batch processes are used to manufacture a large number of different products, with a number of grades with minor differences. Frequent product and process changes are constituent characteristic of batch/mix processes, which allow relatively flexible process adjustments (ASM Consortium 2012).

Austin (1984) explains that early chemical processing was usually done in batches and much continues to be done in that way. Only with some exceptions do continuous processes require smaller, less expensive and less material in process than batch processes, and have more uniform operating conditions and products (Austin 1984). Continuous processes require concise control of flows and conditions, in which computer control has proven to be most valuable (Austin 1984). Small quantities of chemicals are usually made by batch/mix processes. When markets enlarge, operations change continuous processing, as the reduction in plant costs per unit of production is often the major force behind the change. In summary, process/flow and batch/mix industries are contrasted in Table 2.4.

End of digression

What is the relevance for skill and knowledge acquisition?

I would like to give a first impression on how these production conditions are relevant for training design. It is very useful for the training designer to at least deal to some extent with the particularities of process control of a respective company in order to understand the particularities of process control. Major differences among process industries exist, such as number of routings, number of raw materials, number of finished goods, equipment type, equipment flexibility, formulation multiplicity, and product variety (Dennis and Meredith 2000b). The following list provides a selection of potentially relevant issues to consider by way of example:

- The forms of production affect the required knowledge about the "recipes" because variation in raw material leads to variations in recipes for producing.

- Operators in batch/mix processes start up plants more frequently and modify them more frequently; operators in process/flow industries do so very rarely, which is relevant in order to decide whether, for example, the start-up of a plant is more of a routine or a non-routine task (see further below).
- Computer control and automation are found much more prominently in process/flow industries, and control operators, for instance in refineries, are more remote from the process they control than, for instance, operators in pharmaceutical production. This has an effect on how disclosed the process is for the operator and consequently also on how abstract the operator needs to conceive the process itself to be.

These reflections are taken up again in Chap. 3 and pursued further for the derivation of the required knowledge and skills.

After introducing the organisational setting from a management and macroergonomics point of view and the observable task, in the following I will translate the description of that which operators do using a terminology which should later allow us, in Chap. 3, to first of all derive requirements from the task description, and arising from this to develop training goals. It stands to reason that the task to handle a complex technical system is in itself equally not simple but complex. However, a complex task is defined through different features than a complex system. In the following, therefore, the constituents of a complex task are introduced.

2.3 Clarifying the Term "Complex Tasks"

When employing the term complex task, I was confronted with the issue of working out the central features of a complex task from the psychological literature of cognitive psychology, cognitive engineering psychology and human factors, because the term complex task is predominantly used without a clear definition. Frequently, the terms complex task and complex skill are also used synonymously (e.g. Lee and Anderson 2001).

2.3.1 Complexity as "Multiple Components"

Unfortunately, a precise definition of a complex task is lacking in the literature. Proctor and Dutta (1995) provide a useful distinction between simple and complex tasks from which to start. Although they do not explicitly define what "simple" and "complex" tasks are actually composed of, their example gives us some useful cues. A simple task, for instance, is to make simple associations between stimuli and responses (Proctor and Dutta 1995), for example to press a specified key in response to the onset of a designated stimulus (Proctor and Dutta 1995, p. 18; Johnson in press). Performing a simple task includes distinguishing between stimuli, integrating stimuli, and naming, comparing, choosing and making simple actions (Bainbridge 1995).

A more complex task, according to Proctor and Dutta's description, is proving geometric theorems, which are made up of multiple components that must be integrated before performance is highly skilled. Complex tasks additionally have perceptual or motor components or depend on background knowledge (Johnson in press). Finally, Proctor and Vu (2006) prescribe that "complex tasks have multiple elements that need to be executed successfully if performance is to be optimal" (p. 276), for example in dual-task performance.

To perform a complex task, the organisation of a sequence of actions is needed (Bainbridge 1995). With regard to process control, sequences of plant activity typically occur in batch processing (see above), during start-up and shutdown and after a fault has been eliminated, and the operator needs to know the general form of the sequence (Bainbridge 1998). The organisation of several sequences is also called multi-tasking (Bainbridge 1995). Multi-tasking requires the interleaving of sequences, especially if a person has several concurrent responsibilities. Loukopoulos et al. (2009) argue that multitasking involves processes in ways that go beyond the requirement of performing each part-task separately.

To organise or integrate several part-tasks into one whole task means choosing between a limited number of options in attempting to perform the part-tasks competing for attention, for example simultaneous execution and interleaving steps of one task with steps of another task (Loukopoulos et al. 2009), which requires tasks to be scheduled appropriately. For the operator it is not enough to know what should be done, but also when it should be done (Kerstholt and Raaijmakers 1997).

The integration of several part-tasks is coordinated by processes of selective attention (devote attention to one task or another, as a notion of attention switch), by divided attention or attention sharing in order to perform, for instance, two tasks simultaneously (Vicente 2007; Wickens and McCarley 2008). To master situations that call for multitasking, operators need a sense of time to enable them to switch between tasks (Rußwinkel et al. 2011). Rußwinkel et al. (2011) as well as de Keyser (1995) assume that task coordination requires a sense of time to cope with the demands of integrating part-tasks into a whole task in terms of timeliness and correctness of actions.

What is the relevance for knowledge and skill acquisition?

In order to provide an initial example and to convey an idea of the extent to which these aspects are relevant for training design, it should be pointed out that ideally, the acquisition of a complex task contains a *process of composition in which multistep procedures are collapsed into a macro procedure* (Lee and Anderson 2001). Additionally, without reaching too far ahead into the chapter on training design to come, according to Wickens and McCarley (2008), for the learning process, it is for example necessary to find the parts of the whole task that can be automated due to their consistency because "these make strong candidates to be uncoupled from full task and submitted to extensive part-task training" (p. 19).

2.3.2 *Complexity as Element Interactivity*

For this book, which addresses issues of knowledge and skill acquisition in an applied organisational setting for HROs, the definition of a complex task from an instructional perspective by Sweller (2006) is additionally valuable. A complex task defined by Sweller (2006) is characterised by a single construct called "element interactivity". An element is assumed to be everything that needs to be understood or learned (Sweller 2006, p.13), for example the parts and elements of a refinery as well as the chemical processes involved.

To understand the meaning of element interactivity, it is helpful to briefly address mental models here. As briefly introduced above, these are generally used to describe a person's representation of some physical system, and are based on an analog representation of causal relationships and interactions between plant components. Mental models are defined as "mechanisms whereby humans are able to generate descriptions of system purpose and form explanations of a system functioning and observed system states, and prediction of future states" (Rouse and Morris 1985, p. 7; Endsley 2006). As will be explained in Chap. 3, mental models play a fundamental role in controlling complex technical systems (e.g. Kragt and Landweert 1974; Wickens and Hollands 2000), because performance in an organisational context is supposed to be goal-directed (see above "conflicting goals"), for example goals such as production maximisation with the least possible resources needed. Mental models can help to inertly visualise performance strategies and their consequences in relation to the organisational goals. Mental models embody stored long-term knowledge about the system represented, which can be called on to direct applications, for example in non-routine/normal and non-routine/abnormal situations (see below).

When the concern is with acquiring mental models, if elements that need to be understood and learned, for example the process in a refinery unit, interact greatly with each other, they have to be processed and considered simultaneously. Therefore, in cases of high element interactivity, they exceed the limits of the human working memory capacity (Sweller 2006). Working memory holds only the most recently activated, or conscious, portion of long-term memory, and it moves these activated elements in and out of brief, temporary memory storage (Dosher 2003; Sternberg 2009).

The complexity in terms of high element interactivity is *not synonymous with task difficulty*, although it does affect task difficulty. According to Sweller (2006), for instance, for an apprentice in a refinery, learning a large number of chemical elements in the periodic table is probably difficult in the sense that it is effortful, because many elements must be learned. However, it does not contain high element interactivity, elements do not need to be considered simultaneously, and therefore it is not a complex task.

Furthermore, a complex task according to Fisch (2004) needs to be distinguished from a *complicated* task. Playing chess is a complicated task, because one has to learn and apply the rules for each pawn in the game, but it is not considered complex as it is

- not characterised by non-transparency and is in turn considered as transparent (the playing field is visible to everyone, the number of figures is clearly defined, the rules are known by both players in advance),
- not characterised by interconnectivity (the rule on how the knight is allowed to move does not depend on where the queen is or does not change because a pawn has been eliminated) and is
- not characterised by dynamic effects (the chess figures do not move around of their own accord while the player is still thinking about his next move).

What is the relevance for knowledge and skill acquisition?

Element interactivity refers, in the definition by Sweller (2006), not to the task per se, but to the content to be learned. As the complex task of the operator consists of operating a complex system, knowledge is of course also required about the operation of the plant and the process which is being controlled. The understanding of the plant requires the simultaneous processing of interconnected variables because, as described above, interconnectivity constitutes a feature of a complex system and places a strong burden on working memory during learning. In the acquisition of knowledge, it is therefore important to consider that such instructional techniques are selected that optimally support rather than overtax working memory during the processing of learning information.

2.3.3 A Definition of a Complex Task for This Book

Looking at the manifold occupations in HROs, it becomes clear that there is no such thing as "the" complex task. One complex task, such as process control, can be quite different from another complex task, such as piloting.

What we can say overall as a commonality of different applications of complex tasks, that which is a generalised lowest common denominator, *is that a complex task is composed of various part-tasks*. This does not emerge explicitly from the precise definition of a complex task, but rather implicitly from the descriptions above as well as from training approaches examined to date, in which a distinction was drawn between part-task and whole-task training (e.g. Patrick 1992). One assumes that a complex task (as a whole task) can be broken down into parts, for example by means of a task decomposition (Frederiksen and White 1989).

A part-task frequently consists of several steps or *sequences*. Mostly, the part-tasks are performed *in parallel* and have to be *integrated* into a joint flow of action. A *coordination of the part-tasks* ensues through attention selection, attention switching, and attention sharing (Wickens and McCarley 2008). Finally, in HROs, which form the focus of this book, workers performing complex tasks are working in teams and also have to coordinate and orchestrate their individual tasks

Table 2.5 Characteristics of a complex task

Characteristics
A complex task consists of part-tasks
Part-tasks include sequences of steps
Part-tasks have to be integrated
Part-task integration requires coordination based on attentional processes
Coordination requires simultaneous processing of interacting knowledge elements in order to reach a predefined goal
An individual complex task needs to be orchestrated into an interdependent team task

into an *interdependent team task* (Roth and Woods 1988) as outlined in the section on Collaborative complex problem solving (Sect. 4.4.1) in non-routine/abnormal situations. The characteristics of a complex task are listed in Table 2.5.

In summary, *a complex task can be decomposed into part-tasks that include sequences of steps, which need to be integrated and coordinated based on attentional processes and need to be orchestrated based on the simultaneous processing of knowledge elements (mental model) into a interdependent team task to meet the organisational goals.*

In the following chapter, the concern is with the situational conditions under which the control room operator performs his or her tasks. These situational conditions, the routine, non-routine/normal and non-routine/abnormal situations still belong on the one hand to organisational and task analysis (see Preface), but equally provide indications of which conditions need to be considered for transfer, which are in turn important for the derivation of training objectives and evaluation criteria.

2.4 Conditions for Knowledge and Skill Application: Routine, Non-routine/normal and Non-routine/abnormal Situations

In this book, I will distinguish between routine and non-routine as well as between non-routine/normal and non-routine/abnormal situations, in which in the latter case it is no longer possible to continue operating a plant using normal procedures (Fig. 2.13). Although widely used, the terms routine, non-routine, normal and abnormal are not well defined in the human factors and ergonomics publications.

Based on the often used distinction between the two poles of routine and nonroutine/abnormal situations, process control tasks are characterised as "hours of intolerable boredom punctuated by a few minutes of pure hell" (Wickens and Hollands 2000, p. 517), or "99 % boredom and 1 % sheer terror" (Vicente et al. 2004, p. 362).

The "hours of intolerable boredom" (although a little overstated) are seen as the times in which the human operator is monitoring a plant that is automatically controlled. This is the routine situation, routine control and regulation of the process which is well handled by Standard Operating Procedures (SOPs). The "pure hell" refers to the task of timely detection, diagnosis, and corrective action in situations in

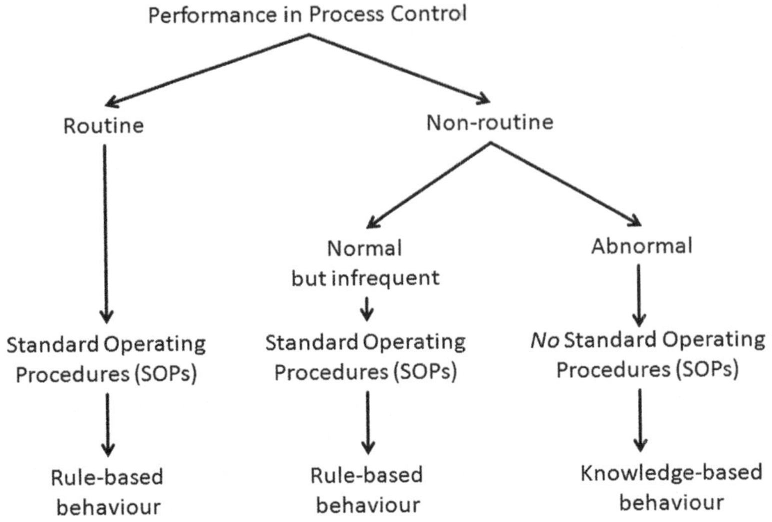

Fig. 2.13 Overview of the conditions of performance, own illustration

which infrequent malfunctions occur that can be fixed by using SOPs (non-routine/normal) or for which operators have no procedures at hand (non-routine/abnormal).

In terms of deriving strategies for learning and instruction later on, it is relevant to distinguish **routine** from **non-routine** tasks as well as **normal** from **abnormal** situations as the conditions under which the operator has to perform his/her tasks (Fig. 2.13).

Conditions for knowledge and skill application in routine situations

Routine situations as defined by Wickens and Hollands (2000) require normal control and regulation of the process which is well handled by Standard Operating Procedures (SOPs). Normal situations include tasks such as process monitoring, or scheduled testing of routine equipment. Routine tasks are rule-based behaviour (Rasmussen and Jensen 1974; Rasmussen 1990). Most of the time, routine situations occur, in which the automation works well and the process is well handled by the operator through SOPs. The main task is to monitor system instruments and periodically adjust control settings to maintain production quantities within certain boundaries (Reinartz 1993; Wickens and Hollands 2000).

In this book, routine stands for a property of the task, in the sense of frequency with which it is performed. Routine therefore stands for the number of repetitions per day, week or year. Moreover, routine stands for a defined, unchanging process. Additionally, from an organisational point of view, Ahuja and Carley (1999) define the degree of routineness as a function of the extent to which the task contains no or low variety (Perrow 1967), a small number of exceptions over time (Daft and Macintosh 1981) and therefore represent predictability and sameness (Ahuja and Carley 1999). Organisational routines in terms of SOPs develop in response to recurring questions (Gersick and Hackman 1990).

Condition for knowledge and skill application in non-routine/normal situations

Non-routine tasks are infrequent, for example the start-up and shutdown of the plant or a unit before and after a revision. But also for non-routine but infrequent tasks, standard procedures exist and can still be considered as normal (Reinartz 1993). In this book, I define non-routine/normal situations as situations in which operators encounter, for example, a malfunction of the automation and have to draw on skills and procedures which have not been used for a longer period of time. In line with Wickens and Hollands (2000), non-routine tasks might be fairly standardised and can be handled by following a set of procedures (SOPs), for example the start-up or shutdown of a plant is called non-routine, since shutdowns and start-ups occur rarely. Non-routine/normal situations also encompass rule-based behaviour (Rasmussen and Jensen 1974; Rasmussen 1990). SOPs are designed to support operators to store and process information correctly in the correct order (Kluge et al. 2013). SOPs include sequences of actions which need to be performed in a fixed sequence of actions or in parallel or dependent (contingent) on specific decision points (see Chap. 2).

Due to the infrequent occurrence, these might be carried out with less automaticity (Reinartz 1993; Schneider 1999). This means that non-routine tasks are less robust to distraction and need more attentional resources accompanied by conscious control and high mental workload, with less reserve capacity (Vidulich 2003), for example for coping with stress, compared to tasks performed with high automaticity. Additionally, these non-routine situations frequently require a so-called "first-shot" performance (Hammerton 1967, p. 63), in which the concern is with initial performance after a retention interval or a period of non-use. There is no second chance or a second attempt. It has to be as close to perfect as possible at the first attempt (Patrick 1992, p.78).

And finally, also from an organisational and economic perspective, for example in the petrochemical industries, non-routine situations are of interest because they cost 3–8 % of capacity, which amounts to approx. 10 billion $ annually in lost production (Bullemer and Laberge 2010, p. 10)

Condition for knowledge and skill application in non-routine/abnormal situations

In an *abnormal* situation, a disturbance or series of disturbances in a process cause plant operations to deviate from their normal operating state. They include "unfamiliar sequences of unplanned and unexpected sequences and either not visible or not immediately comprehensible" (Perrow 1984, p. 78), as introduced above to explain effects of interconnectivity and coupling. The nature of the abnormal situation may be of minimal or catastrophic consequence. It is the job of the operator or the control room crew to identify the cause of the situation and execute compensatory or corrective actions in a timely and efficient manner. Abnormal situations extend, develop, and change over time in the dynamic process control environments, increasing the interconnectivity of the intervention requirements (ASM® Consortium, Abnormal Situation Management Consortium 2012).

Non-routine/abnormal situations include, for example, a fault or situation that has never occurred before and there is a need for problem solving (an extreme example is the case of the tsunami that swept over the NPP of Fukushima). In such cases, knowledge-based behaviour is required (Rasmussen and Jensen 1974; Rasmussen 1990), which expresses itself in complex problem solving (Funke and Frensch 2007; Fischer et al. 2012; Reinartz 1993) and dynamic decision making (Brehmer 1992). An abnormal situation is considered to be a problem because the human operator has several goals (see definition of "multiple goals" above) but does not know how these goals can be reached. If the operator cannot go from the given situation to the desired situation simply by predefined actions (e.g. SOPs), "there has to be a recourse to thinking" (Duncker 1945, p. 1; Fischer et al 2012). Based on the work by Brehmer (1992) and Edwards (1962), dynamic decision making (DDM) "has been characterized by multiple, interdependent, and real-time decisions, occurring in an environment that changes independently as a function of a sequence of actions" (Gonzales et al. 2003, p. 591).

In this book, abnormal situations are what Stachowski et al. (2009, p. 1536) and Gladstein and Reilly (1985), in line with Hermann (1963), define as a "crisis situation", which is (a) *ambiguous* and includes (b) *unanticipated* major (c) *threats* to system survival coupled with (d) *limited time* to respond (Hermann 1963). Non-routine/abnormal tasks are less predictable and require creativity (Ahuja and Carley 1999). Abnormal situations "are *low-probability, high-impact* events that threaten the reliability and accountability of organizations and are characterized by ambiguity of cause, effect, and means of resolution" (Yu et al. 2008, p. 452 based on Pearson and Clair 1998). They are unusual, out-of-the-ordinary, or atypical (Weinger and Slagle 2002, p. 59). Ambiguity is correlated with uncertainty, incomplete and noisy information (Vicente et al. 2004). Grote (2009) distinguishes between several types of uncertainty, such as:

- Source of uncertainty: Incomplete information, inadequate understanding, undifferentiated alternatives
- Content of uncertainty: State uncertainty, effect uncertainty, response uncertainty
- Lack of control: Lack of transparency, lack of predictability and lack of influence.

The main problem in this respect is that in case of the situation in which the system state is uncertain (Vicente et al. 2004), it is unclear which SOPs there even are, and if there is no SOP, which actions lead to a suitable solution.

Looking at the disasters and accidents of the past few years, such as the "Deepwater Horizon" in 2010 and Fukushima 2011, it becomes clear that such non-routine/abnormal situations contain these aforementioned uncertainties, which can also occur simultaneously. A dramatic example of the requirement is provided by the disaster management in Fukushima in 2011. The plant personnel had to handle the situation with "loss of all the safety systems, loss of practically all the instrumentation, necessity to cope with simultaneous severe accidents on four plants, lack of human resources, lack of equipment, lack of light in the installations, and general conditions of the installation after the tsunami and after damage of the fuel resulted in hydrogen explosions and high levels of radiation" (IAEA Report 2011, p. 43).

Table 2.6 Summary and delimitation of the terms routine, non-routine/normal and non-routine/abnormal situation

Conditions for transfer	Description
Routine situations	Require routine control and regulation of the process Based on rule-based behaviour The situation is well handled by Standard Operating Procedures (SOPs) e.g. "daily business", plant monitoring and control
Non-routine/normal situations	Require drawing on skills which have not been used for a longer period of time, Rule-based behaviour The situation is well handled by Standard Operating Procedures (SOPs) e.g. "exceptional business", fault repair or start-up of plant, but is still rule-based behaviour
Non-routine/abnormal situations	Require problem-solving skills and knowledge-based behaviour Situation is (a) *ambiguous* and includes (b) *unanticipated* major (c) *threats* to system survival coupled with (d) *limited time* to respond e.g. low-probability, high-impact situation, an explosion in a subunit of the plant caused by a safety-related rule violation or natural disasters such as earthquakes, tsunami.

In Table 2.6, the transfer conditions are concisely summarised.

Although the transitions between routine, non-routine/normal and non-routine/abnormal are not discrete but continuous, the artificially clear-cut distinction is assumed to be helpful in order to better understand and design knowledge and skill acquisition processes, as will be explained in the following chapters.

Delimitation of the human factors perspective from the plant operations perspective on normal and abnormal situations

The distinction between routine, non-routine/normal and non-routine/abnormal situations is a psychological one. From a learning and training psychological perspective, the distinction between routine and non-routine reflects the frequency of opportunities to use a skill (Ford et al. 1992), i.e. the skill is routine and performed with a minimal use of cognitive and attentional resources. Opportunity to perform is the extent to which a trainee is provided with or actively obtains work experiences relevant to the tasks for which he/she was trained (Ford et al. 1992, p. 512). From that perspective, non-routine and routine tasks are distinguished according to the number of times trained tasks have been applied (Ford et al. 1992), so that a certain level of task experience has been achieved (Tesluk and Jacobs 1998). The longer the period of non-use is because of a lack of opportunity to perform, the more skill decay will occur (Arthur et al 1998; Kluge et al. 2012). If the work environment (e.g. due to high automated processes keeping the human operator not "in the loop") offers no opportunity to perform – also not artificially in immersive environments or with low-cost alternatives such as symbolic rehearsal (Driskell et al. 1994; Kluge et al. 2012) – the lack of opportunity to perform and apply trained skills is a strong negative predictor of the skill retention

Table 2.7 Operational modes and critical systems perspective defined by the ASM (Bullemer and Laberge 2010)

Operational modes	Plant states	Critical systems	Operational goals	Plant activities
Emergency	Disaster	Area emergency response system	Minimise impact	Fire fighting
	Accident	Site emergency response system		First aid rescue
Abnormal	Out of control	Physical and mechanical containment system Safety shutdown Protective systems Hardwired emergency alarms	Bring to safe state	Evacuation
	Abnormal	DCS alarm system Decision support system Process equipment	Return to normal	Manual control & troubleshooting
Normal	Normal	DCS, automatic controls Plant management systems	Keep normal	Preventative monitoring & testing

DCS distributed control system

and performance level (Bjork and Bjork 2006; Burke and Hutchins 2007; Farr 1987).

The distinction between normal and abnormal is equally a psychological one and refers not to the plant state (as in the ASM or IAEA definition in Tables 2.7 and 2.8), but rather to the familiarity to the human operator. It refers to whether a task has, in principle, already been trained and executed and for which there is an SOP which one could use (= normal), which requires a so-called temporal transfer, or whether there was no training for this task and also no SOPs (= abnormal), which then requires an adaptive transfer (Kluge et al 2010).

From a continuous flow operations perspective (e.g. of refineries and petrochemical plants), the distinction between normal and abnormal is a different one and in terms of plant states, critical systems, operational goals and plant activities as displayed in Table 2.7.

The consequences of abnormal situations, for example in a chemical plant, depend on the nature of the materials, for example hazardous vs. non-hazardous chemicals, solids, liquids or gases; flammable vs. non-flammable substance being processed (ASM Consortium 2012). The definition in Nuclear Safety is different (IAEA 2007) and deviates from the ASM Definition. The IAEA (2007) distinguishes between "Operational states" and "Accident conditions" (Table 2.8).

Normal operation in NPP is defined as operation within specified operational limits and conditions, which includes start-up, power operation, shutting down, maintenance, testing and refuelling. Accident conditions are defined as deviations from normal operation that are more severe than anticipated operational occurrences, including design basis accidents and severe accidents, for example major fuel failure or loss of coolant accident. Accident Management includes prevention of escalation of the event into a severe accident, mitigation of consequences of a

Table 2.8 Plant states defined by the IAEA (2007) for NPP

Plant states		Characteristics
Operational states		*Normal operation*
		Operation within specified operational limits and conditions (includes startup, power operation, shutting down, maintenance, testing and refuelling)
		Anticipated operational occurrences[a]
		Operational process deviates from normal operations, which is expected to occur at least once during the operating lifetime of a facility, but which in view of appropriate design provision does not cause any significant damage to items important to safety or lead to accident conditions (e.g. loss of normal electrical power, faults such as turbine trip, malfunction of individual items of a normally running plant, failure of function of single items of control equipment, loss of power to main coolant pump)
Accident conditions	Within design basis accidents	*Design basis accidents* (is designed against a facility and for which the damage to the fuel and the release of radioactive material are kept within authorised limits)
		Not design basis accidents, but encompassed by them
	Beyond design basis accidents...	*Severe accidents* (more severe than design basis accidents)
		...Without severe accidents

[a]Some organisations use the term *abnormal* situation instead of anticipated operational occurrences (IAEA 2007, p. 145)

severe accident and achieving a long-term safe and stable state, and is defined as the taking of actions during the evolution of a beyond design basis accident (IAEA 2007, p. 145).

In summary, this means that the terms routine, non-routine, normal and abnormal from the human factors and the operations perspective are also differently viewed and defined according to the respective branch. In this book, the starting point is the consideration of required knowledge and skills, and situations and conditions under which they need to be applied.

To give some examples and an outlook on the coming chapters, it is important that as a training designer, one is, or becomes, one is aware of what routine, non-routine/normal, and non-routine/abnormal situations are for the organisation for which the training is conceived. Which SOPs exist? Which processes are rather frequent, and which rather rare? In batch/mix processes, the start-up, for instance, is more routine than in continuous/flow industries. Which tasks are performed every day, every week, or only once a year or once every 10 years? And what serious consequences can arise if a procedure is not correctly mastered?

Answers to these questions and the distinction between routine, non-routine/normal and non-routine/abnormal are important, for example, in order to later conduct a so-called DIF analysis (Difficulty-Frequency-Importance analysis, Buckley and Caple 2007), which, in turn, is important in order to define training method, duration or repetition (see Chaps. 4 and 5).

Moreover, from the distinction between routine, non-routine/normal and non-routine/abnormal, it can be derived under which mental workload conditions an operator has to perform his/her task. Waller et al. (2004) assume routine tasks to be moderate-workload and non-routine to be high-workload situations. Additionally, I assume non-routine/abnormal situations to be situations with high mental workload under stress. Therefore, additionally, the answers to the question of what non-routine/normal and non-routine/abnormal situations are need to be used to consider particular training methods such as stress exposure training (Driskell and Johnston 1998; Driskell et al. 2008, see Chaps. 4 and 5).

In addition to the cognitive aspects of dealing with abnormal situations on a knowledge-based level as introduced above, the handling of abnormal situations requires coping with high stress. The purpose of Stress Exposure Training based on Driskell et al. (1998, 2001, 2008) is to provide the operator with the skills and tools necessary to maintain effective performance when operating in high-stress situations (Salas et al. 2006). This training is especially important when the consequences of errors are high, as stress increases the likelihood of errors.

After "setting the scene" by introducing and describing complex technical systems, the task, duties and responsibilities of operators and operator crews and conditions under which performance has to be shown, in Chap. 3, I go into detail regarding the aspects which I have so far only touched on by way of example, by deriving knowledge and skills that need to be acquired for performing complex tasks in routine, non-routine/normal and non-routine/abnormal situations.

References

Ahuja, M. K., & Carley, K. M. (1999). Network structure in virtual organizations. *Organization Science, 10*, 741–757.

Arthur, W., Bennett, W., Stanush, P. L., & McNelly, T. L. (1998). Factors that influence skill decay and retention: A quantitative review and analysis. *Human Performance, 11*, 57–101.

ASM Consortium. (2012). *Process factors*. Retrieved November 12, 2012. http://www.asmconsortium.net/defined/sources/Pages/ProcessFactors.aspx

Austin, G. T. (1984). *Shreve's chemical process industries* (5th ed.). New York: McGraw-Hill.

Bainbridge, L. (1983). Ironies of automation. Increasing levels of automation can increase, rather than decrease, the problems of supporting the human operator. *Automatica, 19*, 775–779.

Bainbridge, L. (1995). *Processes underlying human performance: Complex tasks*. Retrieved September 7, 2012. http://www.bainbrdg.demon.co.uk/Papers/EmbrRid/EmbrRidB.html

Bainbridge, L. (1998). *Planning the training of a complex skill*. Retrieved January 11, 2012. http://www.bainbrdg.demon.co.uk/Papers/PlanTrain.html

Bjork, R. A., & Bjork, E. L. (2006). Optimizing treatment and instruction: Implications of the new theory of disuse. In L. G. Nilsson & N. Ohta (Eds.), *Memory and society. Psychological perspectives* (pp. 109–134). Hove, UK: Psychology Press.

Blech, C., & Funke, J. (2005). *DYNAMIS review: An overview about applications of the DYNAMIS approach in cognitive psychology* (Research Report). Heidelberg: Department of Psychology, University of Heidelberg.

Brehmer, B. (1992). Dynamic decision making: Human control of complex systems. *Acta Psychologica, 81*, 211–241.

Brehmer, B., & Dörner, D. (1993). Experiments with computer-simulated microworlds: Escaping both the narrow straits of the laboratory and the deep blue sea of the field study. *Computers in Human Behavior, 9*, 171–184.

Buckley, R., & Caple, J. (1990/revised 5th edition 2007). *The theory and practice of training*. London: Kogan Page.

Bullemer, P., & Laberge, J. (2010, November 30). *Abnormal situation management and the human side of process safety*. Paper presented at the ERTC 15th annual meeting, Istanbul, Turkey. Retrieved November 12, 2012. http://www.asmconsortium.net/Documents/HumanSideofSafety_ERTC%20Forum_Bullemer_30Nov10.pdf

Bullemer, P. T., Cochran, T., Harp, S., & Miller, C. (1997). Managing abnormal situations II: Collaborative decision support for operations personnel. *ASM Consortium*. Retrieved November 11, 2012. http://www.asmconsortium.net/Documents/Managing%20ASM%20Dec%20Support.pdf

Burke, L. A., & Hutchins, H. M. (2007). Training transfer: An integrative literature review. *Human Resource Development Review, 6*, 263–296.

Carvallo, P. V. R., dos Santos, I. L., & Vidal, M. C. R. (2005). Nuclear power plant shift supervisors' decision making during microincidents. *International Journal of Industrial Ergonomics, 35*, 619–644.

Connor, S. J. (1986). *The process industry thesaurus*. Falls Church: American Production and Inventory Control Society.

Craik, K. (1943). *The nature of explanation*. Cambridge: University Press.

Crossman, E. R. F. W. (1974). Automation and skill. In E. Edwards & F. P. Lees (Eds.), *The human operator in process control* (pp. 1–25). London: Taylor & Francis.

Daft, R. M., & Macintosh, N. (1981). A tentative exploration into the amount and equivocality of information processing in organizational work units. *Administrative Science Quarterly, 26*, 207–224.

De Keyser, V. (1995). Time in ergonomics research. *Ergonomics, 38*, 1639–1661.

Dennis, D. R., & Meredith, J. R. (2000a). An analysis of process industry production and inventory management systems. *Journal of Operations Management, 18*, 683–699.

Dennis, D. R., & Meredith, J. R. (2000b). An empirical analysis of process industry transformation systems. *Management Science, 46*, 1085–1099.

Dörner, D. (1989/2003). *Die Logik des Misslingens. Strategisches Denken in komplexen Situationen* [The logic of failure. Strategic thinking in complex situations] (11th ed.). Reinbeck: rororo.

Dosher, B. A. (2003). Working memory. In L. Nadel (Ed.), *Encyclopedia of cognitive science* (pp. 569–577). London: Nature Publishing Group.

Driskell, J. E., & Johnston, J. H. (1998). Stress exposure training. In J. A. Cannon-Bowers & E. Salas (Eds.), *Making decisions under stress. Implications for individual and team training* (pp. 191–217). Washington, DC: APA (Reprinted in 2006).

Driskell, J. E., Copper, C., & Moran, A. (1994). Does mental practice enhance performance? *Journal of Applied Psychology, 79*, 481–492.

Driskell, J. E., Johnston, J. H., & Salas, E. (2001). Does stress training generalize to novel situations? *Human Factors, 43*, 99–110.

Driskell, J. E., Salas, E., Johnston, J. H., & Wollert, T. N. (2008). Stress exposure training: An event-based approach. In P. A. Hancock & J. L. Szalma (Eds.), *Performance under stress* (pp. 271–286). Aldershot: Ashgate.

Duncker, K. (1945). The structure and dynamics of problem-solving processes. *Psychological Monographs, 58*(5), 1–112.

Edwards, W. (1962). Dynamic decision theory and probabilistic information processing. *Human Factors: The Journal of the Human Factors and Ergonomics, 4*, 59–74. doi:10.1177/001872086200400201.

Emery, F. E. (1959). *Characteristics of socio-technical systems* (Tavistock Documents # 527), London. Abridged in F. E. Emery, *The emergence of a new paradigm of work*. Canberra: Center for Continuing Education.

Endsley, M. R. (2006). Expertise and situation awareness. In K. A. Ericsson, N. Charness, P. J. Feltovich, & R. R. Hoffmann (Eds.), *The Cambridge handbook of expertise and expert performance* (pp. 633–652). Cambridge: Cambridge University Press.

Farr, M. J. (1987). *The long-term retention of knowledge and skills. A cognitive and instructional perspective*. New York: Springer.

Fisch, R. (2004). Was tun? – Hinweise zum praktischen Umgang mit komplexen Aufgaben und Entscheidungen (Titel des Kapitels auf S. 319)/Was tun angesichts komplexer Aufgaben (Titel im Inhaltsverzeichnis, S. 6) [What to do? Guidelines for the practical management of complex tasks and decisions]. In R. Fisch & D. Beck (Hrsg./Eds.), *Komplexitätsmanagement. Methoden zum Umgang mit komplexen Aufgabenstellungen in Wirtschaft, Regierung und Verwaltung* (pp. 319–345). Wiesbaden: VS Verlag für Sozialwissenschaften.

Fischer, A., Greiff, S., & Funke, J. (2012). The process of solving complex problems. *The Journal of Problem Solving, 4*, 19–42.

Ford, J. K., Quinones, M. A., Sego, D. J., & Speer -Sorra, J. (1992). Factors affecting the opportunity to perform trained tasks on the job. *Personnel Psychology, 45*, 511–527.

Fransoo, J. C., & Rutten, W. G. M. M. (1994). A typology of production control situations in process industries. *International Journal of Operations and Production Management, 18*, 47–57.

Frederiksen, J. R., & White, B. Y. (1989). An approach to training based upon principled task decomposition. *Acta Psychologica, 71*, 89–146.

Funke, J. (1985). Steuerung dynamischer Systeme durch Aufbau und Anwendung subjektiver Kausalmodelle [Control of dynamic systems via construction and application of subjective causal models]. *Zeitschrift für Psychologie, 193*, 443–465.

Funke, J. (2010). Complex problem solving: A case for complex cognition? *Cognitive Processing, 11*, 133–142.

Funke, J., & Frensch, P. A. (2007). *Complex problem solving: The European perspective-10 years after* (pp. 25–47). Mahwah: Lawrence Erlbaum Associates.

Gaddy, C. D., & Wachtel, J. A. (1992). Team skills training in nuclear power plant operations. In R. W. Swezey & E. Salas (Eds.), *Teams: Their training and performance* (pp. 379–396). Norwood: Alex.

Gersick, C. J., & Hackman, R. (1990). Habitual routines in task performing groups. *Organizational Behavior and Human Decision Process, 47*, 65–97.

Gladstein, D. L., & Reilly, N. P. (1985). Group decision making under threat: The Tycoon game. *Academy of Management Journal, 28*, 613–627.

Gonzales, C., Lerch, J. F., & Lebiere, C. (2003). Instance-based learning in dynamic decision making. *Cognitive Science, 27*, 591–635.

Grauel, B., Kluge, A., & Adolph, L. (2012). *Analyse vorausgehender Bedingungen für die Unterstützung makrokognitiver Prozesse in Teams in der industriellen Instandhaltung*. Paper presented at the 2nd workshop "Kognitive Systeme", Universität Duisburg-Essen, 18–20 September 2012.

Grote, G. (2009). *Management of uncertainty. Theory and application in the design of systems and organizations*. Dordrecht: Springer.

Hagemann, V., Kluge, A., & Ritzmann, S. (2012). Flexibility under complexity: Work contexts, task profiles and team processes of high responsibility teams. *Employee Relations, 34*, 322–338.

Hammerton, M. (1967). Measures for the efficiency of simulators as training devices. *Ergonomics, 10*, 63–65.

Hansez, I., & Chmiel, N. (2010). Safety behavior: Job demands, job resources, and perceived management commitment to safety. *Journal of Occupational Health Psychology, 15*, 267–278.

Hermann, C. F. (1963). Some consequences of crisis which limit the viability of organizations. *Administrative Science Quarterly, 8*, 61–82.

Hollnagel, E., & Woods, D. D. (2005). *Joint cognitive systems. Foundations of cognitive systems engineering*. Boca Raton: Taylor & Francis.

IAEA. (2007). *IAEA safety glossary. Terminology used in nuclear safety and radiation protection* (2007 edn). Retrieved November 13, 2012. http://www-pub.iaea.org/MTCD/publications/PDF/Pub1290_web.pdf

IAEA. (2011). IAEA international fact finding expert mission of the Fukushima Dai-ichi NPP accident following the great east Japan earthquake and tsunami. Report to the IAEA member states. Retrieved December 3, 2012, from http://www-pub.iaea.org/mtcd/meetings/pdfplus/2011/cn200/documentation/cn200_-final-fukushima-mission_report.pdf

Johnson, A. (in press). Procedural memory and skill acquisition. In A. F. Healy & R. W. Proctor (Vol. Eds.), & I. B. Weiner (Ed.-in-Chief), *Handbook of psychology: Vol. 4. Experimental psychology* (2nd edn). Hoboken: Wiley.

Johnson-Laird, P. N. (1983). *Mental models. Towards a cognitive science of language, inference, and consciousness*. Cambridge: Cambridge University Press.

Kerstholt, J. H., & Raaijmakers, J. G. W. (1997). Decision making in dynamic task environments. In R. Ranyard, W. R. Crozier, & O. Svenson (Eds.), *Decision making. Cognitive models and explanations* (pp. 205–217). London: Routledge.

Kim, J. H., & Seong, P. H. (2009). Human factors engineering in large-scale digital control systems. In H. P. Seong (Ed.), *Reliability and risk issues in large scale safety-critical digital control systems* (Springer series in reliability engineering, III, pp. 163–195). London: Springer. doi:10.1007/978-1-84800-384-2_8.

Kluge, A., Schüler, K., & Burkolter, D. (2008). Simulatortrainings für Prozesskontrolltätigkeiten am Beispiel von Raffinerien: Psychologische Trainingsprinzipien in der Praxis. *Zeitschrift für Arbeitswissenschaft, 62*(2), 97–109.

Kluge, A., Sauer, J., Burkolter, D., & Ritzmann, S. (2010). Designing training for temporal and adaptive transfer: A comparative evaluation of three training methods for process control tasks. *Journal of Educational Computing Research, 43*, 327–353.

Kluge, A., Burkolter, D., & Frank, B. (2012). "Being prepared for the infrequent": A comparative study of two refresher training approaches and their effects on temporal and adaptive transfer in a process control task. In *Proceedings of the Human Factors and Ergonomics Society 56th annual conference* (pp. 2437–2441), Boston. Thousand Oaks: SAGE.

Kluge, A., Grauel, B., & Burkolter, D. (2013). Job aids: How does the quality of a procedural aid alone and combined with a decision aid affect motivation and performance in process control? *Applied Ergonomics, 44*, 285–296.

Kluwe, R. H. (1997). Acquisition of knowledge in the control of a simulated technical system. *Le Travail Human, 60*, 61–85.

Kragt, H., & Landweert, J. A. (1974). Mental skills in process control. In E. Edwards & F. P. Lees (Eds.), *The human operator in process control* (pp. 135–145). London: Taylor & Francis.

Lee, F. J., & Anderson, J. R. (2001). Does learning a complex task have to be complex? A study in learning decomposition. *Cognitive Psychology, 42*, 267–316.

Loukopoulos, L. D., Dismukes, R. K., & Barshi, I. (2009). *The multitasking myth. Handling complexity in real-world operations*. Farnham: Ashgate.

Moray, N. (1987). Intelligent aids, mental models, and the theory of machines. *International Journal of Man-Machine Studies, 27*(5), 619–629.

Moray, N. (1996, October). A taxonomy and theory of mental models. *Proceedings of the Human Factors and Ergonomics Society Annual Meeting, 40*(4), 164–168. Sage.
Moray, N. (1997). Human factors in process control. In G. Salvendy (Ed.), *Handbook of human factors and ergonomics* (pp. 1944–1971). New York: Wiley.
Ormerod, T. C., Richardson, J., & Shepherd, A. (1998). Enhancing the usability of a task analysis method: A notation and environment for requirements specification. *Ergonomics, 41*(11), 1642–1663.
Patrick, J. (1992). *Training: Research and practice*. San Diego: Academic.
Pearson, C. M., & Clair, J. A. (1998). Reframing crisis management. *Academy of Management Review, 23*, 59–76.
Perrow, C. (1967). A framework for the comparative analysis of organizations. *American Sociological Review, 32*, 194–208.
Perrow, C. (1984). *Normal accidents: Living with high risk technology*. New York: Basic Books (Reprint 1999, by Princeton University Press, Princeton).
Proctor, R. W., & Dutta, A. (1995). *Skill acquisition and human performance*. Thousand Oaks: Sage.
Proctor, R. W., & van Zandt, T. (2008). *Human factors in simple and complex systems* (2nd ed.). Boca Raton: CRC Press.
Proctor, R. W., & Vu, K.-P. L. (2006/reprint 2009). Laboratory studies of training, skill acquisition, and retention. In K. A. Ericsson, N. Charness, P. J. Feltovich, & R. R. Hoffman (Eds.), *The Cambridge handbook of expertise and expert performance* (pp. 265–286). Cambridge: Cambridge University Press.
Rasmussen, J. (1990). Mental models and the control of action in complex environments. In D. Ackermann & M. J. Tauber (Eds.), *Mental models and human computer-interaction 1* (pp. 41–69). Amsterdam: North-Holland.
Rasmussen, J., & Jensen, A. (1974). Mental procedures in real-life tasks: A case study of electronic troubleshooting. *Ergonomics, 17*, 293–307.
Reason, J. (2008). *The human contribution. Unsafe acts, accidents, and heroic recoveries*. Surrey: Ashgate.
Reinartz, S. J. (1993). An empirical study of team behaviour in a complex and dynamic problem-solving context: A discussion of methodological and analytical aspects. *Ergonomics, 36*, 1281–1290.
Reinartz, S. J., & Reinartz, G. (1992). Verbal communication in collective control of simulated nuclear power plant incidents. *Reliability Engineering and System Safety, 36*, 245–251.
Rice, J. W., & Norback, J. P. (1987). Process industries production planning using matrix data structures. *Production and Inventory Management Journal, 28*, 15–23.
Rippin, D. W. T. (1991). Batch process planning. *Chemical Engineering, 98*, 100–107.
Roth, E. M., & Woods, D. D. (1988). Aiding human performance I: Cognitive analysis. *Le Travail Humain, 51*, 39–64.
Rouse, W. B., & Morris, N. M. (1985). *On looking into the black box: Prospects and limits in the search for mental models* (No. DTIC#AD-A159080). Atlanta: Center for Man-Machine system Research, Georgia Institute of Technology.
Rußwinkel, N., Urbas, L., & Thüring, M. (2011). Predicting temporal errors in complex task environments: A computational and experimental approach. *Cognitive Systems Research, 12*, 336–354.
Salas, E., Wilson, K. A., Priest, A., & Guthrie, J. W. (2006). Design, delivery, and evaluation of training systems. In G. Salvendy (Ed.), *Handbook of human factors and ergonomics* (pp. 472–512). Hoboken: Wiley.
Schneider, W. (1999). Automaticity. In R. A. Wilson & F. C. Keil (Eds.), *The MIT encyclopedia of the cognitive science* (pp. 63–64). Cambridge, MA: MIT Press.
Stachowski, A. A., Kaplan, S. A., & Waller, M. J. (2009). The benefits of flexible team interaction during crisis. *Journal of Applied Psychology, 94*, 1536–1543.

Sterman, J. D. (1994). Learning in and about complex systems. *System Dynamics Review, 10*, 291–330.

Sternberg, R. J. (2009). *Cognitive psychology*. Wadsworth: Cengage Learning.

Sweller, J. (2006). How the human cognitive system deals with complexity. In J. Elen & R. E. Clark (Eds.), *Handling complexity in learning environments. Theory and research* (pp. 13–27). Amsterdam: Elsevier.

Tesluk, P. E., & Jacobs, R. R. (1998). Toward an integrated model of work experience. *Personnel Psychology, 51*, 321–355.

Van Donk, D. P., & Fransoo, J. C. (2006). Operations management research in process industries. *Journal of Operations Management, 24*, 211–214.

Veland, O., & Eikas, M. (2007). A novel design for an ultra-large screen display for industrial process control. In M. J. Dainoff (Ed.), *Ergonomics and health aspects. HCII 2007* (LNCS 4566, pp. 349–358). Berlin: Springer.

Verschuur, W., Hudson, P., & Parker, D. (1996). *Violations of rules and procedures: Results of item analysis and test of the behavioural model. Field study NAM and shell expro Aberdeen*. Leiden: Report Leiden University of SIP.

Vicente, K. J. (2007). Monitoring a nuclear power plant. In F. Kramer, D. A. Wiegmann, & A. Kirlik (Eds.), *Attention. From theory to practice* (pp. 90–99). Oxford: Oxford University Press.

Vicente, K. J., Mumaw, R. J., & Roth, E. M. (2004). Operator monitoring in a complex dynamic work environment: A qualitative cognitive model based on field observations. *Theoretical Issues in Ergonomic Science, 5*, 359–384.

Vidulich, M. A. (2003). Mental workload and situation awareness. Essential concepts in aviation psychology. In P. S. Tsang & M. A. Vidulich (Eds.), *Principles and practice of aviation psychology* (pp. 115–147). Mahwah: Lawrence Erlbaum.

Walker, G. H., Stanton, N. A., Salmon, P. M., Jenkins, D. P., & Rafferty, L. (2010). Translating the concepts of complexity to the field of ergonomics. *Ergonomics, 53*, 1175–1186.

Wallace, T. F. (1984). *APICS dictionary* (5th ed.). Falls Church: American Production and Inventory Control Society.

Waller, M. J., Gupta, N., & Giambatista, R. C. (2004). Effects of adaptive behaviors and shared mental models on control crew performance. *Management Science, 50*, 1534–1544.

Weinger, M. B., & Slagle, J. (2002). Human factors research in anesthesia patient safety: Techniques to elucidate factors affecting clinical task performance and decision making. *Journal of the American Medical Informatics Association, 9*, 58–63.

Wickens, C. D., & Hollands, J. G. (2000). *Engineering psychology and human performance* (3rd ed.). Upper Saddle River: Prentice Hall.

Wickens, C. D., & McCarley, J. S. (2008). *Applied attention theory*. Boca Raton: CRC Press.

Wilson, J. R., & Rutherford, A. (1989). Mental models: Theory and application in human factors. *Human Factors: The Journal of the Human Factors and Ergonomics Society, 31*(6), 617–634.

Woods, D. D. (1984). Visual momentum: A concept to improve the cognitive coupling of person and computer. *International Journal of Man-Machine Studies, 21*, 229–244.

Woods, D. D., O'Brien, J. F., & Hanes, L. F. (1987). Human factors challenges in process control: The case of nuclear power plants. In G. Salvendy (Ed.), *Handbook of human factors* (pp. 1725–1770). New York: Wiles.

Woods, D. D., Roth, E. M., Stubler, W. F., & Mumaw, R. J. (1990). Navigating through large display networks in dynamic control applications. In *Proceedings of the Human Factors and Ergonomics 34th annual meeting* (pp. 396–399). doi:10.1177/154193129003400435.

Woodward, J. (1965). *Industrial organization: Theory and practice*. London: Oxford University Press.

Yu, T., Sengul, M., & Lester, R. H. (2008). Misery loves company: The spread of negative impacts resulting from organizational crisis. *Academy of Management Review, 33*, 452–472.

Chapter 3
Required Knowledge and Skills to Control a Complex Technical System – Job Analysis Related to Training

After introducing process control in the framework of the organisational context in the second chapter, in this chapter, we will look at the subdivision into routine, non-routine/normal and non-routine/abnormal situations in more detail. From this, we can then derive the knowledge and skill requirements, formulate training goals and demonstrate possibilities for their evaluation. The subsequently derived aspects of knowledge and skills are meant as a job description of the control room operator's job and the tasks included. As Salas and Cannon-Bowers (2001) point out, historically, job/task analysis has been used to identify the information necessary to create the learning objectives (Goldstein 1993). A job/task analysis results in a detailed description of the work functions to be performed on the job, the conditions under which the job is to be performed, and the knowledge and skills needed to perform those tasks (Salas and Cannon-Bowers 2001).

The rationale behind the kind of job description developed in this book is, according to Folley (1964a, b), to define the presence of specified human activities immediately relevant to training. Folley's (1964a, b) view of a task is that it can be described in five classes of attributes (Fleishman and Quaintance 1984):

1. The extent to which each of five types of ongoing activities is required. The five types are: Procedure following, continuous motor activity, monitoring, communicating, decision making and problem solving
2. The temporal, sequential, and causal relationships among these activities
3. Characteristics of the detailed behaviours that constitute the activities
4. Contingencies that might affect task performance
5. Disruptive conditions under which the task might have to be performed

As introduced in the previous chapters, which reflected upon the constituents of a complex technical system, in line with Kragt and Landweerd (1974), as well as Kluwe (1997), Vicente et al. (2004), and Bainbridge (1992), it can be assumed that control room operators need a mental model (Johnson-Laired 1983; Moray 1996; Wilson and Rutherford 1989) of the interconnectedness and dynamics of parts, units, and sub-processes, the equipment to manage the process, for example automation and its displays, and the extent of non-transparency which this entails, in

A. Kluge, *The Acquisition of Knowledge and Skills for Taskwork and Teamwork to Control Complex Technical Systems*, DOI 10.1007/978-94-007-5049-4_3,

which the conflicting goals of the organisation are also integrated. Moreover, this chapter will also show the collaborative problem-solving skills requirements within the control room crew and supporting and supervisory roles. Additionally, the operators require knowledge about the SOPs in routine, non-routine/normal and also in abnormal situations and need to be aware of the situations and conditions of their application. This means that the focus of this chapter is on the transfer conditions, which should be of special importance for the applied community (Wickens et al 2012).

In the following, I will present the knowledge and skills requirements in routine, non-routine/normal and non-routine/abnormal situations in a contrasting manner. However, by way of introduction, I will begin with general aspects of mental models which are deemed important as foundations of action in all three situations.

3.1 Mental Models for Process Control

Kragt and Landeweerd (1974) as well as assume that control room operators need a mental model or situation model (Vicente et al. 2004) of the invisible process which influences their actions and decisions. Mental models are organised knowledge structures that operators construct to understand and explain their experiences (Johnson-Laird 2001; Sternberg 2009) representing a specific task or knowledge domain (Uitdewillingen et al. 2010). The origin of the mental model concept is attributed to Craik (1943) (Darabi et al. 2009; Hodgkinson and Healy 2008), who suggested that a mental model is a spontaneous internal representation of the relevant information about immediate problems for the purpose of construction a solution (Darabi et al. 2009). Mental models describe a person's representation of some physical system, and are based on an analog representation of causal relationships and interactions between plant components (Rouse and Morris 1985). Darabi et al. (2009) define mental models as spontaneously generated internal representation of the conceptual and causal interrelations among elements of a problem that enable the problem solver to explore potential solutions.

The mental models are constrained by the operator's implicit theories about his/her experiences, which can be more or less accurate (Sternberg 2009). Therefore, the operator's mental or situational model is an incomplete mental representation that integrates the operator's current understanding of the state of the system (both physical and functional aspects of the plant and the automated control system, Vicente et al. 2004). Figure 3.1 displays a mental model of my doctoral student working in a steel plant on factors affecting the outcome of steel in tons.

With relevance for skill and knowledge acquisition, Norman (1983) suggests considering four aspects concerning mental models, on which I will primarily concentrate in this book:

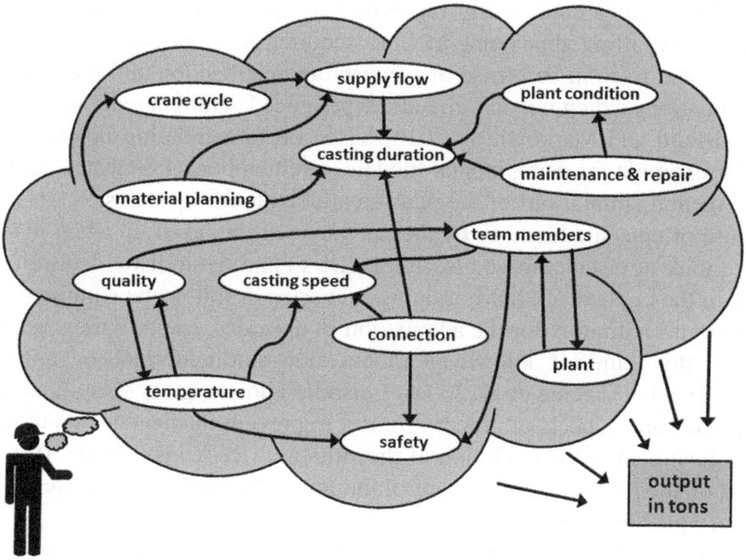

Fig. 3.1 Example picture of a mental model of my doctoral student representing the process in a steelwork (Groß and Kluge 2012)

- The target system, which is the system the operator is learning, e.g. a plant
- The conceptual model of the target system, which is supposed to provide an appropriate and accurate representation thereof
- The scientist's conceptualisation of the mental model used by instructors, designers, scientists and engineers
- The user's mental model, which is a naturally evolving model through interaction and experiences with the target system (Norman 1983, p. 7)

With respect to Norman's (1983) and Darabi et al.'s (2009) assertion that mental models develop through interaction and experiences with the target system, mental models develop through experiences and emerge with repeated generation and progression which are stored in episodic memory (Tulving 2002). Episodic memory captures real and simulated operating experience with the plant, acquired from actual operating experience and from training scenarios. Episodic memory (Tulving 2002) makes mental time travel possible. "Episodic memory is about 'what', 'where' and 'when'" (Tulving 2002, p. 3). It is assumed to share many features with semantic memory but also possesses features that semantic memory does not (Tulving and Markowitsch 1998). Semantic memory stores general knowledge about the world and serves as the memory to remember facts that are not unique to the operator and that are not recalled in a particular temporal context (Sternberg 2009). Episodic memory enables mental time travel through subjective time, thus allowing the operator to re-experience previous experiences (Tulving 2002). Episodic memory brings the past into the present and enables us – in contrast to all other non-human beings in the world – not only to learn from experience in principle but also to consciously remember the point in time when we had this experience. Recalling this point in time requires an "episodic retrieval mode" (Tulving 2002, p. 5) in the sense of a conscious recollection and remembering of similar situations which one has already experienced. Thinking and memory act in concert (Brand and Markowitsch 2010) based on remembering biographical episodes, for example for using mental models to remember relationships and events, to "run" mental simulations of the plant to anticipate future states.

The use of episodic memory by the operator will be taken up again in Chap. 4, when we look at instance-based learning (IBLT) and naturalistic decision making (NDM). In the context of NDM, training scenarios in full-scope simulator training are important facilitators for the acquisition of episodes, because they are the only source of this kind of knowledge about non-routine/normal or non-routine/abnormal events (Vicente et al. 2004). Episodic knowledge is also important as it contains temporal aspects of process control to prevent inadequate and to facilitate correct adjustment to the evolution of the situation (Rußwinkel et al. 2011).

Based on the relevant process control literature, the following features of mental models of operators were carved out:

What does such a mental model contain? An operator's mental model includes:

- Knowledge about the technical systems to be controlled (Veldhuyzen and Stassen 1977),
- Knowledge of the plant's physical systems and their characteristics and interconnectivity (Vicente et al. 2004),
- Knowledge about the properties of disturbances likely to affect the systems (Veldhuyzen and Stassen 1977), and
- Knowledge about the criteria and strategies associated with the control task (Veldhuyzen and Stassen 1977).

How can a mental model be helpful? An operator's mental model:

- Serves as a mnemonic device for remembering relationships and events (Williams et al. 1983),
- Supports the operator in integrating separate indications and accounting for all data (Vicente et al. 2004),
- Supports the operator in developing cause-and-effect relationships in explaining plant behaviour and indications (Vicente et al. 2004),
- Provides the basis for estimating the "state" of system variables that are invisible and not directly displayed (Williams et al. 1983),
- Supports the understanding of unexpected phenomena that occur as the task progresses (Veldhuyzen and Stassen 1977), and
- Aids the operator in developing a description that includes plant state at a higher level than single indications, such as process performance and goal achievement (Vicente et al. 2004).

What does the operator use mental models for in concrete terms? The operator uses his/her mental model:

- To make inferences in order to find causes of observed events (Rasmussen and Goodstein 1985),
- For calculations of expected control performance (Rouse and Morris 1985),
- To perform internal experiments (Rasmussen and Goodstein 1985) and to "run" mental simulations of the plant in order to anticipate future states of the plant or to evaluate plant performance under various configurations (Vicente et al. 2004),
- To develop and adopt control strategies and select proper control actions (Veldhuyzen and Stassen 1977),
- To determine whether or not actions led to desired results (Veldhuyzen and Stassen 1977), and
- To inertly visualise performance strategies and their consequences in relation to the organisational goals such as production and safety.

To summarise the characteristics listed above, the common themes in mental model research have been *describing, explaining and predicting system behaviour* (Rouse and Morris 1985). "Mental models are the mechanism whereby humans are able to generate descriptions of system purpose and form, explanations of system functioning and observed system states and future system states" (Rouse and Morris 1985, p. 7, Fig. 3.2). Moray (1996) raises the issue in this respect that in the field of human factors, operators of process industries such as NPP, chemical factories or petroleum distillation plants are working "with many degrees of freedom, hundreds or even thousands of displays and controls, and computer driven automation with hundreds of pages of display" (p. 166). Such systems are far too large for an operator to be able to track the exact value of all variables at once, also due to time lags and phase lags in response to inputs and too many levels of automation. For this reason, mental models of operators of process control are not comparable to the mental model research in general and in cognitive psychology, for example by Johnson-Laird or Gentner and Stevens (1983), in which described investigations are conducted in laboratory settings using reasoning tasks or physical devices (Moray 1996, p. 164). Moray (1996) proposes that operators in such complex industrial plants normally operate at a high level of abstraction, because only then can they handle the workload of these complex systems. Mental models are therefore also considered the means for simplification of complex systems (Darabi et al. 2009).

In Fig. 3.2, the relationship between the purposes of mental models and Rasmussen's taxonomy of mental models (1983; Rasmussen and Goodstein 1985) is displayed. The taxonomy moves from concrete to abstract perspectives in five types of mental models:

- The physical form: Physical appearance and anatomy, material and form, locations,
- The physical function: Electrical, mechanical, chemical processes of components and equipment,
- Functional structure: "Standard" functions and processes, control loop, heat transfer, etc.

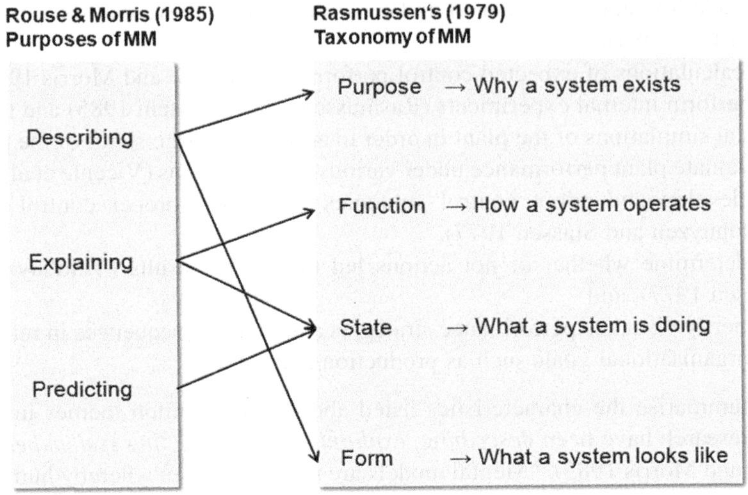

Fig. 3.2 A combined consideration of purposes of Mental Models (MM) according to Rouse and Morris (1985) and Rasmussen's Taxonomy (1979)

- Abstract function: General structure, mass, energy, information flow topology, and
- Functional meaning/purpose: Production flow models, system objectives.

According to Rasmussen and Goodstein (1985) and Vicente et al. (2004), by using their mental models, operators need to be able to move up and down to different levels of abstraction (Wickens and Hollands 2000): In the case of a failure of a part or subsystem, the operator needs to think on a very concrete level in terms of variables such as steam or water flows, valve settings or heat measurement. At other times, he/she must conceptualise on more abstract levels, for example relating to thermodynamics of energy conversion, which requires thinking about the appropriate balance between mass and energy. Finally, the mental model must allow for thinking on an even more abstract level, defined in terms of concepts like plant safety, human risk and company profits (Wickens and Hollands 2000).

Relevance for Knowledge and Skill Acquisition

For skill acquisition, three questions arise in relation to mental models: How can they be meaningfully (1) acquired, (2) differentiated, and (3) corrected in the complex technical system environment?

Concerning the acquisition, according to Norman (1983), mental models are constrained by such things as the user's technical background and previous experiences with similar systems, and the structure of the human information processing system (p. 8). For the training designer, it makes a great deal of sense, for example, to familiarise oneself with the particularities of process control of a respective organisation and the specific process industry, as in Chap. 2, in order to understand the important aspects of the general mental model for the respective process control task, the so-called target system. The target system of the mental model is the system which an operator is using or operating. As was introduced above, major differences exist among process industries as target systems, such as number of routings, number of raw materials, number of finished goods, equipment type, equipment flexibility, formulation multiplicity, and product variety (Dennis and Meredith 2000). Wickens and Hollands (2000) stress that there are clear differences between experts and novices with regard to their respective mental models, as experts have a superior mental model of the process, its time constraints, and interconnectivity, are better at anticipating the future, and have a broader spotlight of attention, which guards against cognitive tunnelling. They also use a conscious setting of the speed-accuracy trade-off to go slow, because experts know that rapid actions carried out with sluggish and complex systems can be an invitation to error and instability (Wickens and Hollands 2000).

Concerning the elaboration and differentiation of a mental model, according to Norman (1983), the more prior experiences somebody has with this type of technical system or a similar one, the more differentiated the manner in which experiences on the job or simulator experience can be integrated into the existing mental model. The method of task fractionation introduced in Chap. 4, in which the task of controlling a mental model is broken down into simpler mental models, which are then acquired in a series of increasing complexity through simulated experience, might be an effective training approach here, and we will elaborate on this in Chap. 5. During formal basic training, the operator has developed some form of mental model of the idealised plant, which focuses on the original plant design and theoretical foundations (Vicente at al. 2004). However, this idealised model will change and become differentiated during his/her time in the control room. Shift-accompanying evaluations of events can, for instance, be helpful in terms of utilising on-the-job experiences for the differentiation of one's own mental model.

Finally, experience is a useful tool for the repair of faulty mental models (Greene and Azevedo 2007; Sternberg 2009, p. 284). In this regard, it is particularly important that before gathering the concrete experience, for example in simulation/simulator-based training, the learner explicitly names his/her hypotheses, for instance regarding the dynamic development or the interconnectedness of a situation. Through the concrete experience, the mental models can then be corrected through the comparison of the expected result with the actual result.

3.2 Knowledge and Skills for Routine Situations

Routine situations (see Chap. 2) as defined by Wickens and Hollands (2000) require normal control and regulation of the process which is well handled by standard operating procedures (SOPs). Routine situations include tasks such as process monitoring or scheduled testing of routine equipment. The routine tasks addressed in this book are called supervisory control in recognition of the fact that the operator's role in process control is one of monitoring automatically controlled

Fig. 3.3 A control room operator monitoring the plant (Photo courtesy of BP Gelsenkirchen/Ruhr Oel GmbH)

systems for the purpose of detecting, diagnosing, and compensating for system failures (Rouse and Morris 1985) by using SOPs. Most of the time, operators maintain vigilant over the process that changes relative infrequently and changes slowly when it does (Gaddy and Wachtel 1992, see Fig. 3.3). In contrast to an airline crew task, the level of stimulation in an NPP is lower, performance feedback is less apparent and less immediate and the degree of control is less whereas the responsibility is potentially greater in terms of risk to public health and safety (Gaddy and Wachtel 1992). Hollnagel and Woods (2005) describe that in process industries with approx. 2,000–10,000 process variables, the frequency of operator actions is 5–6 per hours with less than 1 min of time allowed for operator actions; in nuclear power generating stations with 10,000–20,000 process variables, the frequency of operator actions is 1 per hour and 1–30 min time allowed for operator actions.

As was already described in Table 2.2 in Chap. 2, in routine situations, the main task consists of monitoring, keeping records of events, adjusting the system with regard to disturbances or to counteract unwanted deviations, and applying appropriate strategies to support both safety and productivity. A study by Yin and Laberge (2010) outlines the routine tasks of an operator in a refinery and the way in which operators use their mental models.

Digression: How process operators derive, update, and apply mental models

Yin and Laberge (2010) vividly describe how process control operators of a chemical plant use and apply their mental models during a shift. Based on a ethnographic approach, 10 male expert console operators with work experience ranging between 13 and 30 years (at least 8 as field operators) were observed from

Table 3.1 Typical weekday day shift (Yin and Laberge 2010)

Parts of day shift	
Coming on shift (6–7 am)	Shift handover and discussion with outgoing operator, review shift log for clarification, email updates for operational matters and updates, check system console displays for critical system notifications such as bypasses and alarms
Morning (7–10 am)	Shift meeting/briefing by supervisor, "virtual rounds" done from the console, mentally visualising what he/she would see if he/she was out in the unit, scrolling through the displays to observe process set-up for an overview of the unit's conditions, updates for production planning, request and monitor lab results
Late morning (10–12 noon)	Submit request for quality checks and monitor lab results Manage process, update shift log
Afternoon (12 noon–5 pm)	Manage process, update shift log, request and monitor lab results
Prior to end (5–6 pm)	Prepare and await shift handover

the start of their shift (6 am) to the end (6 pm), amounting to120 h of observation in total. The work day of the console operators is illustrated in Table 3.1.

Operators observed in the study attributed much of their system and process knowledge included in their mental model to the *many years of practical experience* as field operators. The field experience and experienced incidents and upsets serve as a major source *for deriving and developing their mental models, so that they know the plant outside in order to work inside* (Yin and Laberge 2010), including, for instance, knowledge about the line-up, the layout of the plant, how the process works internally, why the equipment is at certain places, what is happening in each component, what the operating procedures are. The field experience was assumed to be useful as operators were able to quickly relate newly encountered scenarios to past events in order to support their decision making.

The "up-to-the minute model" (Vicente at al. 2004) or the mental model of the current situation ensued, for example, through the shift handover, when operators were informed by outgoing operators about any operational changes such as equipment failure, faults or bypasses. As equipment conditions change during a shift, operators returning back to work 12 h after their previous shift may find that the process units are in a different set-up or operation mode (Yin and Laberge 2010).

Mental models are used by the console operators when they apply efficient scanning strategies and monitoring priorities, for example to critical production areas and in terms of where to look, what to look out for, what values to expect, and why the values are as they are (Yin and Laberge 2010). As in the description by Vicente et al. (2004), experienced operators quickly filter and point out cues and problems on the displays; this is termed proactive monitoring and has already been described by Hollnagel (2007). In addition to specific monitoring strategies, when taking actions, console operators do not "blindly follow a sequence of instructions" (Yin and Laberge 2010, p. 1949) but rather visualise the current process flow and initiate systematic action in close consultation with field operators while monitoring

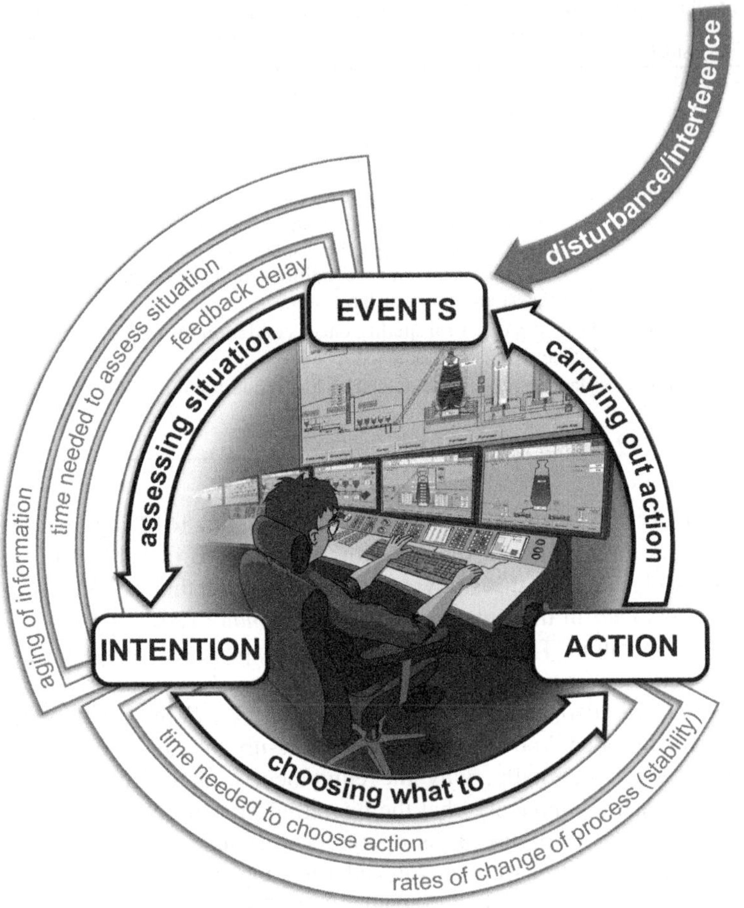

Fig. 3.4 The contextual control model (COCOM) by Hollnagel (2007)

the reaction of the process towards achieving the desired state. In summary, console operators require a strong sense of spatial mapping and causal relationships within the units being monitored and controlled in order to strategically monitor the process and to coordinate with field operators (Yin and Laberge 2010).

End of digression

According to Hollnagel (2007) and Hollnagel and Woods (2005), the control task is a cyclical one. In the contextual control model (COCOM, Hollnagel 2007; Hollnagel and Woods 2005), controlling and adjusting a system contains a cyclical relation linking events, followed by the assessment of the situations, followed by intentions, followed by choosing what to do, and actions taken (Fig. 3.4).

To illustrate the knowledge requirements included in the COCOM, I refer to two additional publications by Kluwe (1997) and Vicente et al. (2004), which adapt it

Table 3.2 Types of knowledge for process control (Kluwe 1997) applied to the COCOM by Hollnagel

Epistemic structure (data and rules)	
System knowledge	
Plant level:	Device knowledge (→ assessing the situation)
Interface level:	Display knowledge (→ assessing the situation)
	Indicator available (Vicente et al. 2004)
Control knowledge	
Plant level:	Causal knowledge (→ choosing what to do)
Interface level:	Operating knowledge (→ choosing what to do)
Heuristic structures (cognitive processes)	
Cognitive processes for the acquisition and generation of knowledge	
Cognitive processes for the transformation of knowledge	

more strongly to process control in routine situations. Kluwe (1997) proposes four knowledge types to be relevant for process control (Table 3.2).

To evaluate and assess the situation (Fig. 3.4), the operator needs *system* knowledge about facts relating to the technical system such as components, the structure, the organisation and behaviour of the plant (Kluwe 1997); this is equivalent to the operator's mental model. Knowledge about plant behaviour includes knowledge about temporal aspects such as response or reaction time or duration of processes (de Keyser 1995). It also contains knowledge about the cause-and-effect relations between parts and units as well as their functions ("how-it-works knowledge", Kluwe 1997).

System knowledge comprises knowledge on the plant level, called *device knowledge*, and on the interface level, called *display knowledge* (Kluwe 1997, p. 66).

- *Device* knowledge refers to the concrete physical plant and the technical system "behind" the interface.
- *Display* knowledge represents the organisation and function of the interface, knowledge about location and meaning of input and output units and the information displayed (Kluwe 1997).

System knowledge can be described in terms of semantic networks with a hierarchical structure made up of relations such as "is a…"-relation, "has a…"-- relation, part-whole relations, spatial relations and temporal relations (Kluwe 1997, p. 66). At the beginning of each shift, the mental model is updated by the operator into an *up-to-the-minute* mental model, for example by updating status, operating mode, ongoing maintenance activities (Yin and Laberge 2010; Vicente et al. 2004).

As proposed above, system knowledge is required for what Hollnagel (2007) calls "assessing the situation" and what Vicente et al. (2004) calls situation assessment. *Situation assessment* refers to general diagnosis and the process of constructing an explanation to account for observations (Vicente et al. 2004). Diagnosis refers to searching for the causes of non-routine/normal and non-routine/abnormal symptoms and consequently at the same time determines what, for the operator, is a normal or abnormal situation. Situation assessment is supported by monitoring activities such as confirming expectations about plant state, pursuing unexpected findings, checking the likelihood of problems, validating initial indications, and determining an appropriate referent for a specific indication (Vicente et al. 2004). For assessing the situation, Vicente et al. (2004) considers knowledge about the set of indicators available (declarative), location of indicators (declarative), how to read indicators, how they work and how they fail (procedural) as well as how to assess and configure displays (procedural) as important. Finally, the operator also holds knowledge about priorities and frequencies with which relevant indicators should be monitored (Vicente at al. 2004).

Instead of situation assessment, many authors (e.g. Flin et al. 2008; Patrick et al. 2006a; Stachowski et al. 2009; Uitdewillingen et al. 2010; Waller et al. 2006) also speak of situation *awareness*. In a very global sense, as Salmon et al. (2009) define it, situation awareness is an "individual's dynamic awareness of the ongoing external situation" (p. 8). Situation assessment is also defined as the "up-to-the-minute comprehension of task-relevant information that enables appropriate decision making under stress" (p. 59). Endsley (1995, 2000) defines situation awareness as "the perception of the elements in the environment within a volume of time and space, the comprehension of their meaning and the projection of their status in the near future" (1995 p. 36). It is understood as including three levels: (1) perception, (2) comprehension and (3) projection, and is defined as a state of knowledge about a dynamic environment, which is assumed to be different from the *process of situation assessment* to achieve that knowledge (Endsley 2000). On the whole, most of the studies on situation awareness were conducted with regard to rather dynamic processes in aviation, air traffic control or military operations, capturing dynamic changes within seconds, minutes or a few hours (Wickens 2008). In its origins, it was developed less for rather slow dynamic environments such as process control, and more for military cockpits (Prince and Salas 2000). Durso and Sethumadhavan (2008) propose that the process of achieving situation awareness is situation assessment, with the latter providing information about how an operator acquires information guided by the use of his/her mental models, scripts and schemas which include a time constant of hours, days and years. The operator's system knowledge and mental models are assumed to aid the understanding and comprehension of the current state via top-down processes and the user's mental model as the most critical element for the prediction of how the situation is going to develop (see Sect. 3.1 and Endsley 2000).

In the further course of the text, I will favour the term *situation assessment* as used by Vicente et al. (2004), as situation assessment provides a more behaviour-related term for that which an operator "does", which knowledge he/she requires for this, and how one might observe or measure it in terms of a later evaluation. Situation awareness (product) would then be the product of the situation assessment (process) (Endsley 2000).

Turning back to the situation assessment, the time needed to evaluate and assess the current situation and the time needed to select from action alternatives must be considered in relation to the time that is available for carrying out the action, which is expressed as the window of opportunity (Hollnagel 2007, p. 7). Therefore, according to Hollnagel (2007), time plays an important role in process control. The assessment of the situation is susceptible to delays in feedback or responses from the process, or applications being controlled, as well as to the aging of information (Hollnagel 2007, p. 7). The aging of information is itself dependent on how long the evaluation takes, which leads to an intricate coupling of the two (Hollnagel 2007, p. 7).

For "choosing what to do" (Fig. 3.4), *response planning* is required to decide on a course of action based on the situation assessment (Vicente et al. 2004). Monitoring activities support response planning by the assessment of goal achievement, assessment of potential side effects of considered actions, assessment of means for goal achievement, obtaining feedback on actions and assessing preconditions for action. From Kluwe's (1997) knowledge perspective, "choosing what to do" requires *control knowledge*. Control knowledge includes input-output-rule knowledge about how to perform changes of system states, how to interact with the system and how to reach control goals (Kluwe 1997), for example "if a given state s (t) and action o, than state s(t + 1) will result" or "if goal state s(t + 1) and given state s(t), then perform action o". Control knowledge as *causal knowledge* enables the operator to use specific cause-and-effect relations to select a control action, for example a sequence (Bainbridge 1991, 2012) in order to achieve, for instance, a certain production goal.

On the interface level, control knowledge equals *operating knowledge* such as input sequences performed on the interface (Kluwe 1997), for example where one adjusts a target value, closes a valve, or to put it simply "which buttons to press".

The choice of action depends on the stability of the process and on the window of opportunity. Depending of the type of process industry, it might be more important to do something quickly than to invest time finding the optimal solution. This means that based on their target state mental models, operators need to derive, for example, the correct timing for action to be performed (not too early, not too late), the speed (not too slow, not too fast) and also the duration of an action (neither too long nor too brief).

Looking at the cyclical process in flow, according to Hollnagel (2007), operators are aware of the dynamic dependencies with the aim of reducing the time needed to assess the current state and to choose an action. Therefore, operators balance *proactive* and *reactive* monitoring and control. Operators look ahead in order to be able to react more quickly. Through the use of anticipation, the operator gains time by reducing the need to evaluate the situation in detail in terms of what happened and the need for feedback (Hollnagel 2007). By being prepared for control actions, actions may be taken faster and the necessary resources may be made be available ahead of time.

Referring back to Kluwe's (1997) knowledge classification, the heuristic structure is not explained in detail. I interpret his remarks such that the heuristic structure, i.e. the cognitive processes, are decisive for acquiring further knowledge from practical experience in routine, non-routine/normal and non-routine/abnormal situations as well as, for example, in simulator training with a technical system.

Moreover, they are also important for differentiating and generalising one's own knowledge with increasing experience, for example on-the-job, i.e. through assimilation and accommodation processes (Proctor and Dutta 1995; Patrick 1992; Johnson in press). This was described in the chapter about mental models and their evolution.

Taking up the remarks in Chap. 2, the COCOM process also needs to be put in the context of the introduced "recipe knowledge". Due to the varying nature of the raw materials that are processed, as described in Chap. 2, and depending on the respective process industry, knowledge about the "recipes" in the production of products is relevant, especially in steel and chemical companies. This is because (a) variation in raw material leads to variations in recipes for producing the final products, and (b) especially in the chemical industry, for example, from a small number of raw materials (such as crude oil, salt or water) tens of thousands of products are synthesised. This recipe knowledge contains declarative and procedural knowledge of how, in terms of with which ingredients, with which plant, in which sequence, and with which quality certain production steps need to be performed.

Finally, after introducing the requirements for controlling the technical process in terms of technical and taskwork skills, it should be pointed out that the operator needs non-technical personal and teamwork skills.

Non-technical skills "are cognitive, social and personal resource skills that complement technical skills and contribute to safe and efficient task performance" (Flin et al. 2008, p. 1).

For routine situations, non-technical skills of the operator include regulating his/her workload so that the tasks are cognitively more manageable (Vicente et al. 2004). Workload regulation by the operator deals with issues such as task prioritisation, job scheduling, allocating tasks and personnel (Vicente et al. 2004). If operators can effectively regulate their workload so that it is well calibrated to their cognitive capabilities, then they will rarely put themselves in a position where errors will occur. Although Vicente et al. (2004) points out the importance of these non-technical skills for the control room operator, no training contents or offers for these skills can usually be found in the training of the control room operator.

Taking all of the remarks on mental models and routine control situations according to the COCOM together, the following training objectives emerge for a training program which should enable the operator to master routine tasks (Table 3.3): *Training objectives are a statement about the knowledge and skills an operator is supposed to apply after a phase of deliberately designed learning experiences (e.g. on-, off- and near-the-job) for knowledge and skill acquisition, and include a statement about the conditions under which the knowledge and skills are supposed to be applied (e.g. under conditions of high mental workload*) (Kluge and Burkolter 2013). Ideally, training objectives are stated in such a way that they simultaneously inform about the operationalisation in the form of measurement instruments or procedures (Goldstein and Ford 2002; Salas et al. 2006). This is difficult in the case of this book, as the training objectives should be tailored to the respective application situation. In this sense, they should be used as the starting

Table 3.3 Training objectives for routine tasks in accordance with the tasks described in the COCOM (Hollnagel 2007)

To be able to assess the situation:

The operator possesses an accurate *mental model* of the target system for which he is responsible.

The operator must be able to describe, explain and predict system behaviour of the target system.

The operator applies

- display knowledge about the interface,
- knowledge about indicators, location of indicators and how to configure displays,
- knowledge about priorities and frequencies with which relevant indicators should be monitored,
- knowledge about the properties of disturbances likely to affect the systems,
- diagnosis skills, in terms of skills for searching for causes of deviations,
- knowledge about plant states and criteria of safe states,
- monitoring skills in terms of strategies to confirm expectations and pursue unexpected findings,
- strategies for proactive and reactive monitoring.

For choosing what to do/response planning

The operator applies

- skills to choose the correct control actions in the case of routine adjustments,
- knowledge on variations in raw material and how this requires certain adjustments,
- control knowledge on the plant level: Input-output-rule knowledge,
- control knowledge on interface: Level operating knowledge (input sequences).

The operator

- inertly visualises performance strategies and their consequences in relation to the organisational goals such as production and safety,
- calculates expected control performance,
- determines whether or not actions led to desired results,
- applies knowledge about the criteria (e.g. safety and productivity) associated with the control action.

Non-technical skills

The operator is able to regulate his/her workload by

- prioritising tasks,
- scheduling jobs,
- allocating tasks and personnel.

point for the formulation of training goals for the training designer with a specific target group in mind.

One more comment to conclude: In most process industries, operators who monitor and manage from behind a console workstation (a distributed control system, DCS) are required to possess a certain level of expertise in terms of field experience as a field operator (Yin and Laberge 2010; Bullemer et al. 1997). In many plants of interest in this book, operators had been working for 10 years before being picked to work in the control room (Yin and Laberge 2010), because field experience is assumed to lead to a more accurate cognitive representation of the plant layout, and to a more accurate mental model of the performance of plant units and control actions in terms of SOPs. For example, in refineries and petrochemical plants, the console operator is supposed to be required to first be certified as a field operator in all field areas (Bullemer et al. 1997).

3.2.1 Evaluation Possibilities

As introduced in the Chap. 1, for each of the respective training goals, the corresponding evaluation possibilities/options should also be presented. In this respect, only a few examples are shown in order to provide an impetus regarding the direction one can take when thinking about the development or use of evaluation instruments. I do not address psychometric properties or advantages and disadvantages of using methods in this regard. The procedures and methods listed under "evaluation possibilities" should provide food for thought regarding training evaluation and criteria. Crandall et al. (2006) also provide an overview concerning the use of Cognitive Task Analysis for the development of measurement and evaluation tools (see Chap. 5). However, these need to be adapted for each area of application, or even tailor-made. The specific implementation modalities and the concrete application can be found in the cited literature. Let us recall at this point that evaluation means the systematic, scientific, empirical, hypothesis-oriented investigation of effectiveness and efficiency of an intervention, with the aim of using the evaluation results to (re)design and apply the findings in the socio-technical context of training decisions (Goldstein 1993, p. 147; Mittag and Hager 2000, p. 103). The book will address the aspects of how to assess training effectiveness in terms of measuring training results by providing ideas on how to measure learning improvements.

Interesting aspects of the evaluation for routine tasks include the consideration of the training goals and the assessment of the operator's mental model. However, for the evaluation or measurement of training effectiveness, it is necessary to note that mental models are differently accessible to conscious verbal description or concrete retrieval. Depending on the nature of the task, the operator is more or less aware of his or her manipulation and usage of mental model. According to Rouse and Morris (1985), one is likely to be totally unaware of manipulating one's own neural network representation, whereas the start-up of a plant or problem-solving in a non-routine/abnormal situation is likely to be very open to awareness and verbalisation. Rouse and Morris term this distinction the implicitness or explicitness of the model manipulations (Fig. 3.5). The second distinction is the distinction between the levels of discretion, meaning the extent to which an operator has a choice as opposed to being dictated by the task (Rouse and Morris 1985, p. 21). Figure 3.5 displays the distinction of the direct access to one's own mental models in line with Rouse and Morris (1985). The less accessible the mental model, the more laborious the measurement of the matching mental model.

In the following, different evaluation possibilities for the measurement of mental models are introduced, which we and others (Funke 1992; Kersting 1999; Kluwe 1997; Meyer 2008) have already tested in applied research. Our experience has

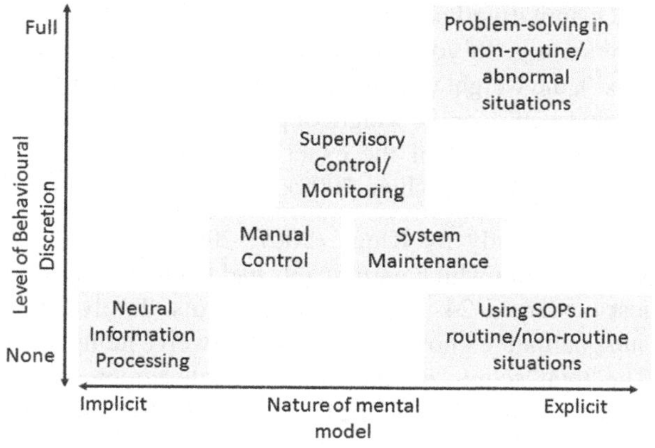

Fig. 3.5 Distinctions between the nature of mental models and level of discretion as indicators of their conscious accessibility with assessment instruments

found them to be valid and reliable and they can also be developed for organisations with a reasonable expenditure and are economical to implement.

Assessing mental models with traditional knowledge tests: From my perspective, Kluwe's (1997) classification lends itself very well to the measurement of training effectiveness in order to derive concrete forms of knowledge. For instance, a display knowledge test on the system knowledge/interface level can construe where operators have to answer questions about the location and meaning of interface units, for example "Which units of the interface serve to operate the mineral silos?" An operating knowledge test (control knowledge/interface level) would require the recollection of standard input sequences like SOPs, for example how to control crude gas temperature. The answers should provide a sequence of inputs to be performed on the interface. Device and causal knowledge could contain questions about the components of the plant, their characteristics and interconnections, for example "Which temperature must the crude gas have when filler is to be released from the filler silo by the dust arrester?" The study by Kluwe (1997) showed that the type of knowledge acquired by operators is strongly affected by the type of training they have undergone.

Assessing knowledge about cause-and-effect relationships as a component of mental models: These knowledge tests for measuring mental models can be developed on different levels of precision of the answers, as shown by an example from the work of Kluge (2008). Mental models may be assessed in terms of semi-qualitative, qualitative and quantitative knowledge (Kluge 2008):

- Semi-qualitative knowledge requires the *identification* of a relationship between input and "invisible" variables and between "invisible" as well as output variables (e.g. "If you alter the values of x, z, and y, those of a and b will change as well.")
- Qualitative knowledge requires the *identification of features* such as dynamic changes (exponential growth or decline, e.g. "a increases by itself") and parallel effects ("The value of b influences a") or identification of the relationship's direction ("a influences c")

- Quantitative knowledge requires the *specification of the exact weight* of influence (e.g. "If you change the value of x, then a increases by 10 times the value of x"), the weight of dynamics (e.g. "a increases by 90 % of the value reached in the next step"), or the weight of parallel effects ("a influences b by a factor of 0.25"); or recognition of the exact simulation algorithm (e.g. "$a_{t+1} = 2 * y_t + 0.5 * z_t + 0.9 * a_t$", Kluge 2008).

In the study by Kluge (2007, 2008), each item consisted of six alternative answers from which participants had to choose one correct answer. The knowledge test contained 24 multiple-choice items. Twelve items required semi-qualitative and qualitative knowledge; the other twelve items required quantitative knowledge. The total scores on the knowledge test represented the percentage of correct answers. The idea of measuring qualitative, semi-quantitative and quantitative aspects of the mental models goes back to the work of Kersting (1991/1999). The knowledge test scores showed substantial correlations with the control performance in a complex technical system, with quantitative knowledge being the strongest predictor (Kluge 2008).

Assessing mental models using graphics. Mental models are assumed to be frequently pictorial and image-like rather than symbolic in a list-processing sense (Rouse and Morris 1985). This is supported by Wickens and Hollands (2000, p. 514), who state that although controls are often adjusted in a discrete fashion, the variables that are being controlled are essentially analog, continuous processes. Thus, the operator's mental model of the process and the complex system should be analog and continuous rather than discrete and symbolic (Wickens and Hollands 2000, p. 514).

An assessment tool that addresses the pictorial aspect in greater detail is the measurement of mental models using the diagnosis of structural knowledge as proposed by Funke (1992). Funke (1992) uses the diagnosis of structural knowledge in the form of a causal diagram analysis. In order to save the trainees from recalling the exact quantitative structure of relationships, Funke (1992) assumes that the graphical form enables a facilitated presentation of the different relationships between components (see Fig. 3.6).

Additionally, the trainees have to indicate the causal structure which they suspect in graphical form. The trainees join boxes which depict the input and "invisible" throughput and output variables with arrows or connecting lines, between which they suspect a link. If the trainees are only aware of the link, they only draw a line, while if they know the operating direction (positive or negative), they draw in a "+" or "–" at the tip of the arrow; if the numerical effect factor is known, this can also be entered on the arrow.

To evaluate the mental model, the number of correct assumptions is then related to the total number of all assumed relationships and the number of correct relationships to the total number of correct relations. Quality of the mental model (QMM) is described by:

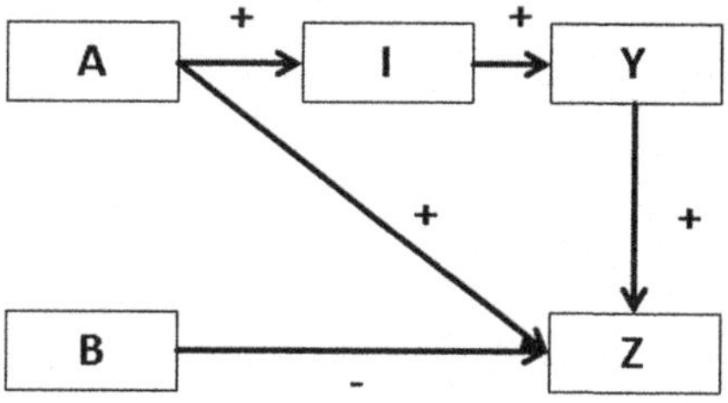

Fig. 3.6 Example of a drawn mental model of an artificial system, with A and B as input variables and Y and Z as output variables and I as "invisible" (endogenous) variable, which cannot be controlled directly, but effects the output variables as well

$$QMM = \frac{C}{C+I} \times \frac{C}{C_{\max}}$$

C = Number of correct elements, I = Number of incorrect elements, C_{max} = Maximum number of correct elements

QMM can assume values between zero (no correct element recognised) and one (all correct elements recognised). Additionally, a decomposition of the data can be undertaken if a differentiated analysis is being pursued (Funke 1992).

Measuring the quality of anticipation of future states (QaF)

In the investigation by Funke and Müller (1988, Funke 1992), besides the QMM for measuring knowledge, the authors also use the predictive quality. Analogously to the control power, *QaF is calculated as the distance of the cyclical predictions to the actually resulting state values.* According to the authors, while the QMM measures "knowledge as abstraction power" (Funke and Müller 1988, p. 180), in the sense of the projection of perceived system properties on a causal diagram, the *QaF* requires, in each case, quantitative predictions of the system behaviour without the participants having to identify the causal structure. Following a knowledge and skill acquisition phase at the target system, the trainees can, for instance, be presented with different system states and system interventions as screenshots. They are then required to predict the degree of the state variables to the next cycle. *QaF* is seen by Funke and Müller (1988) as dependent on QMM. This assumption has been confirmed, as QMM proves to be the strongest predictor of *QaF*.

Computer-based testing of mental models

In one of our own studies investigating knowledge and skill acquisition for process control tasks, we explored the potential of computer-based testing of mental models (Burkolter et al. 2010) by using the Association Structure Test (AST, Meyer 2008). This covers the way in which operators organise and interrelate concepts within a knowledge domain. The AST integrates an association task and Pathfinder network scaling on the basis of relatedness ratings into one information technology-

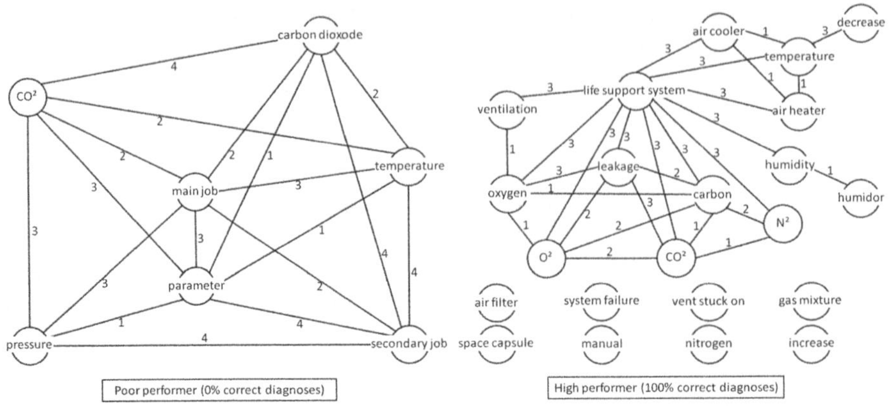

Fig. 3.7 Operators' knowledge measured by the AST (Meyer 2008) in the study by Burkolter et al. (2010) for poor and high performers in a process control task. 1 = strong relationship, 4 = no or weak relationship. Concepts that were associated in the association task but not included in the graph are displayed at the *bottom*

based test system (Fig. 3.7). There are two parts: an *association task* and *relatedness ratings*. In the association task, participants are asked to associate concepts that they think belong to a specified knowledge domain. In addition to the participants' associated concepts, thinking times during the word associations are logged. Drawing from the theory of spreading activation by Anderson (1983), semantically closely related terms are thought to follow quickly after each other, whereas semantically less related terms are assumed to result in longer pauses in thought between associations.

For the *relatedness ratings,* the associated concepts are presented as pairs, and their relatedness is rated. The maximum number of concepts that is selected for pairwise comparisons can be determined in the configuration of the AST. In our own study, a limit of 15 concepts was employed (Burkolter et al. 2010). If the number of terms entered during the first stage of the AST exceeds the specified maximum, the total number of terms selected for pairwise comparison in the second stage is equal to the specified maximum (i.e. 15). The sample of terms is chosen from clusters formed in the first stage: The very first term in each cluster enters the second stage; the remaining terms are selected randomly from each of the clusters in proportion to the cluster size. In this way, the selected terms represent the terms entered in the first stage, and a preservation of the cognitive structure is maintained. These relatedness ratings require neither a complex process nor a high degree of conscious processing. Therefore, the AST is thought to elicit relationships between knowledge elements that are difficult or impossible to verbalise and thus to capture a part of unconscious access to structural knowledge. For more details, see Burkolter et al. (2010).

Whether a person can regulate his/her workload cannot, of course, be measured by the procedures introduced so far. However, possibilities are provided by procedures such as the Subjective Management Test and observations in simulator exercises, which will be introduced in the upcoming chapters on non-routine/normal and non-routine/abnormal situations.

3.3 Knowledge and Skills for Non-routine/normal Situations

Non-routine tasks are infrequent, for example the start-up and shutdown of the plant or a unit before and after a revision. But standard procedures also exist for non-routine but infrequent tasks and can still be considered as normal. In this book, I define *non-routine/normal* situations as situations in which operators encounter, for example, a malfunction of the automation and have to draw on skills and procedures which have not been used for a longer period of time. The non-routine/normal sequences include, besides the start-up and shutdown, the controlling of the plant during maintenance and repair works, when special tests are conducted, or under particular weather conditions, for example when it is particularly hot or cold.

What renders a task a non-routine task? According to my definition, it is above all the rarity with which it is performed. This rare performance creates a so-called retention interval, or rather a period of non-use, which leads to the fact that due to processes of forgetting, which are expressed in a very low strength of retrieval (Bjork and Bjork 1992; Bjork 2009), the performance level is no longer present in the necessary manner. Or to put it more simply, as the saying goes: One is "rusty".

In what way and why are various tasks performed only rarely? As reported at the outset, the period of non-use depends, among other things, on the type of plant and the process industry. Operators in batch/mix processes start up plants more frequently and modify them more frequently; operators in process/flow industries do so very rarely. Thus, the start-up of a plant is a rather routine task in batch/mix processes and a rather non-routine task in process/flow industries.

Referring back to Table 2.3 in Chap. 2 and the COCOM introduced earlier in Fig. 3.4 in its basic version, non-routine/normal tasks can be divided into *planned actions* to handle scheduled tasks (Fig. 3.8), and *reactions to unexpected disturbances* (Fig. 3.9). *Planned actions* have their starting point in the COCOM with "actions" (Fig. 3.8) or rather with response planning (Vicente et al. 2004). *Planned actions* include activities such as scheduled testing of equipment to ensure that back-up and safety systems are in an acceptable state, manual changes or changing the program of automated controllers, special actions during handover at the end of the shift or during special operations such as start-up or shutdown.

Reactions to unexpected disturbances have their starting point in the COCOM in situation assessment after the unexpected disturbance has occurred, for example when alarms go off (Fig. 3.9). Referring back to Table 2.3 in Chap. 2, these tasks include the fact that disturbances and their consequences must be (1) detected and (2) communicated to the crew members (or field operator or maintenance, safety

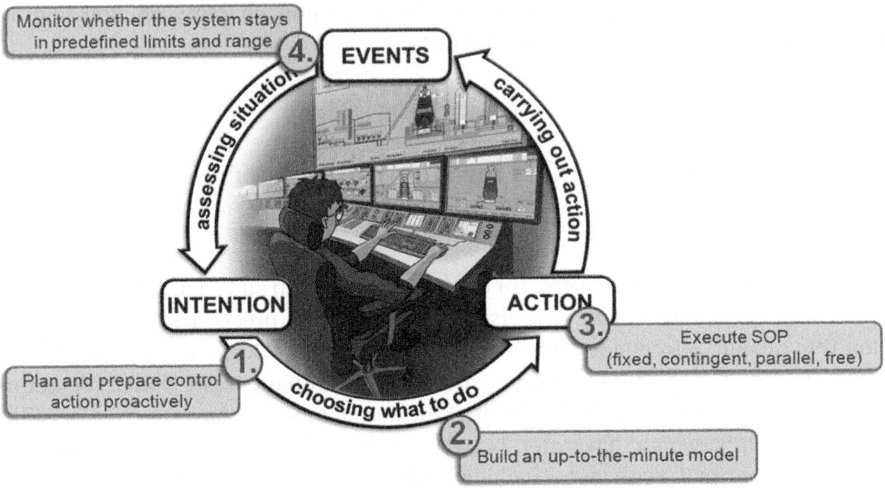

Fig. 3.8 The COCOM applied to planned action in non-routine/normal tasks

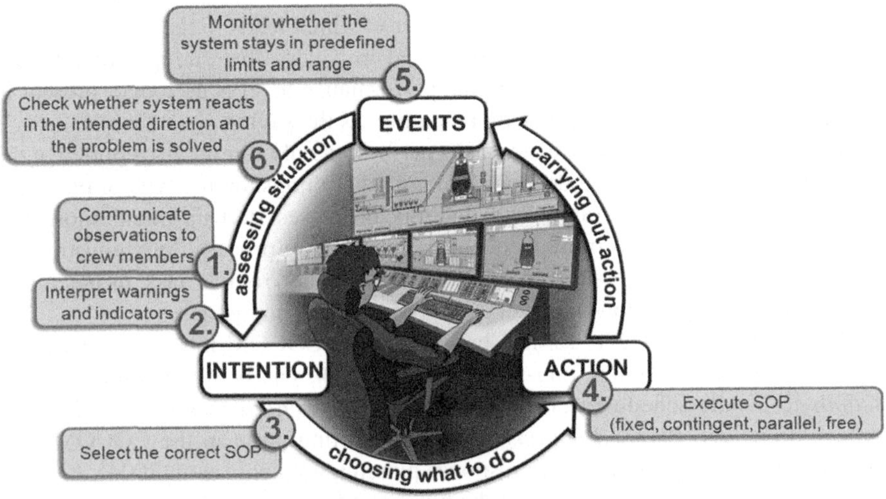

Fig. 3.9 The COCOM applied to reactions to unexpected disturbances

department, shift supervisor). Moreover, (3) the causes of faults must be diagnosed, (4) the SOP must be consulted and implemented, and (5) special inspections in the plant must be organised.

As already stressed, *planned actions* can be prepared, for example by consulting the standard operating procedures (SOPs) and being performed as control actions

Fig. 3.10 Cupboard with SOPs of a nuclear power plant in Germany (Photo courtesy of GfS/KSG, Essen)

(Gaddy and Wachtel 1992, see Fig. 3.10). SOPs are job aids which are designed "to extend human capability to store and process information" (Swezey 1987, p. 1040). They are procedural aids which provide step-by-step instructions for completing a task, and guide the user through sequences of actions (Kluge et al. 2013; Salas et al. 2006; Swezey 1987). SOPs prove to be especially useful for tasks in process control that are (a) infrequent and (b) complex or have several steps, and when (c) the costs of errors are high, and (d) task performance depends on knowing a large amount of information (Kluge et al. 2013; Rossett and Gautier-Downes 1991). But there are also poorly defined SOPs (Carvallo et al. 2005). It depends on how well SOPs are designed or problems arise from not knowing which SOP to select and implement or also the problem of incompatibility of procedures (Carvallo et al. 2005).

Using SOPs requires operating knowledge in Kluwe's sense, and which is subsequently the performance of "sequences" defined by the Sub-Goal Template method (SGT) by Ormerod, Richardson and Shepherd (1998) and Ormerod and Shepherd (2004). The SGT is a task-analysis technique in order to derive and specify learning requirements. Sub-Goal Templates (SGTs) are a *set of standard task elements that capture most of the tasks that control operators encounter in any process plant* (Ormerod et al. 1998). Our research (e.g. Burkolter et al. 2007; Kluge and Burkolter 2012) suggests that important insights for the development of training objectives and training design can be gained by using the SGT method. Sequence elements distinguish between

- *Fixed sequences*: "If S1 then x",
- *Contingent sequences*: "S2 either z then x or not z then y",
- *Parallel sequences* :"S3 then do x and y", and
- *Free sequences*: "S4 in any order x and y".

The SGT method also helps to define the declarative and procedural knowledge as the prerequisites for performing a fixed, contingent, parallel or free sequence. The knowledge of possible sequences as well as their proficient performance is an important precondition, for instance, for mental flexibility and problem-solving skills (Kluge and Burkolter 2012). For example, in cases of contingent sequences, one needs to know what the constituent characteristics of "S2" are, what "z" represents and what follows as "x" or if not "z" what "y" could be. The SGT method therefore also helps to elicit the necessary knowledge to perform and choose among the sequences.

SOPs can also be distinguished according to the number of procedural steps, the dependencies of procedural steps and the adherence to them (Fleishman and Quaintance 1984). As stated in Chap. 2, such procedures consist of part-tasks, which in turn frequently consist of several steps or sequences. Mostly, the part-tasks are performed in parallel and have to be integrated in a joint flow of action. A coordination of the part-tasks ensues through attention selection, attention switching, and attention sharing (Wickens and McCarley 2008). For this book and the training design addressed therein, it is important to be clearly aware of what, in the organisation for which the training is conceived, non-routine/normal situations actually are. Which SOPs exist? Which tasks are performed every day, every week, or only once a year or once every 10 years? Which skill level does this task then require? And which serious consequences can result if a procedure is not correctly mastered?

From my experiences with process industries and as outlined in Chap. 2, in the case of *reactions to unexpected disturbances*, a single operator does not assess the situation alone and does not decide alone how to respond to an unexpected disturbance. Rather, he discusses and consults with the other control room operators on his shift. In these unexpected disturbances, the task frequently changes from an individual problem detection to a joint problem definition and solution-finding (see below and Fig. 3.11). The reactions to unexpected disturbances are usually the

Fig. 3.11 Two control room members consulting a field operator on the telephone to clarify their observations (Photo courtesy of GfS/KSG, Essen)

scenarios which are run through in the so-called incident training in the simulator. Here, the concern is with rare events, or events which have occurred in other plants (NPPs, refineries) and which are incorporated into the training program because they could, in principle, occur in one's own plant, for example due to similar or the same type of build of the plant.

What renders the non-routine/normal situations a particular execution condition in terms of the training objectives? From the management and plant operations perspective, the human operator is requested to follow the SOPs at all times (Bullemer and Kiff 2011):

- In routine and non-routine/normal situations, operators are expected to know and follow the procedure.
- In non-routine/abnormal situations, operators are expected to use the procedure for planning and execution, and to know the initial steps and then refer to the procedure in completing the remaining steps (Bullemer and Kiff 2011).

This means that operators are required to know the SOPs, without their direct consultation in most cases, or else with their support and help.

From the human factors perspective, a particularity emerges here, in the sense that first, the non-routine/normal and abnormal situations which were described at the outset occur rather rarely and are thus less automated and proceduralised than routine tasks, which are frequently repeated. "Automaticity is a characteristic of cognitive processing in which practice-consistent component behaviors are performed rapidly, with minimal effort or with automatic allocation of attention"

(Schneider 1999, p. 63). Automatic processing is contrasted with controlled or attentive processing (Schneider 1999). Controlled processing is serial, whereas automatic processing requires minimal-effort multitask processing and is robust and highly reliable relative to controlled processing (Schneider 1999).

Second, it is precisely such sequences that frequently have to be performed in process control in non-routine situations that are, moreover, particularly susceptible to skills decay and performance decrements after periods of non-use (Arthur et al. 1998; Farr 1987; Kluge and Frank 2014). This is unfortunate, as due to the high automation and process stability in many industries, these are primarily rarely used.

Third, the non-routine/normal tasks are also special because they are performed under a higher mental workload than the routine and more procedural tasks (Waller et al. 2006), because, due to the lack of application on the job, they are less strongly proceduralised (see Fig. 3.12). Mental workload is high when the amount of information elements (see also element interactivity, Chap. 2) that needs to be processed simultaneously reaches or exceeds the information-processing resources available (Vidulich 2003). Based on the remarks of Fitts (1962/1990) as well as Proctor and Dutta (1995), it can be very justifiably assumed that in non-routine/normal situations, due to the low automaticity of the task, for example the concentration on the execution of an SOP, the total available information-processing resources are already completely drawn upon and there is no more reserve capacity (Vidulich 2003). The reserve capacity results from the total resources available minus the demands for the task that is currently being conducted (working through the SOPs). In terms of the SOPs that are not highly practised, the operator will steer his/her total available resources to information processing and attending to the conducting of the SOPs. He/she may then overlook, for example, important feedback cues or fail to hear a request or instruction from another crew member, as there is no more reserve capacity available. Therefore, during the non-routine/normal tasks, not very much is allowed to "go wrong", as the reserve capacity, which is only very small due to the high mental workload of the non-routine task, is possibly no longer sufficient for reacting appropriately to unexpected disturbances. This combination of low automaticity, low reserve capacity and skill decays makes non-routine/normal tasks more susceptible to errors than routine tasks (Fitts 1962/1990), as they are carried out on the level of involvement of conscious cognitive processes and high attentional demands while performing the task (Proctor and Dutta 1995; Johnson in press). Errors are likely to occur, accompanied by a longer performance time in comparison to routine tasks. Here, there is therefore a danger of human errors, as described, for instance, by Hollnagel (1998). Hollnagel and Woods (2005) list undesired strategies in high mental workload situations such as omissions, reduced precision, queuing, filtering, and defective parallelisation during situation assessment, simplifications in deciding what to do, applying short cuts with the intention of gaining back control over the process.

This can be illustrated by an anecdote from an employee's perspective: An older employee of a petrochemical plant once told me that he had asked his superior to

Fig. 3.12 Two operators adjusting the plant (Photo courtesy of GfS/KSG, Essen)

take him out of the control room and that he would rather work in the plant as a field operator again, as he found the "stress" even under normal conditions too great, particularly during the night shift or at the weekend when there is barely anybody else there. He was afraid that something might happen when he was alone, and he could no longer endure this mental burden in the long term. This personal portrayal demonstrates that the tension in such rarely occurring situations is indeed great, also in view of the fact that one then has to perform control actions that are rarely performed and which are therefore more liable to errors. According to Wickens and McCarley (2008, p. 4), for performance in such situations, it is important that the human mental resources which are necessary to operate the system are lower than those that are available overall, so that reserves remain available for unexpected tasks. With an increased stress level (e.g. due to a worry concerning safety), it can happen that this, in turn, limits the available resources in comparison to normal situations (Kramer and Weber 2005, p. 803).

Based on the remarks made above, training objectives can be summarised as in Table 3.4.

3.3.1 Evaluation Possibilities

What can one do to ascertain whether one has the required skills to react confidently in non-routine/normal situations? Building on the measurements of the mental models of the operator, in non-routine/normal tasks, added to this are

Table 3.4 Training objectives for non-routine/normal tasks

To implement planned actions in non-routine/normal tasks, under *conditions of higher mental workload*, the operator must be able to:
Plan and prepare the control activity proactively by having the correct SOP at hand based on the control knowledge on the plant and interface level
Build up an up-to-the minute model before the control actions are initiated
Work through the SOPs in terms of fixed, contingent, parallel or free sequences correctly without any sequence error
Monitor the system and plant behaviour so that the processes remain safe and in the predefined limits based on the system knowledge on the plant and interface level
To adequately react to unexpected disturbances, under *conditions of higher mental workload*, the operator must be able to:
Communicate observations to the plant operations team members (→described in more detail in the next chapter)
Interpret warnings and indicators correctly based on the system knowledge on the plant and interface level in order to define the problem
Choose what to do based on control knowledge on the plant and interface level
Select the correct SOP
Work through die SOPs in terms of fixed, contingent, parallel or free sequences correctly without any sequence error
Monitor the system and plant behaviour so that the processes remain safe and in the predefined limits based on the system knowledge on the plant and interface level
Check whether the systems react in the intended direction and the problem is solved
To react to unexpected disturbances, the operator must be able to use his/her mental model under *conditions of higher mental workload* to:
Integrate separate indications and accounting for all data
Develop cause-and-effect relationships in explaining plant behaviour and indications (Vicente et al. 2004)
Estimate the "state" of system variables that are invisible and not directly displayed
Understand unexpected phenomena that occur as the task progresses
Develop a description that includes plant state at a higher level such as process and safety performance
***Under conditions of higher mental workload*, the operator must be able to apply non-technical skills to:**
Effectively communicate with control room crew members
Manage workload (as in routine tasks)
Evaluate his own performance in order to avoid error due to low automaticity

specific skill aspects. For an assessment of the skills of *planned actions*, knowledge test tasks can be developed which ask what needs to be taken into account in the preparation and planning of a specific control action, for example what needs to be considered in a planned maintenance. Prior to the preparation and planning question, it can also be asked which SOP should be applied in a planned action such as a scheduled repair. Which concrete cues need to be in place for one to begin with the execution of the SOPs? What might need to be considered in particular with an SOP? To what events might the execution lead? Within which limits must the plant remain? Which errors might be made in the execution of the SOP?

To this aim, for the assessment contents, so-called Situational Judgement Tests (SJTs) can be developed, which are also commonly described as low-fidelity situations (Motowidlo et al. 1990). SJTs typically contain depictions of work-related scenarios which describe challenging scenarios that require the application of trained skills (Ritzmann 2012). The scenarios can be given in written or oral form, as videos or computer-based, and in addition to open questions, can contain a selection of possible reactions to the described situation (Christian et al. 2010; Ritzmann 2012). SJTs have already proven their worth as training evaluation instruments (Fritzsche et al. 2006; Ritzmann 2012; Ritzmann et al. 2011).

Whether a person feels confident in dealing with *reactions to unexpected disturbances* can also be measured on the basis of SJTs, but should also definitely be evaluated through concrete observation and assessments of the actual behaviour in the simulator. In contrast to the SJT, the simulator offers the possibility to observe the actual behaviour under conditions of higher mental workload. This higher workload cannot be generated "on paper", but only through a so-called immersive environment such as a full-scope simulator. "Immersion" is the subjective impression that one is participating in a holistic and realistic experience (Dede 2009). The more a virtual immersive experience is generated by behavioural, symbolic and sensory factors, the stronger the trainees' feeling of actually being "in" the setting and experiencing a higher mental workload. Furthermore, the interaction and communication with other control crew members becomes more important, which can also only be observed in the simulator.

What exactly, then, should be observed and evaluated? Firstly, the correct selection and execution of the SOPs as well as possible human errors which can arise. In an evaluation by Bullemer et al. (2010), an analysis of 32 incident reports in process industries showed that in all most 60 % of the incidents, procedures were followed incorrectly, that the wrong procedure was selected or the situation was not covered, and in many cases that the procedure was not followed or used. Bullemer and Kiff (2011) conclude that ineffective procedure use is a significant contributor to process safety incidents. Reasons include, for example, the lack of procedure classification, which leaves the decision of which SOP to be used to the judgement of the operators and supervisors.

We have tried this out in our own studies (Kluge et al. 2013; Weyers et al. 2012) and were positively surprised to find that the evaluation of errors in the execution of SOPs on the basis of Hollnagel's CREAM approach (1998, pp. 166 and onwards) is not labour-intensive to implement. With regard to *planned actions*, the focus of the assessment of training success can lie, for example, on the following errors (Hollnagel 1998):

- Planning: Inadequate plan (incomplete plan, wrong plan), priority error (wrong goal selected)
- Distraction: Task suspended, task not completed, goal forgotten, loss of orientation
- Inattention: Signal missed
- Memory failure: Item forgotten, incorrect recall, incomplete recall
- Sequence error: Omission, jump forward, jump backward, repetition, reversal

With regard to *reactions to unexpected disturbances*, the following errors, for example, are interesting for an assessment of training success (Hollnagel 1998):

- Observation missed: Overlook cue/signal, overlook measurement
- False observation: False reaction, false recognition
- Wrong identification: Mistaken cue, partial identification, or incorrect identification
- Faulty diagnosis: Wrong diagnosis, incomplete diagnosis
- Wrong reasoning: Induction error, deduction error, wrong priorities
- Decision error: Decision paralysis, wrong decision, partial decision
- Delayed interpretation: No identification, increased time pressure
- Incorrect prediction: Unexpected state change, unexpected side effects, process speed misjudged
- Communication: Is required for the joint diagnosis with the other team members' memory failures and sequence errors (as mentioned above in the planned actions).

A detailed description of the above-listed errors can be found in Hollnagel (1998), which can be used for the development of a classification system for the analysis of qualitative data such as observations or written answers to SJT as described above. There are also other error classifications; those of Hollnagel, however, are already in large-scale use and are known to engineers and psychologists alike. Consequently, they should be easier to use in training design as they are not unknown.

In addition, in these non-routine/normal situations, skills of situation assessment gain in importance. Although I prefer the term situation assessment over awareness, authors like Hogg et al. (1995) decided to measure situation awareness and developed the procedure of SACRI (Situation Awareness Control Room Inventory) (Hogg et al. 1995), which addresses the three levels of SA according to Endsley (1995a). Question wording is based on the concept of SA as a temporal state within dynamic decision making (see below). Freezing the simulator allows the investigation of a snapshot of the operator's SA, and response categories refer to qualitative trends in the state of process parameters over time. SACRI relates to:

- **Level 1** SA in terms of operators answering past or normal questions in response to directly observed readings of parameters, e.g. "In comparison to the recent past (normal status), how has the average reactor temperature developed?"
- **Level 2** SA relates to past and normal questions about parameters that cannot be observed directly, e.g. "In comparison to the recent past (or with the normal status), how has the level in the steam generators developed?"
- **Level 3** SA relates to three types of questions (past, normal, future) since prediction of future is done on the basis of what is observed directly and what has been inferred, e.g. "In comparison to now, predict how the process parameter, e.g. the temperature of the pressurizer, will develop over the next few minutes."

Response categories are: (Parameter) increases, decreases, stays the same, or increase in more than one, increase in one, decrease in one, decrease in more than one and drift in both directions (Hogg et al. 1995). Moreover, one could think further and implement procedures for measuring mental workload. In the literature, subjective (workload ratings or workload judgements), objective (e.g. secondary task performance) and physiological measures (electrocardiogram/ECG, heart rate, electroencephalogram/EEG measurement or event-related potentials/ERP, Positron Emission Tomography/PET) are suggested for the measurement of MW (Kramer and Weber 2005; Marshall 2007; Tsang and Vidulich 2006), and with the technical developments of eye tracking, pupillometric determinations of mental workload have also been suggested (Rosch and Vogel-Walcutt 2012).

3.4 Knowledge and Skills for Non-routine/abnormal Situations

In this sub-chapter, the concern is with situations which occur very rarely as very high safety standards have already been implemented, but which, due to their consequences and the associated damages to humankind and the environment, remain in our memory. Such situations include BP's Texas City refinery explosion in 2005, the explosion of the Deep Water Horizon in 2010, the explosion in Chernobyl in 1986, and the tsunami of Fukushima in 2011. Even though these situations are rare, their retrospective analysis has very frequently shown that besides factors such as rule or procedure violations, or management commitment to safety issues, the communication and cooperation of the actors on site can also be described as very problematic. Recommended reading for further information is the accident investigations report, for example on the website of www.csb.gov or the IAEA pages. In the following, I will concentrate on certain points of the collaborative problem-solving processes which are important in such abnormal situations.

Complex problem solving and dynamic decision making

Non-routine/abnormal situations include, for example, a fault or situation that has never occurred before and where there is a need for problem solving (to give an extreme example, for example, in the case of the tsunami that swept over the NPP of Fukushima) and decision making. *Decision making is a part of the attempt to gain control* (Brehmer 1992) in order to achieve some form of safe plant state, especially in HROs. What causes loss of control? According to Hollnagel and Woods (2005), the loss of control is caused by unexpected events, acute time pressure, lack of knowledge and skill, for example not knowing what has happened, what happens and what will happen, not knowing what to do and not having the necessary resources. For problem solving and decision making, knowledge-based behaviour is required (Rasmussen and Jensen 1974), which is expressed in complex problem solving (Funke and Frensch 2007; Fischer et al. 2012) and dynamic decision making (Brehmer 1992). An abnormal situation is considered to be a problem, because the human operator has several goals (see Definition of "multiple goals" Chap. 1) but does not know how these goals can be reached (Fischer et al. 2012). *Problem solving* is defined as successfully searching for an operation or a series of operations in order to transfer a given actual state of a system to a goal state (Fischer et al. 2012, p. 22). For problem solving, a *representation* must be generated or a pre-existing experienced-based representation must be recalled leading to the situation assessment (Simon 1999). "A representation includes (1) a *description* of the given situation, (2) *operators* or actions for changing the situation, and *tests* to determine whether the goal has been achieved. Applying operators creates new situations, and potential applications of all permissible operators define a branching tree of achievable situations, the *problem space*" (Simon 1999, p. 674).

Complex problem solving means "to overcome barriers between a given state and a desired goal state by means of behavioral and/or cognitive *multistep* activities" (Frensch and Funke 1995; Funke and Frensch 2007, p. 28). Complex problem solving shares the aspect of multistep activities or decisions with dynamic decision making.

Dynamic decision making means that a series and sequence of decisions is required to reach the goal. These decisions are not independent and the state of the decision problem changes, both autonomously and as a consequence of the operator's action (Brehmer 1992; Edwards 1962; Gonzales et al. 2003). In dynamic decision making in predicting the future system state, the decision maker has to take both the dynamic system developments and the effects of his/her own actions into account (Kerstholt and Raaijmakers 1997). An accurate mental model of the target systems therefore needs to represent the relation between the system parameters and their temporal characteristics (Kerstholt and Raaijmakers 1997). Dynamic decision making also contains the characteristics which have already been described in the COCOM (see above), with the aspects of aging of information, time needed to choose a course of action, windows of opportunity and feedback delay (Hollnagel 2007).

From the human factors perspective on skill acquisition, non-routine/abnormal situations are interesting, because skills and knowledge, as described, for example, by Kluwe (1997) and Vicente et al. (2004) for routine and non-routine/normal tasks are now presupposed, and the skills for dealing with non-routine/abnormal situations need to be added on top of this. The basic assumption is that one can only solve non-routine/abnormal situations if one also masters or is able to perform the other two situations and tasks.

To elucidate the procedure of the operator in non-routine/abnormal situations, the Decision Ladder by Rasmussen is frequently drawn on (Fig. 3.13 for a simplified version without the rule-based short cuts applied by experienced workers), for example by Naikar (2005). The decision ladder encompasses the information processes sequence in dealing with an abnormal situation (or problem, Rasmussen and Goodstein 1985) and identifies what needs to be done. It can be considered as a normative, rational model of decision making.

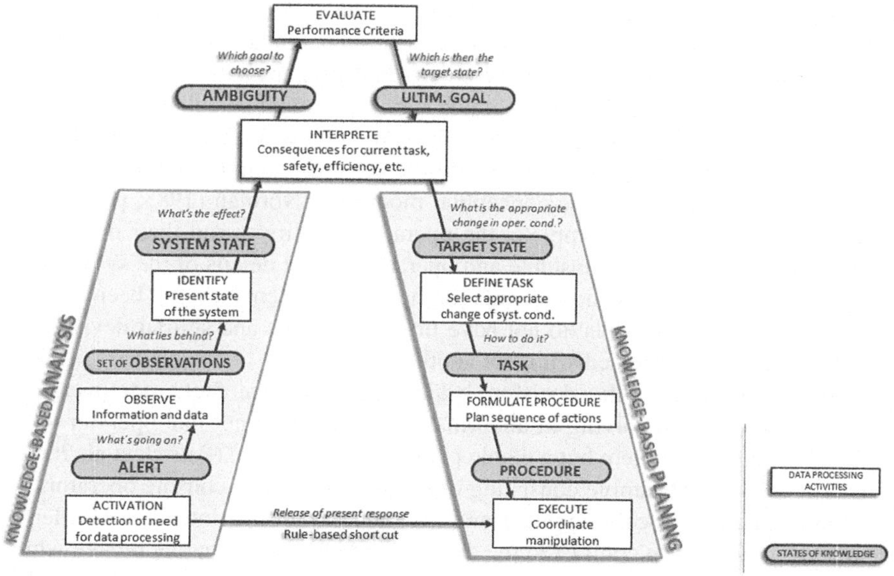

Fig. 3.13 Simplified version (without the rule-based short cuts applied by experienced workers) of Rasmussen's Decision Ladder (Rasmussen and Goodstein 1985)

The novice to the situation is expected to follow the decision ladder in a linear fashion whereas experts are expected to link the two halves by shortcuts (Jenkins et al. 2010).

The operator "climbs up the ladder" on the left-hand side while observing, identifying, interpreting implications and prioritising goals. In this regard, in each case, interim knowledge states such as "alert" or "system state" are reached, each of which enter into the next processing step. After the evaluation of the current states with reference to predefined performance criteria and goal setting, the operator subsequently climbs down the ladder in connection with planning and carrying out the appropriate set of actions in order to achieve or reach the chosen target state. The decision ladder serves, and has served, as the basis for decisions about the design of decision support systems that are not only effective during routine situations but also effective in unforeseen situations (by the designer, Naikar 2005) and as a framework known as cognitive work analysis (Naikar 2005). I am aware that the decision ladder did not lay claim to this, and was and is not conceived for the application case outlined here. The decision ladder is not concerned with who, the operator or the automation, carries out the activities that are required (Jenkins et al. 2010). Nevertheless, I use it as a starting point because many readers are likely to be familiar with it and it forms part of the basic knowledge of this domain. I have included the decision ladder in this chapter because it plays a great role in cognitive ergonomics and engineering psychology as well as in the area of automation. However, for the theme of skill acquisition, the decision ladder is problematic for two reasons: Firstly, the human operator is only a limited rational decision maker (O'Hare 2003; Carvallo et al. 2005; Greitzer et al. 2008); and secondly, an abnormal situation is worked through collaboratively in the plant operation team (Patrick et al. 2006a; Reinartz and Reinartz 1992).

With regard to (1) the human operator is not a rational calculator: The knowledge that is acquired in each case in the problem-solving sequence is probably not as available as the decision ladder would desire. For example, the user's mental models are not identical to the conceptual model. As Norman (1983, p. 8) points out, mental models are incomplete, the operator's ability to run their models are limited, mental models are unstable and operators forget details of the system they are using, especially when those details for the whole system have not been used for some period, mental models do not have firm boundaries and similar devices and operations become confused with one another.

With regard to (2), the decision ladder overlooks the fact, moreover, that especially in problem-solving in abnormal situations, it is not one operator alone who is solving the problem but a whole plant operations *team* (Patrick et al. 2006a; Reinartz 1993), for example consisting of the supervisor, the console operator, the field operator, the process engineer and the operations superintendent (Bullemer et al. 1997). Finally, in contrast to the decision ladder as a normative model, which focuses on decisions that could be made, NDM, which is described below, describes how decisions are actually made (Jenkins et al. 2010). But Jenkins et al. (2010) also show that the two models can be integrated and combined and are not mutually exclusive.

Digression: Collaborative problem solving in a steel plant

If a problem is discerned in a plant, firstly, the persons in the control room ask what the problem is and/or warn the workers on site that there is a problem. Generally speaking, the foundry foreman is informed first, who establishes an overview of the situation and possesses the actual "decision-making power". As the foundry foreman is responsible, for example, for three plants, it might be the case that one has to first wait until he is there, because there are long distances between the plants. The foremen are directly responsible for the plant and then describe the situation to the foundry foreman. He then decides whether the plant potentially needs to be switched off and the whole process interrupted. If this is the case, first of all, the steel work material planning team is informed in order to initiate changes in the process. However, this generally only occurs when the situation really is dangerous for the workers. The foundry foreman also always has the possibility to call so-called "duty workers", in particular after 5 pm or at the weekend. These are engineers who switch on a weekly basis. Generally, this path is chosen more by young foremen and less by very experienced foremen. If even experienced foremen choose this path, the concern is mostly with really critical situations. If the problem cannot be remedied by the production alone, the maintenance team is informed. The control room or the foreman then rings maintenance. The maintenance team then comes to the respective plant and takes a look at the situation. Based on whether the problem can be directly classified as electrical or mechanical, workers of the respective side come out, or if it is unclear, then representatives of both sides come out. Then, it is again decided, generally together with the colleagues from production, whether the problem can be solved with the plant running or whether the plant has to be stopped for a certain time and taken out of production. A combination of the two is also possible, i.e. the symptom is bridged over until the sequence has finished casting or an unplanned maintenance is initiated. In this latter case, the steel plant material planning team again has to be informed. For the situation assessment, the electricians mostly remain in the control room and look around in the plant control, while the metalworkers in many cases go to the plant to look at the problem directly on site.

End of digression

3.4.1 Teamwork Skills for Collaborative Complex Problem Solving

From the skill acquisition perspective, the concern with non-routine/abnormal situations is not with "high art", i.e. the highest level of skills which take place on the level of the individual operator, but rather on the level of *collaborative* problem-solving and collaborative dynamic decision making, which encompasses collaborative reasoning of the plant operations *team* and requires macrocognitive processes (see below).

A *team* is defined "as two or more people who interact interdependently with respect to a common goal and who have been assigned specific roles" (Cooke et al. 2008, p. 51; Salas et al. 1992). Teams exist within the context of a larger organisation and share responsibility for a team product or service (Edmondson et al. 2008). Teamwork also means that based on team members' common valued organisational goals (e.g. safety and productivity), multiple tasks have to be performed with the team members' complementary and interdependent skills, being mutually accountable for methods, resource use and outcomes, and taking on extended managerial responsibility (Langan-Fox et al. 2004). The plant operations team, which is required to collaborate, is composed in a refinery, for example, as introduced in Chap. 2, of console operator, shift leader, field operator, shift coordinator, operations superintendent and process engineer (Bullemer et al. 1997) or in an NPP of its shift supervisor, control room supervisor, primary operator, secondary operator, third reactor operator and shift technical advisor (Waller et al. 2006).

According to the classification of Hollenbeck et al. (2012), in abnormal situations, these plant operations teams become "decision making teams" (De Dreu and Weingart 2003). Decision making teams are teams working together to reach consensus on issues with no right answer (De Dreu and Weingart 2003). One of the most important tasks in non-routine/abnormal situations is to understand together what is currently happening and why it is happening in order to make a decision which satisfies the goals (multiple goals, see Chap. 2) of safety and productivity. Through the high interconnectivity of the parts of the technical system (see Chap. 2), the main problem is to comprehend what is currently occurring in the plant: For example, in a refinery, due to energy integration, several heat exchangers are interconnected and networked. This means that if there is a loss of heating capability, it becomes challenging to isolate the root cause of the problem (ASM 2012). Another example is that relief valves of several units discharge to the same flare. When the flare is found to burn at a higher than normal rate, it becomes difficult to identify which specific unit is operating abnormally (ASM Consortium 2012). In this respect, the plant operations team – although it is called a team – only engages to form a decision-making team in the non-routine/abnormal situation. As these non-routine/abnormal situations rarely occur, these teamwork episodes are very rare in the entire life cycle of the plant operations team (Zijlstra et al. 2012), which might work together in routine situations for years.

Plant operation teams in non-routine/abnormal situations engage in collaborative problem solving and collaborative dynamic decision making (see Fig. 3.14). *Collaboration* is defined as "*a coordinated, synchronous activity that is the result of a continued attempt to construct and maintain a shared conception of a problem*" (Roschelle and Teasley 1995, p. 70). *Collaborative problem solving* is seen as the mutual engagement of team members in a coordinated effort to solve a problem together (Roschelle and Teasley 1995). Collaboration is contrasted with cooperation. Cooperative work is assumed to be accomplished by the division of labour among interdependently working team members with different roles, as an activity where each person is responsible for a portion of the problem solving (Roschelle and Teasley 1995). *Collaborative reasoning* means that two or more individuals deliberately coordinate their thinking for the shared purpose of achieving justifiable results (Moshman and Geil 1998). Reasoning may be defined "as a deliberate effort to coordinate inferences so as to reach justifiable conclusions, which includes collaborative as well as individual forms of cognitive action" (Moshman and Geil 1998, p. 231). As will be described below, this contains collaborative reasoning on the basis of shared mental models (Uitdewillingen et al. 2010). Collaborative reasoning requires top-down information processing in the sense that accumulated knowledge from past experiences is used to make sense of information environments and to guide actions (Uitdewillingen et al. 2010).

Taken together, collaborative problem solving and decision making are required in these non-routine/abnormal situations which are ill-defined, with dynamic information, and contain information knowledge uncertainty (see Chap. 2 uncertainty by Grote 2009). Non-routine/abnormal situations require the processing and making sense of large amount of knowledge (Patrick et al. 2006a), which leads to a high mental workload, accompanied by human-agent interface complexity (Warner and Letsky 2008). The team's task is to reach a decision for a choice of action after the development of a shared understanding of the situation in order to gain (back) control over the situation (Brehmer 1992).

To avoid losing the focus on skill acquisition, at this point, I will briefly address what the relevance for knowledge and skill acquisition is. As introduced above, safety in process control in process industries is based on the one hand on the adherence to SOPs as well as the high standardisation of sequences, as described

Fig. 3.14 Collaborative problem solving in an NPP control room (Photo courtesy of GfS/KSG Essen)

above, even in abnormal situations. Nevertheless, despite the high standardisation in the teams, with highly trained, role-occupying members such as in the plant operations team, the team members still exhibit a wide range of behaviours and interactions during task performance and decision making, leading to different levels of team effectiveness (Zijlstra et al. 2012). For example, Wickens and Hollands (2000) point out that expert operators in terms of non-technical skills have a better ability to communicate and coordinate with other operators and team members in the complex, multitask environment in the control room. Moreover, in collaborative problem solving and reasoning, communication and coordination failures are apparent in the process industries, which contribute to a problem not being effectively solved (Laberge et al. 2008), for example within shift teams, between shift teams, between functional groups, as well as coordination failures for example in planning activities, team execution, work direction and supervision, or activity assessment, which can possibly then lead to incidents. Patrick et al. (2006a) report that the most frequent team performance decrements in several accidents analysed were a deficiency in communication followed by an overly strong belief in one's own procedure, and deficiencies in task management. This means that teamwork in a plant operations team places further demands, beyond the application of SOPs, and precisely on the non-technical teamwork skills in the form of information exchange and communication.

Collaborative complex problem solving as a non-technical skill

Derived from the teamwork requirement formulated at the outset, my proposition in this book is that in non-routine/abnormal situations, macrocognitive processes are required. *Macrocognition is defined "as the internalized and externalized high level mental process employed by teams to create new knowledge during complex, one-of-a-kind, collaborative problem-solving"* (Warner and Letsky 2008, p. 18). Macrocognition as an interaction process of communication and coordination is involved in team activity (Cooke et al. 2008). The individual specialists in the team must communicate to the others their suspicions, generated on the basis of their mental models, about the problem causes. The others' suspicions and hypotheses are aligned with one's own mental model, and through further communicative acts with all involved, are used to reach a joint conclusion as to which course of action should then be adopted. Each individual works with his/her mental model to understand unexpected phenomena, to infer causes of observed events, mental simulations of technical processes to anticipate the course of situation, inertly visualise performance strategies and courses of action. At the same time, each team member must include the suspicions and assumptions of the others in his/her reflections and align his understanding in a manner that relates to the other team members' reference and interpretation and knowledge system (Warner and Letsky 2008). In the following, we will only look in part at the individual macrocognitive process stages in relation to the COCOM; details on macrocognition can be found in Warner and Letsky (2008) as well as Fiore et al. (2008).

Assessing the situation

During situation assessment, it must be recognised in the team that the situation is developing from a normal into an abnormal situation. The detection of the abnormal requires the recognition of the normal, deviations from the normal and patterns in terms of constellations of cues. Pattern recognition is defined as the ability to discriminate between familiar classes of objects (Gonzales and Quesada 2003) and to detect configurations of cues (Klein and Hoffman 1992), also including trend analysis (Fiore et al. 2008). Pattern recognition is proposed to include the recognition of single cues or the constellation of cues which must be discriminated amongst a large number of other cues in order for idiosyncratic salience to be detected (Fiore et al. 2008, p. 148). Operator and team members collect information about system cues and try to comprehend and interpret whether cues of situation are normal or abnormal based on their mental models (Waller et al. 2006).

In the context of collaborative problem solving, the next task of the team consists in developing a Joint Problem Space (JPS, Roschelle and Teasley 1995). The JPS is a shared knowledge structure that supports problem solving activity by integrating: (a) goals; (b) descriptions of the current problem state; (c) awareness of available problem-solving actions; and (d) associations that relate goals, features of the current problem state, and available actions (Roschelle and Teasley 1995). Similarly, Fiore et al. (2008) state that the team must develop a shared problem conceptualisation, which means involving the identification of initial problem states, goals and actions. With the joint development of a JPS, the team exchanges information, comprehensions and interpretations of the received information and knowledge based on referential communication (Fiore et al. 2008) and sharing mental models.

Fig. 3.15 Collaborative problem solving II (Photo courtesy of GfS/KSG, Essen)

Particularly during non-routine/abnormal situations, the collection of new information plays a critical role in the collaborative problem solving success (Waller et al. 2006). This is the collection and restructuring of data (Fiore et al. 2008) in order to reduce uncertainty associated with these data arising from either incompleteness, source confusion and/or lack of clarity (see Fig. 3.15). The skill of the plant operations crew is to quickly collect and assemble cues and pieces of information into a joint problem space, thus quickly and efficiently gaining control over the situation before it cascades through the tightly coupled, interconnected system (Waller et al. 2006). A control team's failure to detect a symptom of a problem can exacerbate the situation due to the momentum, and a critical factor will be how long a symptom remains undetected (Patrick et al. 2006a, p. 1397). Particularly in abnormal situations in process control, the timely recognition of cues signalling abnormal situations and the incorporation of these cues into the collective team-level pre-presentation is critical to plant operations teams' success (Hogg et al. 1995; Sebok 2000; Uitdewillingen et al. 2010).

Sharing mental models is proposed to be a process of uncertainty reduction by comparing assumptions about cause-and-effect relations among cues against the external source of data, for example displays and screens. Through collaborative problem solving, team members combine, sort, filter new information and cues based on their mental models in order to share the insights gained with the other team members, for example with the field operator and supervisor, through verbal communication. While Warner and Letsky (2008) refer to sharing mental models, some other authors also speak here of a *team situation awareness*. Team situation awareness is a team's awareness and understanding of a complex and dynamic situation at any point in time (Endsley 1995). Mental models are assumed to influence the content of team SA because top-down cognitive information processing leads to focusing attention on specific aspects of the situation and determines how a team understands what is going on and how this information is interpreted (Uitdewillingen et al. 2010).

In the phase of assessing the situation, the team must, above all through communication, manage the hypotheses about the causes of the problem and coordinate the individual contributions regarding the cues, possible patterns and indications to form a collaborative reasoning (see Fig. 3.15).

Choosing what to do

To choose a course of action and gain control over the situation, in addition to the individual operators' mental model of the target system, for collaborative problem-solving, the operator and all other control room and plant operations team members fall back on *team knowledge* (Wildman et al. 2012), which should orchestrate and coordinate the actions. Coordination refers to team activities that aim at attuning team members' activities towards to concerted common goal-directed behaviour of the team as a unit (Cannon-Bowers et al. 1995; Uitdewillingen et al. 2010). Team knowledge contains knowledge that is *task-, team-, process- and goal-related* (Wildman et al. 2012).

Task-related team knowledge represents relatively unchanging knowledge about the task and duties for which the team in the plant is responsible during the time that the shift is performing.

Team-related team knowledge refers to the mental structures concerning the characteristics and qualities of one's teammate or of the team as a holistic social entity (Wildman et al. 2012), for example whether the console or field operator is new and inexperienced or an "old hand" who can keep calm under stress.

The *process-related team knowledge* refers to the mental representation of the teamwork and interpersonal, team interaction processes involved, for example the sequence in which team members have to be informed and included, who can decide what and who has to grant which approval. The concern here is not only with communication in general but with knowledge about who has which authorities, and in which order and sequence particular persons must be incorporated into the problem-solving process – also by virtue of legal-formal reasons alone.

Finally, *goal-related team knowledge* refers to the mental representation of goals and how to achieve them, for example strategic consensus (Wildman et al. 2012), for instance how to bring the plant into a safe state. In particular, abnormal situation management requires operators to think at varying levels of abstraction, ranging from the more abstract organisational goals such as safety and production goals to the highly concrete knowledge about the physical state, for example of a part or unit (Wickens and Hollands 2000). High, medium and low levels of abstraction might be information about profit and risk, information about mass and energy, and information about specific pumps and pipes in operation, respectively (Wickens and Hollands 2000).

Before choosing a course of action, the team engages in interaction processes to resolve opposing interpretations, for example by team negotiation (Warner and

Letsky 2008). The team needs skills for conflict resolution to find solutions for technical and interpersonal areas of disagreement (Gaddy and Wachtel 1992). The negotiation process includes *critical thinking*, whereby goal accomplishment requires an active exchange of ideas, self-regulatory judgement, and systematic consideration of evidence, counter-evidence and context in order to prepare the decision making under conditions of uncertainty.

What is important about critical thinking? Experienced decision makers collect and critically evaluate the available evidence, seek inconsistencies, and test assumptions underlying their assessment of the problem (Helsdingen et al. 2010). Critical thinking includes the testing of the created joint problem space (see above) for conflicting or missing information, evaluating its plausibility and finding contingencies, and a quick consideration of the need to decide immediately or spend more time on the critical thinking process (Cohen et al. 1998; Helsdingen et al. 2010). Critical thinking skills incorporate questions (Cohen et al. 1998/2006) which are raised during the course of collaborative complex problem solving: First, the application and usefulness of critical thinking is questioned: Is the cost of a delay (caused by applying critical thinking skills) acceptable? Is the cost of an error high? Is the situation unfamiliar and problematic? In case these questions are answered with yes, a search for incompleteness such as missing arguments for a hypothesis or stated cause-and-effect relation is started. In the case of missing arguments, several options are faced: More data is collected, the focus is shifted and more knowledge is retrieved, or assumptions are added or dropped. In parallel, the problem solvers are engaging in looking for conflicts such as arguments with contradictory conclusions. Additionally, the collaborative problem solvers are encouraged to look for unreliabilities such as arguments that depend on unconsidered assumptions (Cohen et al. 1998/2006). Critical thinking requires blending deep domain expertise and situational nuances (Stanton et al. 2011).

It is assumed that the quality and quantity of team knowledge and team skill application is positively related to team communication and team performance. Especially during abnormal situations and high stress levels, the opportunity for communication is reduced so that it becomes essential for a team to communicate only the task-relevant aspects as it can be confident that the other team members share a similar understanding of the situation (Uitdewillingen et al. 2010). Additionally, team knowledge reduces a team's efforts for reaching consensus, decreases the occurrence of friction due to misunderstandings, and reduces time for clarifying and agreeing upon strategies (Uitdewillingen et al. 2010).

The processes of collaborative dynamic and complex problem solving applied to the COCOM by Hollnagel (2007, Fig. 3.4) are displayed in Fig. 3.16.

What is interesting about non-routine/abnormal tasks from a human factors and skill acquisition perspective?

In abnormal situations, the part of so-called non-technical and teamwork skills gains considerably in importance. Patrick et al. (2006a) found a significant variability and difference between control room teams even when the plant teams were using SOPs. In order to detect a problem quickly, a team has to monitor the control

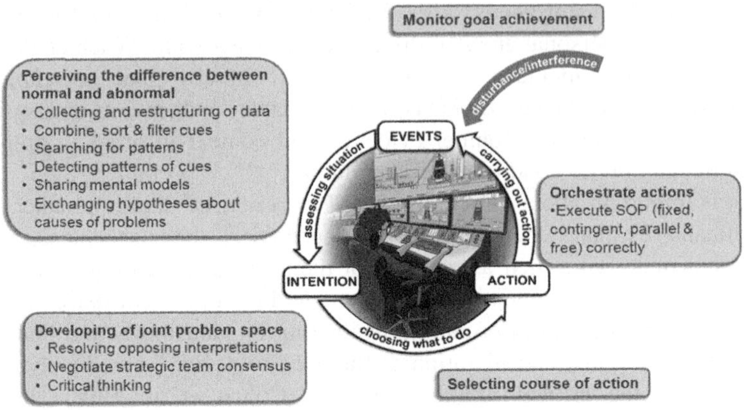

Fig. 3.16 Combining of the COCOM and macrocognitive processes in non-routine/abnormal situations

panels and remain vigilant in addition to the attention required by routine tasks, because operators and supervisors seem to become distracted because they are so fixated on a procedure that nobody monitors the control panels. Moreover, supervisors fail to monitor the operators to ensure that an adequate monitoring strategy is applied because they also become absorbed by the SOPs. Patrick et al. (2006a) also found that control room teams do not formulate sufficient hypotheses regarding what the problem might be. Hypothesis generation is also assumed to be critical and there is a danger that control room teams act too much in a control-oriented manner and too little in a hypothesis-generating manner. In another study, Patrick et al. (2006b) showed that inadequate communication, lack of attention/distraction, misperception and inadequate initial knowledge and/or reasoning are main problems of collaborative problem solving in the control room.

As the concern here is with non-routine situations that have frequently never previously arisen, in very few cases are practised scripts available for the tackling of technical problems and their solution or for the collaboration of the control room crew. This is why one speaks here of knowledge-based behaviour and procedures. Moreover, these situations are experienced as stressful because on the one hand, the operators are aware of the importance, urgency and necessity of a quick problem solution, but on the other hand there is not yet any available solution. Stressors taken from a list by Moore et al. (2012) relevant to non-routine/abnormal tasks are too much information, sensory overload, ambiguity, uncertainty, time pressure, unpredictability, and difficult judgements. The stress encountered in non-routine/abnormal situations is caused by cognitive overload (Orasanu and Backer 1996a, b) which includes task load and information load (Orasanu and Backer 1996a, b; Salas et al. 1996). *Task load is defined as performing two or more tasks concurrently, which includes divided attention* (Orasanu and Backer 1996a, b; Salas et al. 1996) because tasks compete for specific resources during information processing. One aspect of coping with complexity is to be able to make use of the available information in time, which means fast enough to allow an action to be taken before it is too late (Hollnagel and Woods 2005). This ability is reduced in conditions of information overload in which there is more information than can be handled (Miller 1960). *Information load is characterised by the amount of data handling that must be completed* (Orasanu and Backer 1996a, b). With increasing amounts of data there is the possibility of conflicting or uninterpretable data, which increases the operators load. Time pressure also plays a role in abnormal situations. *Time pressure* is a restriction in time required to perform a task (Salas et al. 1996) and *defined as the ratio of time to perform required tasks divided by the time available* (Orasanu and Backer 1996a, b). Time pressure tempts an operator to accelerate the speed of task execution, for example of an SOP or by speeding up the information integration in order to match the speed with which information is being presented, and by filtration. This is the tendency to restrict information processing (Salas et al. 1996), which might be very dysfunctional in non-routine/abnormal situations which require the situation to be constantly reassessed. Common reactions to information overload range from temporary non-processing of input to abandoning the task completely. Two sensory events relevant for performance in abnormal situations which can happen during periods of acute stress are called tunnel vision and auditory exclusion, also called tunnel hearing (Moore et al. 2012).

The observations by Patrick et al. (2006a, b, further below) reveal this phenomenon. Cognitive overload is most sensitive to individual differences in training and experience (Orasanu and Backer 1996a, b) and is amenable to cognitive skill and resource management training. As outlined by Driskell and Johnston (1998/2006), stress in non-routine/abnormal situations may result in:

- Physiological changes, such as quickened heart beat, laboured breathing and trembling,
- Emotional reactions, such as fear, anxiety, frustration, and motivational losses,
- Cognitive effects, e.g. narrowed attention, decreased search behaviour, longer reaction times to peripheral cues and decreased vigilance, degraded problem solving, performance rigidity,
- Changes in social behaviour, e.g. loss of team perspective, loss in prosocial behaviour and helping (Driskell and Johnston 1998/2006).

Because all of these changes affect individual and team performance degradation, which stems from having to manage multiple tasks in a high-demand stress situation, stress training provides training in time-sharing multiple tasks and in prioritising critical task demands to maintain effective performance under stress (Driskell and Johnston 1998/2006). Stress training is defined as an intervention to enhance familiarity with the stressful environment in order to acquire skills necessary to maintain effective task performance under stress conditions (Driskell and Johnston 1998/2006 see Chap. 5).

Which skills does one need for collaborative complex problem solving?

As already introduced above, the phase of assessing the situation requires communication skills in order to exchange hypotheses and mental models, as well as the coordination of the different hypotheses and assumptions to reach a negotiated team consensus. After the team has chosen what to do, control actions to stabilise the situation and to gain control must be coordinated and orchestrated. The necessary non-technical skills of information exchange and delivery (Smith-Jentsch et al. 1998), which have proven their worth in other team contexts (e.g. Wilson et al. 2010), contain the following aspects:

- Utilising all available sources of information
- Passing information to the appropriate persons without having to be asked
- Providing periodic situation updates which summarise the big picture

Verbal communication plays a significant part in the team's handling of disturbances in the control room (Reinartz and Reinartz 1992). An effective information exchange allows the team to develop and maintain a shared situation assessment (Smith-Jentsch et al. 1998, p. 276), while information exchange addresses what kind of information is passed to whom, and communication involves how that information is delivered. Simplification of communication, brevity and coordination strategies are useful when dealing with urgent situations (Stanton et al. 2011). Communication delivery includes (Smith-Jentsch et al. 1998):

- Proper phraseology
- Completeness of standard reports
- Brevity, avoiding chatter
- Clarity, avoiding inaudible communications

Coordination includes, for example, non-technical skills of supporting behaviour and leadership. *Supporting behaviour* means monitoring and correcting team errors, providing and requesting back-up or assistance to balance workload. *Initiative/leadership* means providing guidance or suggestions to team members and stating clear and appropriate priorities (Smith-Jentsch et al 1998).

There are also industry-specific skills described, for example Gaddy and Wachtel (1992) distinguish between generic team skills for NPP teams and operational team tasks. Generic control room crew skills are communication (Gaddy and Wachtel 1992), feedback, effective influence (e.g. to query courses of action and to persuade other crew members to consider alternatives; Gaddy and Wachtel 1992). A specific NPP team skills taxonomy from a scientific point of view has been proposed, for example, by O'Connor et al. (2008).

Finally, one has to consider that these abnormal situations are described as "pure hell" (Wickens and Hollands 2000) or "sheer terror" (Vicente et al. 2004) (see Chap. 2), in which all warnings go off simultaneously (Chapter on dynamic effects and non-transparency). Therefore, operators also need *emotional coping skills* for abnormal situations/dealing with stress, because non-routine/abnormal situations are situations with high mental workload under stress (Waller et al. 2006). In addition to the cognitive aspects of dealing with abnormal situations on a knowledge-based level as introduced above, the handling of abnormal situations requires coping with high stress and using skills and tools necessary to maintain effective performance when operating in high-stress situations (Salas et al. 2006),

Table 3.5 Training objectives for non-routine/abnormal tasks

For *assessing the situation, under conditions of "pure hell"*, as a member of the control room team, the operator:
Detects deviations from the normal states and pattern constellation of cues
Collects information about cues
Interprets cues as being abnormal (based on their mental models)
Passes information to the appropriate person
Exchanges information, comprehensions and interpretations to establish a shared problem space
Provides periodic situation updates
Formulates and communicates hypotheses about cause-and-effect relations
Uses proper phraseology
Pays attention to completeness of standard reports
Compares assumptions about cause-and-effect relations among cues against the external source
Resolves opposing interpretations by team negotiation
Uses critical thinking
For *choosing what to do under conditions of "pure hell"*, as a member of the control room team, the operator:
Applies team knowledge (task, team process and goal-related team knowledge) to select the course of action
Monitors and supports the actions of others
Provides guidance or suggestions to team members
States appropriate priorities
***Non-Technical Skills* for performing *under conditions of "pure hell"*:**
Under conditions of "pure hell", the operator applies stress coping skills, e.g. to manage cognitive effects of stress such as attention management

because stress increases the likelihood of errors. Possibilities include the acquisition of skills to control negative physiological stress reactions, to manage cognitive effects of stress (e.g. attention management, automation of action) and to develop collective stress-management abilities (Driskell et al. 2008; Orasanu and Backer 1996a, b).

With respect to the following chapters, I introduce the distinction between taskwork and teamwork (Eccles and Tenenbaum 2004; Entin and Serfaty 1999; Salas et al. 1992; Shuffler et al. 2011), at this point in order to summarise the requirements of the non-routine/abnormal situations regarding technical and control aspects as well as team coordination aspects. In the subsequent chapters, *taskwork involves individually performing the technical components of the task based on mental models of the target system, knowing and executing SOPs, whereas teamwork requires the application of non-technical team skills in order to integrate team members' individual contributions into a coordinated team performance for collaborative dynamic problem solving and decision making.*

Training objectives are summarised in Table 3.5.

A whole separate book could be written about the team processes in control rooms or the embedding of teamwork into the whole organisational process, about the delimitation of these teams from other forms of teamwork or about factors which influence team efficacy. Indeed, a whole book could be devoted to the theme of team cognition, team knowledge, shared mental models and team mental models, and shared team or distributed situation awareness. Teamwork requirements in selected High Responsibility Teams have been reported on in detail, for instance by Hagemann (2011). Furthermore, overview works are provided by Cannon-Bowers and Bowers (2011), Uitdewillingen et al. (2010) as well as Mathieu et al. (2008) or Paris et al. (2000). A general taxonomy regarding team tasks can be found in Fleishman and Zaccaro (1992), and general teamwork models can be found in Hinsz et al. (2009). However, in this book, I have decided to derive and describe which team processes occur and are required in non-routine/abnormal situations, and with a focus on the processes that can be detected and trained.

3.4.2 Evaluation Possibilities

Here too, as with the reactions to unexpected occurrences (see above), observation in a control room full-scale simulator presents itself as an option. Examples of this are provided by the works of Waller et al. (2006) and Stachowski et al. (2009). In both works (even though they did not measure training efficacy but were rather descriptive studies), the team behaviour in non-routine/normal situations was observed and coded. Various four-to-six-person NPP control room teams were assigned to different routine and non-routine scenarios. While the control room teams performed their tasks within the scenario, two coders recorded the occurrence of six types of behaviours. Additionally, the team performance and performance deficiencies were measured by the simulator trainers with the following categories: Diagnosis of problems and conditions based on signals and reading, understanding of plant and system response, adherence to and use of procedures, control board operations, crew operations, and communication. General guidelines on how to assess non-technical and teamwork skills after training can be found in Flin et al. (2008).

Patrick et al. (2006a) used the method of process tracking. Process tracking aims at observing and describing how an incident unfolds including available cues, cues actually noticed by participants as well as their interpretation of these cues (Patrick et al. 2006a). In this sense, process tracking tries to capture the situation assessment (Vicente et al. 2004) in its process of development. Process tracking can take place with video recording, verbal reports, eye-tracking or observations, for example in a full-scale simulator. After data collection, data need to be transcribed or coded and segmented into a time-lined representation for further analysis (Patrick et al. 2006a; Woods 1992).

For the analysis of the videotaped observation of control room teams in a non-routine situation, Patrick et al. (2006a) used a coding schema that differentiated between the detection phase and the diagnosis-control phase. For example, the code for the detection phase included implementing procedure and monitoring control panels, interacting with the operator, interacting with the supervisor, supervisor's questions regarding what the operator is doing etc. Codes for the diagnosis control phase included generating hypotheses and discussing the nature of the problem/symptom, interaction between operator and supervisor, testing hypotheses, restatement of hypotheses, interaction with plant personnel, etc.

In another study, Patrick et al. (2006b) worked with an observation which was performed with a rating scale. Team behaviour was observed with regard to inadequate communication, lack of attention/distraction, misperception and inadequate initial knowledge and/or misreasoning and rated on a 7-point Likert scale in three different scenarios (shift handover with a leak on the main feed pump, a start-up with a partial closed valve leading to low flow to a boiler, a bomb explosion and double reactor trip). Patrick et al. (2006b) developed the following categories for analysing behaviours for the team's situation assessment:

- Planning, e.g. discuss contingencies and anticipate problems prior to engaging in operational procedure
- Problem solving, e.g. discuss alternative diagnoses in parallel rather than accepting one hypothesis; examine the consistency of a proposed hypothesis within the available symptoms
- Team coordination, e.g. supervisor allocates roles to team members and checks on these roles
- Attention, e.g. monitor plant appropriately despite distraction, do not become over-focused
- Communication, e.g. communicate future actions
- Knowledge, e.g. demonstrate knowledge of how the plant works

Sebok (2000) and Montgomery et al. (1991) used a measure for non-technical teamwork skills based on the Behaviourally Anchored Rating Scale Technique. Rating scales captured:

- Task focus/decision making
- Coordination as a crew
- Communication
- Openness and team spirit

Each of these was identified with several anchor example behaviours (positive and negative) for raters to observe and use as criteria for their rating. The overall rating was a number between 1 and 7, with 7 being the best team interactions. In addition to team interaction, Sebok (2000) measured team performance with rating criteria:

- Solution path, the team's use of time in recognising the abnormal situation and selecting the correct mitigation strategy
- Control of plant, team's understanding of procedures in their analysis of the transient mitigation and the extent to which they challenged safety equipment
- Communication, extent to which information exchange facilitated transient mitigation
- Confidence, ease with which the crew completed transient mitigation without hesitation, and statement about sureness of their own actions and decisions

Patrick et al. (2006a) state that monitoring performance should be a content of training programs, which not only covers the timely monitoring by operators but also the supervisors' monitoring and evaluation of operators' responsibilities when engaged in tracking SOPs. Mutual performance monitoring (Smith-Jentsch et al. 1998) is essential to team performance in terms of the monitoring of monitoring activities themselves by operators and supervisors.

3.5 Final Remark

It might be criticised that the division into routine, non-routine/normal and non-routine/abnormal is an artificial one. For the practitioners among the readers, this might be a justified objection. For the researcher colleagues and students, this artificial categorisation can be an aid to work out the central differences of the three situations and to derive and develop methods for skill and knowledge acquisition. In this respect, this book and this division simplify the actual facts and circumstances in practice, in order to refer to the relevant core differences for training development. I am aware that the world of process control is much more fluid and multi-faceted than the simplified presentation in the three categories of situations.

References

Anderson, J. R. (1983). A spreading activation theory of memory. *Journal of Verbal Learning and Verbal Behavior, 22*, 261–295.

Arthur, W., Bennett, W., Stanush, P. L., & McNelly, T. L. (1998). Factors that influence skill decay and retention: A quantitative review and analysis. *Human Performance, 11*, 57–101.

ASM (2012). Definition. Retrieved February 5, 2012, from http://www.asmconsortium.net/defined/definition/Pages/default.aspx

ASM Consortium. (2012). Process factors. Retrieved November 12, 2012, from http://www.asmconsortium.net/defined/sources/Pages/ProcessFactors.aspx

Bainbridge, L. (1991). *A proposal for the structure of training in a complex task*. London: Department of Psychology, University College London.

Bainbridge, L. (1992). *Mental Models in cognitive skill: The example of industrial process operations*. Retrieved November 12, 2012. http://www.bainbrdg.demon.co.uk/Papers/MM.html

Bainbridge, L. (2012). *Planning the training of a complex skill*. Retrieved January 11, 2012. http://www.bainbrdg.demon.co.uk/Papers/PlanTrain.html

Bjork, R. A. (2009). Structuring the conditions of training to achieve elite performance: Reflections on elite training programs and related themes in Chapter 10–13. In K. A. Ericsson (Ed.), *Development of professional expertise. Toward measurement of expert performance and design of optimal learning environments* (pp. 312–332). Cambridge: Cambridge University Press.

Bjork, R. A., & Bjork, E. L. (1992). A new theory of disuse and an old theory of stimulus fluctuation. In A. Healy, S. Kosslyn, & R. Shiffrin (Eds.), *From learning processes to cognitive processes: Essays in honour of William K. Estes* (Vol. 2, pp. 35–67). Hillsdale: Erlbaum.

Brand, M., & Markowitsch, H. J. (2010). Thinking and Memory. In A. von Müller, B. M. Glatzeder, & V. Goel (Eds.), *Towards a theory of thinking. Building blocks for a conceptual framework* (pp. 147–160). Heidelberg: Springer.

Brehmer, B. (1992). Dynamic decision making: Human control of complex systems. *Acta Psychologica, 81*, 211–241.

Bullemer, P. T., & Kiff, L. (2011). Retrieved November 21, 2012. *Effective Procedural Practices: A Review of the ASM Consortium Guidelines and Related Studies*. http://www.asmconsortium.net/Documents/2011_ASM%20Webinar_ProcedurePractices.pdf

Bullemer, P. T., Cochran, T., Harp, S., & Miller, C. (1997). Managing abnormal situations II: Collaborative decision support for operations personnel. *ASM Consortium*. Retrieved November 11, 2012. http://www.asmconsortium.net/Documents/Managing%20ASM%20Dec%20Support.pdf

Bullemer, P. T., Kiff, L., & Tharanathan, A. (2010, October 26–27). *Common procedural execution failure modes during abnormal situations*. Paper presented at the Mary Kay O'Conner Process Safety Center international symposium, College Station, TX. Retrieved November 21, 2012. http://www.asmconsortium.net/Documents/Understanding%20Procedural%20Execution%20Failures.pdf

Burkolter, D., Kluge, A., Schüler, K., Sauer, J., & Ritzmann, S. (2007). Cognitive requirement analysis to derive training models for controlling complex systems. In B. Hockey & D. de Waard (Eds.), *Human factors issues in complex system performance* (pp. 475–485). Aldershot: Ashgate.

Burkolter, D., Meyer, B., Kluge, A., & Sauer, J. (2010). Assessment of structural knowledge for training evaluation in process control environments. *Human Factors, 52*, 119–138.

Cannon-Bowers, J. A., & Bowers, C. A. (2011). Team development and functioning. In S. Zehdeck (Ed.), *APA handbook of industrial and organizational psychology building and developing the organization* (Vol. 1, pp. 597–650). Washington, DC: APA.

Cannon-Bowers, J. A., Tannenbaum, S. I., Salas, E., & Volpe, C. E. (1995). Defining competencies and establishing team training requirements. In R. Guzzo & E. Salas (Eds.), *Team effectiveness and decision making in organizations* (pp. 333–80). San Francisco: Jossey-Bass.

Carvallo, P. V. R., dos Santos, I. L., & Vidal, M. C. R. (2005). Nuclear power plant shift supervisors' decision making during microincidents. *International Journal of Industrial Ergonomics, 35*, 619–644.

Christian, M. S., Edwards, B. D., & Bradley, J. C. (2010). Situational judgment tests: Constructs assessed and a meta-analysis of their criterion-related validities. *Personnel Psychology, 63*, 83–117.

Cohen, M. S., Freeman, J. T., & Thompson, B. (1998/2006 reprint). Critical thinking skills in tactical decision making: A model and a training strategy. In J. A. Cannon-Bowers & E. Salas (Eds.), *Making decisions under stress. Implications for individual and team training* (pp. 155–190). Washington, DC: APA.

Cooke, N. J., Gorman, J. C., & Kiekel, P. A. (2008). Communication as team-level cognitive processing. In M. P. Letsky, N. W. Warner, S. M. Fiore, & C. A. Smith (Eds.), *Macrocognition in teams. Theories and methodologies* (pp. 51–64). Aldershot: Ashgate.

Craik, K. (1943). *The nature of explanation*. Cambridge: Cambridge University Press.

Crandall, B., Klein, G., & Hoffman, R. R. (2006). *Working minds. A practitioner's guide to cognitive task analysis*. Cambridge, MA: MIT Press.

Darabi, A. A., Nelson, D. W., & Seel, N. M. (2009). Progression of mental models throughout phases of a computer-based instructional simulation: Supportive information, practice and performance. *Computers in Human Behavior, 25*, 723–730.

De Dreu, C. K. W., & Weingart, L. R. (2003). Task versus relationship conflict, team performance, and team member satisfaction: A meta-analysis. *Journal of Applied Psychology, 88*, 741–749.

De Keyser, V. (1995). Time in ergonomics research. *Ergonomics, 38*, 1639–1660.

Dede, C. (2009). Immersive interfaces for engagement and learning. *Science, 5910*, 66–68.

Dennis, D. R., & Meredith, J. R. (2000). An analysis of process industry production and inventory management systems. *Journal of Operations Management, 18*, 683–699.

Driskell, J. E., & Johnston, J. H. (1998/2006 reprint). Stress exposure training. In J. A. Cannon-Bowers & E. Salas (Eds.), *Making decisions under stress. Implications for individual and team training* (pp. 191–217). Washington, DC: APA.

Driskell, J. E., Salas, E., Johnston, J. H., & Wollert, T. N. (2008). Stress exposure training: An event-based approach. In P. A. Hancock & J. L. Szalma (Eds.), *Performance under stress* (pp. 271–286). Aldershot: Ashgate.

Durso, F. T., & Sethumadhavan, A. (2008). Situation awareness: Understanding dynamic environments. *Human Factors, 50*(3), 442–448.

Eccles, D. W., & Tenenbaum, G. (2004). Why an expert team is more than a team of experts: A social-cognitive conceptualization of team coordination and communication in sport. *Journal of Sport and Exercise Psychology, 26*, 542–560.

Edmondson, A. C., Dillon, J. R., & Roloff, K. S. (2008). Three perspectives on team learning. Outcome improvement, task mastery, and group process. *The Academy of Management Annals, 1*, 269–314.

Edwards, W. (1962). Dynamic decision theory and probabilistic information processings. *Human Factors: The Journal of the Human Factors and Ergonomics, 4*, 59–74. doi:10.1177/001872086200400201.

Endsley, M. R. (1995). Toward a theory of situation awareness in dynamic systems. *Human Factors, 37*, 32–64.

Endsley, M. R. (2000). Theoretical underpinnings of situation awareness: A critical review. In M. R. Endsley & D. J. Garland (Eds.), *Situation awareness analysis and measurement* (pp. 3–33). Boca Raton: CRC Press.

Entin, E. E., & Serfaty, D. (1999). Adaptive team coordination. *Human Factors, 41*, 312–325.

Farr, M. J. (1987). *The long-term retention of knowledge and skills. A cognitive and instructional perspective*. New York: Springer.

Fiore, S. M., Rosen, M., Salas, E., Burke, S., & Jentsch, F. (2008). Process in complex team problem-solving: Parsing and defining the theoretical problem space. In M. P. Letsky, N. W. Warner, S. M. Fiore, & C. A. Smith (Eds.), *Macrocognition in teams. Theories and methodologies* (pp. 143–164). Aldershot: Ashgate.

Fischer, A., Greiff, S., & Funke, J. (2012). The process of solving complex problems. *The Journal of Problem Solving, 4*, 19–42.

Fitts, P. M. (1962/1990). Factors of complex skill training. In M. Venturino (Ed.), *Selected readings in human factors* (pp. 275–295). Santa Monica: Human Factors Society. (Original work by Fitts published 1962)

Fleishman, E. A., & Quaintance, M. K. (1984). *Taxonomies of human performance. The description of human tasks*. Orlando: Academic.

Fleishman, E. A., & Zaccaro, S. J. (1992). Toward a taxonomy of team performance functions. In R. W. Swezey & E. Salas (Eds.), *Teams: Their training and performance* (pp. 31–56). Norwood: Ablex.

Flin, R., O'Connor, P., & Crichton, M. (2008). *Safety at the sharp end. A guide to non-technical skills*. Aldershot: Ashgate.

Folley, J. D. (1964a). *Development of an improved method for task analysis and beginnings of a theory of training* (NAVTRADEVCEB 1218-10). Port Washington: USNTDC.

Folley, J. D. (1964b). *Guidelines for task analysis* (NAVTRADEVCEN 1218-2). Port Washington: USNTDC.

Frensch, P. A., & Funke, J. (Eds.). (1995). *Complex problem solving: The European perspective*. Hillsdale: Lawrence Erlbaum.

Fritzsche, B. A., Stagl, K. C., Salas, E., & Burke, C. S. (2006). Enhancing the design, delivery, and evaluation of scenario-based training: Can situational judgment tests contribute? In J. A. Weekley & R. E. Ployhart (Eds.), *Situational judgment tests. Theory, measurement, and application* (pp. 301–318). Mahwah: Lawrence Erlbaum.

Funke, J. (1992). *Wissen über dynamische Systeme: Erwerb, Repräsentation und Anwendung*. Berlin: Springer.

Funke, J., & Frensch, P. A. (2007). Complex problem solving: The European perspective – 10 years after. In D. H. Jonassen (Ed.), *Learning to solve complex scientific problems* (pp. 25–47). New York: Lawrence Erlbaum.

Funke, J., & Müller, H. (1988). Eingreifen und Prognostizieren als Determinanten von Systemidentifikation und Systemsteuerung. *Sprache & Kognition, 7*, 176–186.

Gaddy, C. D., & Wachtel, J. A. (1992). Team skills training in nuclear power plant operations. In R. W. Swezey & E. Salas (Eds.), *Teams: Their training and performance* (pp. 379–396). Noorwood: Ablex.

Gentner, D., & Stevens, A. L. (Eds.). (1983). *Mental models*. Hillsdale: Lawrence Erlbaum.

Goldstein, I. L. (1993). *Training in organisations. Needs assessment, development and evaluation*. Monterey: Brooks/Cole.

Goldstein, I. L., & Ford, J. K. (2002). *Training in organisations. Needs assessment, development, and evaluation* (4th ed.). Wadsworth: Cengage Learning.

Gonzales, C., & Quesada, J. (2003). Learning in dynamic decision making: The recognition process. *Computational and Mathematical Organization Theory, 9*, 287–304.

Gonzales, C., Lerch, J. F., & Lebiere, C. (2003). Instance-based learning in dynamic decision making. *Cognitive Science, 27*, 591–635.

Greene, J. A., & Azevedo, R. (2007). Adolescents' use of self-regulatory process and their relation to qualitative mental model shifts while using hypermedia. *Journal of Educational Computing Research, 36*, 125–148.

Greitzer, F. L., Podmore, R., Robinson, M., & Ey, P. (2008). Naturalistic decision making for power system operators. In *Proceedings of the NDM9, the 9th international conference on naturalistic decision making*, London, UK. Also available online: http://www.bcs.org/upload/pdf/ewic_ndm09_s1paper2.pdf

Groß, N., & Kluge, A. (2012). "Why should I share what I know?" – Antecedents for enhancing knowledge sharing behavior and its impact on shared mental models in steel production. In *Proceedings of the Human Factors and Ergonomics Society 56th annual conference*, Boston (pp. 403–407).

Grote, G. (2009). *Management of uncertainty. Theory and application in the design of systems and organizations*. Dordrecht: Springer.

Hagemann, V. (2011). Trainingsentwicklung für High-Responsibility-Teams: eine systematische Analyse von High-Responsibility-Team-Arbeitskontexten und Ableitung der High-Responsibility-Team-spezifischen Situationen der Trainingsziele mit anschließender Trainingsevaluation. Pabst Science Publ.

Helsdingen, A. S., van den Bosch, K., van Gog, T., & van Merrienboer, J. J. G. (2010). The effects of critical thinking instruction on training complex decision making. *Human Factors, 52*, 537–545.

Hinsz, V. B., Wallace, D. M., & Ladbury, J. L. (2009). Team performance in dynamic task environments. *International Review of Industrial and Organizational Psychology, 24*, 183–216.

Hodgkinson, G. P., & Healey, M. P. (2008). Cognition in organizations. *Annual Review of Psychology, 59*, 387–417.

Hogg, D. N., Folleso, K., Strand-Volden, F., & Torralba, B. (1995). Development of a situation awareness measure to evaluate advanced alarm systems in nuclear power plant control rooms. *Ergonomics, 38*, 2394–413.

Hollenbeck, J. R., Beersma, B., & Schouten, M. E. (2012). Beyond team types and taxonomies: A dimensional scaling conceptualization for team description. *Academy of Management Review, 37*, 82–106.

Hollnagel, E. (1998). *Cognitive Reliability and Error Analysis Method (CREAM)*. Oxford: Elsevier.

Hollnagel, E. (2007). Decision about “what” and decisions about “how”. In M. Cook, J. Noyes, & Y. Masakowski (Eds.), *Decision making in complex environments* (pp. 3–13). Aldershot: Ashgate.

Hollnagel, E., & Woods, D. D. (2005). *Joint cognitive systems. Foundations of cognitive systems engineering*. Boca Raton: Taylor & Francis.

Jenkins, D. P., Stanton, N. A., Salmon, P. M., Walker, G. H., & Rafferty, L. (2010). Using the decision-ladder to add a formative element to naturalistic decision-making research. *International Journal of Human-Computer Interaction, 26*, 132–146.

Johnson, A. (in press). Procedural memory and skill acquisition. In A. F. Healy, & R.W. Proctor (Vol. Eds), & I. B. Weiner (Ed.-in-Chief), *Handbook of psychology*: *Vol. 4. Experimental psychology* (2nd edn). Hoboken: Wiley.

Johnson-Laird, P. N. (1983). *Mental models. Towards a cognitive science of language, inference, and consciousness*. Cambridge: Cambridge University Press.

Johnson-Laird, P. N. (2001). Mental models and deduction. *Trends in Cognitive Science, 5*, 434–442.

Kerstholt, J. H., & Raaijmakers, J. G. W. (1997). Decision making in dynamic task environments. In R. Ranyard, R. W. Crozier, & O. Svenson (Eds.), *Decision making: Cognitive models and explanations* (pp. 205–217). New York: Routledge.

Kersting, M. (1991). *Wissensdiagnostik beim Problemlösen. Entwicklung und erste Bewährungskontrolle eines kontentvalide konstruierten problemspezifischen Wissenstest. Unveröffentlichte Diplomarbeit*. Berlin: Freie Universität Berlin.

Kersting, M. (1999). *Diagnostik und Personalauswahl mit computergestützten Problemlöseszenarien? Zur Kriteriumsvalidität mit Problemlöseszenarien und Intelligenztests*. Göttingen: Hogrefe.

Klein, G., & Hoffman, R. R. (1992). Seeing the invisible: Perceptual-cognitive aspects of expertise. In M. Robinowitz (Ed.), *Cognitive science foundations of instruction* (pp. 203–226). Mahwah: Lawrence Erlbaum.

Kluge, A. (2007). Experiential learning methods, simulation complexity and their effects on different target groups. *Journal of Educational Computing Research, 36*, 323–349.

Kluge, A. (2008). What you train is what you get? Task requirements and training methods in complex problem solving. *Computers in Human Behavior, 24*, 284–308.

Kluge, A., & Burkolter, D. (2013). Training for cognitive readiness: Research issues and experimental designs. *Journal of Cognitive Engineering and Decision Making, 7*, 96–118. doi:10.1177/1555343412446483.

Kluge, A., Grauel, B., & Burkolter, D. (2013). Job aids: How does the quality of a procedural aid alone and combined with a decision aid affect motivation and performance in process control? *Applied Ergonomics, 44*, 285–296.

Kluge, A., & Frank, B. (2014). Counteracting skill decay: Four refresher interventions and their effect on skill retention in a simulated process control task. *Ergonomics*. doi:10.1080/00140139.2013.869357.

Kluwe, R. H. (1997). Acquisition of knowledge in the control of a simulated technical system. *Le Travail Human, 60*, 61–85.

Kragt, H., & Landweert, J. A. (1974). Mental skills in process control. In E. Edwards & F. P. Lees (Eds.), *The human operator in process control* (pp. 135–145). London: Taylor & Francis.

Kramer, A. F., & Weber, T. (2005, reprint from 2000). Applications of psychophysiology to human factors. In J. T. Cacioppo, L. G. Tassinary, & G. G. Berntson (Eds.), *Handbook of psychophysiology* (pp. 794–814). Cambridge: Cambridge University Press.

Laberge, J. C., Bullemer, P., & Whitlow, S. D. (2008). Communication and coordination failures in the process industries. In *Proceedings of the Human Factors and Ergonomics Society 52nd annual meeting, New York* (pp. 498–502). Santa Barbara: HFES.

Langan-Fox, J., Anglim, J., & Wilson, J. R. (2004). Mental models, team mental models, and performance: Process, development and future directions. *Human Factors and Ergonomics in Manufacturing, 14*, 331–352.

Marshall, S. P. (2007). Identifying cognitive state from eye metrics. *Aviation, Space, and Environmental Medicine, 78*(5 Suppl), B165.

Mathieu, J., Maynard, M. T., Rapp, T., & Gilson, L. (2008). Team effectiveness 1997–2007: A review of recent advancements and a glimpse into the future. *Journal of Management, 34*, 410–476. doi:10.1177/0149206308316061.

Meyer, B. (2008). *The effects of computer-elicited structural and group knowledge on complex problem solving performance*. Open access doctoral dissertation, Humboldt University Berlin, Berlin. Retrieved November 24, 2012, from http://edoc.hu-berlin.de/dissertationen/meyer-bertolt-2008-05-16/PDF/meyer.pdf

Miller, J. G. (1960). Information input overload and psychopathology. *The American Journal of Psychiatry, 116*, 695–704.

Mittag, W., & Hager, W. (2000). Ein Rahmenkonzept zur Evaluation psychologischer Interventionsmaßnahmen. In W. Hager, J.- L. Patry, & H. Brezing (Hrsg.) *Handbuch Evaluation psychologischer Interventionsmaßnahmen. Standards und Kriterien* (S. 102–129). Bern: Huber.

Montgomery, J., Gaddy, C., & Toquam, J. (1991, September). Team interaction skills evaluation criteria for nuclear power plant control room operators. *Proceedings of the Human Factors and Ergonomics Society Annual Meeting*, 35(13), 918–922.

Moore, B. A., Mason, S. T., & Crow, B. E. (2012). Assessment and management of acute combat stress on the battlefield. In C. H. Kennedy & E. A. Zillmer (Eds.), *Military psychology. clinical and operational applications* (pp. 73–92). New York: The Guilford Press.

Moray, N. (1996). A taxonomy and theory of mental models. In *Proceedings of the Human Factors and Ergonomics Society 40th annual meeting* (pp. 164–168). Thousand Oaks: Sage.

Moshman, D., & Geil, M. (1998). Collaborative reasoning: Evidence for collective rationality. *Thinking & Reasoning, 4*, 231–248.

Motowidlo, S. J., Dunnette, M. D., & Carter, G. W. (1990). An alternative selection procedure: The low-fidelity simulation. *Journal of Applied Psychology, 75*, 640–647.

Naikar, N. (2005). *A comparison of the decision ladder template and the recognition-primed decision model*. DSTO Defence Science and Technology Organisation, Air Operations Division, Australia. Retrieved November 24, 2012. http://www.dsto.defence.gov.au/attachments/A comparison of the decision ladder template and the recognition-primed decision model.pdf

Norman, D. A. (1983). Some observations on mental models. In D. Gentner & A. L. Stevens (Eds.), *Mental models* (pp. 7–15). Hillsdale: Erlbaum.

O'Connor, P., O'Dea, A., & Flin, R. (2008). Identifying the team skills required by nuclear operations personnel. *International Journal of Industrial Ergonomics, 38*, 1028–1037.

O'Hare, D. (2003). Aeronautical decision making: Metaphors, models, and methods. In P. S. Tsang & M. A. Vidulich (Eds.), *Principles and practice of aviation psychology* (pp. 201–238). Mahwah: Lawrence Erlbaum.

Orasanu, J. M., & Backer, P. (1996a). Stress and military performance. In J. E. Driskell & E. Salas (Eds.), *Stress and human performance* (pp. 89–125). Mahwah: Lawrence Erlbaum.

Orasanu, J. M., & Backer, P. (1996b). Stress and military performance. In J. E. Driskell & E. Salas (Eds.), *Stress and human performance* (pp. 89–126). Mahwah: Lawrence Erlbaum.

Ormerod, T. C., & Shepherd, A. (2004). Using task analysis for information requirements specification: The sub-goal template (SGT) method. In D. Diaper & N. A. Stanton (Eds.), *The handbook of task analysis for human-computer interaction* (pp. 347–365). Mahwah: Lawrence Erlbaum.

Ormerod, T. C., Richardson, J., & Shepherd, A. (1998). Enhancing the usability of a task analysis method: a notation and environment for requirements specification. *Ergonomics, 41*, 1642–1663.

Paris, C. R., Salas, E., & Cannon-Bowers, J. A. (2000). Teamwork in multi-person systems: a review and analysis. *Ergonomics, 43*, 1052–1075.

Patrick, J. (1992). *Training: Research and practice*. San Diego: Academic.

Patrick, J., James, N., & Ahmed, A. (2006a). Human processes of control: Tracing the goals and strategies of control room teams. *Ergonomics, 49*, 1395–1414.

Patrick, J., James, N., Ahmed, A., & Halliday, P. (2006b). Observational assessment of situation awareness, team differences and training implications. *Ergonomics, 49*, 393–417.

Prince, C., & Salas, E. (2000). In M. R. Endsley & D. J. Garland (Eds.), *Situation awareness analysis and measurement* (pp. 325–349). Boca Raton: CRC Press.

Proctor, R. W., & Dutta, A. (1995). *Skill acquisition and human performance*. Thousand Oaks: Sage.

Rasmussen, J. (1979). Notes on human error analysis and prediction. In G. Apostolakis & G. Volta (Eds.), *Synthesis and analysis methods for safety and reliability studies*. London: Plenum.

Rasmussen, J., & Jensen, A. (1974). Mental procedures in real-life tasks: A case study of electronic trouble shooting. *Ergonomics, 17*(3), 293–307.

Rasmussen, J. (1983). Skills, rules, and knowledge: Signals, signs, and symbols, and other distinctions in human performance models. *IEEE Transaction on System, Man, and Cybernetics, SMC-13*(3), 257–266.

Rasmussen, J., & Goodstein, L. P. (1985). *Decision support in supervisory control*. Roskilde: Risø National Laboratory.

Rasmussen, J., & Goodstein, L. P. (1987). Decision support in supervisory control of high-risk industrial systems. *Automatica, 23*, 663–671.

Reinartz, S. J. (1993). An empirical study of team behaviour in a complex and dynamic problem-solving context: A discussion of methodological and analytical aspects. *Ergonomics, 36*, 1281–1290.

Reinartz, S. J., & Reinartz, G. (1992). Verbal communication in collective control of simulated nuclear power plant incidents. *Reliability Engineering and System Safety, 36*, 245–251.

Ritzmann, S. (2012). *Entwicklung und Evaluation von Crew Ressource Management Training für Flight Attendants* [Development and evaluation of crew resource management training for flight attendants]. Lengerich: Pabst Science Publisher.

Ritzmann, S., Kluge, A., & Hagemann, V. (2011). Using comics as a transfer support tool for crew resource management training. In *Proceedings of the Human Factors and Ergonomics Society 55th annual meeting 2011* (pp. 2118–2122). Santa Monica: HFES.

Rosch, J. L., & Vogel-Walcutt, J. J. (2012, June). A review of eye-tracking applications as tools for training. *Cognition, Technology & Work*. Online first, 21, doi: 10.1007/s10111-012-0234-7

Roschelle, J., & Teasley, S. D. (1995). The construction of shared knowledge in collaborative problem solving. In C. E. O'Malley (Ed.), *Computer-supported collaborative learning* (pp. 69–197). Berlin: Springer.

Rossett, A., & Gautier-Downes, J. (1991). *A handbook of job aids*. San Francisco: Jossey-Bass/Pfeiffer.

Rouse, W. B., & Morris, N. M. (1985). *On Looking into the black box: Prospects and limits in the search for mental models* (Report No 85-2. AD-A 159 080). Atlanta: Center of Man-Machine Systems Research, Georgia Institute of Technology.

Rußwinkel, N., Urbas, L., & Thüring, M. (2011). Predicting temporal errors in complex task environments: A computational and experimental approach. *Cognitive Systems Research, 12*, 336–354.

Salas, E., & Cannon-Bowers, J. A. (2001). The science of training: A decade of progress. *Annual Review of Psychology, 52*, 471–499.

Salas, E., Dickinson, T. L., Converse, S. A., & Tannenbaum, S. I. (1992). Toward an understanding of team performance and training. In R. W. Swezey & E. Salas (Eds.), *Teams: Their training and performance* (pp. 3–29). Norwood: Ablex.

Salas, E., Driskell, J. E., & Hughes, S. (1996). Introduction: The study of stress and human performance. In J. E. Driskell & E. Salas (Eds.), *Stress and human performance* (pp. 1–46). Mahwah: Lawrence Erlbaum.

Salas, E., Wilson, K. A., Priest, H. A., & Guthrie, J. W. (2006). Design, delivery, and evaluation of training. In G. Salvendy (Ed.), *Handbook of human factors and ergonomics* (pp. 472–512). Hoboken: Wiley.

Salmon, P. M., Stanton, N. A., Walker, G. H., & Jenkins, D. P. (2009). *Distributed situation awareness. Theory, measurement, and application to teamwork.* Aldershot: Ashgate.

Schneider, W. (1999). Automaticity. In R. A. Wilson & F. C. Keil (Eds.), *The MIT encyclopedia of the cognitive science* (pp. 63–64). Cambridge, MA: MIT Press.

Sebok, A. (2000). Team performance in process control: Influences of interface design and staffing levels. *Ergonomics, 43*, 1210–36.

Shuffler, M. L., DiazGranados, D., & Salas, E. (2011). There's a science for that: Team development interventions in organizations. *Current Directions in Psychological Science, 20*, 365–372.

Simon, H. A. (1999). Problem solving. In R. A. Wilson & F. C. Keil (Eds.), *The MIT encyclopedia of the cognitive science* (pp. 674–676). Cambridge, MA: MIT Press.

Smith-Jentsch, K. A., Zeisig, R. L., Acton, B., & McPherson, J. A. (1998). Team dimensional training: A strategy for guided team self-correction. In J. A. Cannon-Bowers & E. Salas (Eds.), *Making decisions under stress: Implications for individual and team training* (pp. 271–297). Washington, DC: APA.

Stachowski, A. A., Kaplan, S. A., & Waller, M. J. (2009). The benefits of flexible team interaction during crisis. *Journal of Applied Psychology, 94*, 1536–1543.

Stanton, N. A., Wong, W., Gore, J., Sevdalis, N., & Strub, M. (2011). Critical thinking. *Theoretical Issues in Ergonomics Science, 12*, 204–209.

Sternberg, R. J. (2009). *Cognitive psychology*. Wadsworth: Cengage Learning.

Swezey, R. W. (1987). Design of job aids and procedure writing. In: Salvendy, G. (Ed.), *Handbook of human factors and ergonomics* (pp. 1039–1057). Hoboken: Wiley. doi: http://dx.doi.org/10.1080/135467898394148

Tsang, P. S., & Vidulich, M. A. (2006). Mental workload and situation awareness. In G. Salvendy (Ed.), *Handbook of human factors and ergonomics* (pp. 243–268). Hoboken: Wiley.

Tulving, E. (2002). Episodic memory: From mind to brain. *Annual Review of Psychology, 2002* (53), 1–25.

Tulving, E., & Markowitsch, H. J. (1998). Episodic and declarative memory: Role of the hippocampus. *Hippocampus, 8*, 198–204.

Uitdewillingen, S., Waller, M. J., & Zijlstra, F. R. H. (2010). Team cognition and adaptability in dynamic settings: A review of pertinent work. *International Review of Industrial and Organizational Psychology, 25*, 293–353.

Veldhuyzen, W., & Stassen, H. H. (1977). The internal model concept: An application to modelling human control of large ships. *Human Factors, 19*, 367–380.

Vicente, K. J., Mumaw, R. J., & Roth, E. M. (2004). Operator monitoring in a complex dynamic work environment: A qualitative cognitive model based on field observations. *Theoretical Issues in Ergonomic Science, 5*, 359–384.

Vidulich, M. A. (2003). Mental workload and situation awareness. Essential concepts in aviation psychology. In P. S. Tsang & M. A. Vidulich (Eds.), *Principles and practice of aviation psychology* (pp. 115–147). Mahwah: Lawrence Erlbaum.

Waller, M. J., Gupta, N., & Giambatista, R. C. (2006). Effects of adaptive behaviors and shared mental models on control crew performance. *Management Science, 50*, 1534–1544.

Warner, N. W., & Letsky, M. P. (2008). Empirical model of team collaboration focus in macroicognition. In M. P. Letsky, N. W. Warner, S. M. Fiore, & C. A. Smith (Eds.), *Macrocognition in teams. Theories and methodologies* (pp. 15–34). Aldershot: Ashgate.

Weyers, B., Burkolter, D., Luther, W., & Kluge, A. (2012). Formal modeling and reconfiguration of user interfaces for reduction of errors in failure handling of complex systems. *International Journal of Human-Computer Interaction.*, *28*, 646–665.

Wickens, C. D., & Hollands, J. G. (2000). *Engineering psychology and human performance* (3rd ed.). Upper Saddle River: Prentice Hall.

Wickens, C. D. (2008). Situation awareness: Review of Mica Endsley's 1995 articles on situation awareness theory and measurement. *Human Factors, 50*, 397–403.

Wickens, C. D., & McCarley, J. S. (2008). *Applied attention theory*. Boca Raton: CRC Press.

Wickens, C., Hutchins, S., Carolan, T., & Cumming, J. D. (2012). Attention and cognitive resources load in training strategies. In A. F. Healy & L. E. Bourne Jr. (Eds.), *Training cognition. Optimizing efficiency, durability, and generalizability* (pp. 67–88). New York: Psychology Press.

Wildman, J. L., Thayer, A. L., Pavlas, D., Steward, J. E., & Howse, W. R. (2012). Team knowledge research: Emerging trends and critical needs. *Human Factors, 54*, 84–111.

Williams, M. D., Hollan, J. D., & Stevens, A. L. (1983). Human reasoning about a simple physical system. In D. Gentner & A. L. Stevens (Eds.), *Mental models* (pp. 131–153). Hillsdale: Erlbaum.

Wilson, J. R., & Rutherford, A. (1989). Mental models: Theory and application in human factors. *Human Factors, 31*, 617–634.

Wilson, K. A., Salas, E., & Andrews, D. H. (2010). Preventing errors in the heat of the battle: Formal and informal learning strategies to prevent teamwork breakdowns. In D. H. Andrews, R. P. Herz, & M. B. Wolf (Eds.), *Human factors issues in combat identification* (pp. 1–28). Aldershot: Ashgate.

Woods, D. D. (1992). Process tracing methods for the study of cognition outside of the experimental psychology laboratory. In G. Klein, R. Calderwood, & J. Orasanu (Eds.), *Decision making in action: Models and methods* (pp. 1–26). Norwood: Ablex.

Yin, S., & Laberge, J. (2010, September). How process control operators derive, update, and apply mental models. *Proceedings of the Human Factors and Ergonomics Society Annual Meeting, 54*(23), 1946–1950. Thousand Oaks: Sage.

Zijlstra, F. R. H., Waller, W., & Phillips, S. I. (2012). Setting the tone: Early interaction patters in swift starting teams as a predictor of effectiveness. *European Journal of Work and Organizational Psychology, 21*, 749–777.

Chapter 4
Basic Learning Processes and Supportive Learning Mechanisms for Taskwork and Teamwork to Control Complex Systems

A brief preface to this chapter: When I was planning this book, I imagined developing in this chapter something like a learning theory for controlling complex systems. However, during my research into learning theories, "learning laws" or learning mechanisms, I established that the previous works, for instance on dynamic decision making, complex problem-solving or complex task acquisition, are of very limited help regarding jobs and tasks such as those described in this book. Indeed, many learning processes and the laws and principles of learning and memory derived from them, which are also in the textbooks, frequently prove not to be generalisable for this purpose.

In his review on the "law of memory" and learning, Roediger (2008) establishes that "laws of memory" do not meet the criteria proposed by Teigen (2002) for being a "law", for example the criterion of validity (the law is a well established regularity with no exception) or universality (the law should be independent of place and time). Roediger (2008) declares that a lack of generality of formal laws, or to take it even further "everybody knows" commonsensical generalisations such as "practice improves memory" are either invalid or at least need some qualification (Roediger 2008). Based on a model by Jenkins (1979), Roediger (2008) points out that many phenomena that are extolled as laws originated in very specific experimental surroundings, and were subject to

- a specific *sample* (e.g. specific with regard to age, abilities, knowledge/expertise, disorders and traits),
- specific *encoding* conditions (e.g. context, setting, instruction, activities, strategies),
- specific *learning material*/events (e.g. pictures, words, sounds, sentences, lists of words, videos, life events, general knowledge), and
- specific conditions of *retrieval* (e.g. free recall, cued recall, recognition, transfer, stem completion, fragment completion).

In summary, Roediger (2008, p. 230) states, in the words of Jenkins (1979), that: "The memory phenomena that we see depend on what kinds of subjects we study, what kinds of acquisition conditions we provide, what kinds of materials we choose

A. Kluge, *The Acquisition of Knowledge and Skills for Taskwork and Teamwork to Control Complex Technical Systems*, DOI 10.1007/978-94-007-5049-4_4,

to work with, and what kinds of criterion measures we obtain. Furthermore, the dependencies themselves are complex, the variables interact vigorously with one another" (Jenkins 1979, p. 431). And in this sense, Roediger (2008) shows that such general assumptions as "practice makes perfect", the "deeper the level of processing, the better the retention", "distributed practice is better than massed practice", and the assumption that the generation of information, for example in self-directed learning, supports retention ("generation effect", see below) can be confirmed in some samples and with some material, but there are also many exceptions. According to Roediger (2008), the most fundamental principle of learning and memory is that when making any generalisations about learning and memory, one must add that "it depends".

Why am I writing this here? I refer to Roediger (2008) in order to make it clear that the learning theories used in the following originate for the most part from different contexts, were tested on different tasks, and demonstrated with different subjects than would be precisely fitting for process control. Although there are some theoretical assumptions regarding learning processes in dynamic decision making, here too, one must look closely at the sample, the specific complex systems and the retrieval conditions which the research investigated. For instance, as Osman (2010) and Kerstholt and Raaijmakers (1997) also determined, it can be observed that most of the studies, for instance on dynamic decision making, were conducted with students who had no prior knowledge, or else with chess players, sportspeople or violinists, i.e. persons with expertise, or in the area of piloting or preparations for a deployment in the military context. Moreover, both Osman (2010) and Kerstholt and Raaijmakers (1997) put forward the following criticism: On the one hand, the scientific community is aware that an extremely long phase of practice and exercises is necessary to reach expertise in dynamic decision making (i.e. over a hundred trials or several years). However, on the other hand, the subjects in the laboratory only had a few trials at their disposal in order to actually explore and understand the complex system. In my view, nothing at all is known about how persons who have prior knowledge, for example the field operator with ten years of field experience, learn to control a complex technical system like a subunit in a refinery. And equally, nothing is known about how, exactly, skill retention and decay take place in this very group of people (Sonnentag et al. 2004).

Furthermore, it can be determined that works which deal, for instance, with decision making in "natural settings" such as naturalistic decision making do describe the decision making processes of experts, but they say nothing about the previous learning process, except perhaps that one needs "lots of experience". One still finds isolated training concepts, but no learning theories.

In this respect, in the following remarks, it is important to keep in mind that the theoretical models presented here cannot be applied in a 1:1 manner, but should rather be first carefully and circumspectly transferred to knowledge and skill acquisition for controlling complex technical systems under consideration of the given circumstances of the job. A central emphasis in this regard is on the theme of "experiences", or rather how one becomes an expert, as this book does not aim to focus on general phenomena of learning and retrieval, but on the specific requirements of "becoming an expert through experience on-the-job".

4.1 Components of the Learning Theory Perspective: Acquisition, Retention and Transfer

In the following, we tackle the general principles of knowledge and skill acquisition, which are linked to the acquisition of experiences, for example through particular forms of practice in order to become an expert in controlling a complex technical system.

Basic assumptions about learning processes of core aspects of controlling complex systems, such as mental models, situation assessment and control actions by using SOPs, and collaborative complex problem-solving as introduced in Chap. 3, are described and analysed from a learning theory perspective. A learning theory perspective addresses three fundamental cognitive components of learning (Bourne and Healy 2012):

1. Acquiring new (declarative, procedural) knowledge and skills (Table 4.1)
2. Retention of what has been learned over time (sometimes without further exposure or training)
3. Transfer of acquired knowledge and skills to new contexts (Bourne and Healy 2012)

The three components of knowledge and skill acquisition, retention and transfer as introduced by Bourne and Healy (2012) take place, with some interdependence, across different time spans and in different environments. Nevertheless, it has been shown that optimising one of these components does not necessarily support the other two simultaneously (Bourne and Healy 2012; Roediger 2008), for example conditions that produce rapid skill acquisition do not necessarily produce better retention, and maximum retention does not necessarily ensure maximum transfer. And as we will see in the following, not all researchers are of the opinion that there are actually no laws, as Roediger (2008), Teigen (2002) and Jenkins (1979) see it. Indeed, Bourne and Healy (2012) as well as VanLehn (1996) present laws with which I will work in the following on a very high level of abstraction.

General principles, "laws" of knowledge and skill acquisition, retention and forgetting, and principles of transfer are named "The power law of practice" (skill acquisition), "The power law of forgetting" (skill retention and degradation, respectively) and "Laws relating to similarity" (transfer to abnormal situations), respectively.

Power law of practice: Most tasks have the characteristic that with practice, performance improves with respect to accuracy and speed, with the greatest changes occurring early in practice (Bourne and Healy 2012; Proctor and Dutta 1995; VanLehn 1996). According to the power law of practice (Snoddy 1926;

Table 4.1 Introducing "knowledge" and "skills"

	Description
Declarative Knowledge	Declarative knowledge is the body of facts and information, concepts and models about a domain that a person knows (Anderson 1983; Bourne and Healy 2012; Proctor and Dutta 1995), which is mainly called explicit knowledge (Sun 2002).
Procedural Knowledge	Procedural knowledge is the non-declarative set of skills or knowledge about the sequence of steps a person has to perform (Proctor and Dutta 1995, p. 16; Bourne and Healy 2012), which is mainly called implicit knowledge (Sun 2002). Proceduralisation refers to the process by which learners switch from the explicit use of declarative knowledge to a direct application of procedural knowledge (Anderson 1995, p. 283).
Skill	"Skill is goal-directed, well-organised behaviour that is acquired through practice and performed with economy of effort" (Proctor and Dutta 1995, p. 18).

Newell and Rosenbloom 1981), learning and skill acquisition is described as a linear function of the logarithm of time and trials.

Roediger (2008) demonstrates that the effect of practice and repetition also has exceptions and that repetition alone does not always improve performance. Others, for instance Heathcote et al. (2000), have argued that the power law is misnamed and that an exponential equation fits the data better, while Rickard (1997) states that the type of function obtained depends on the types of task practised. It is not my intention to establish a new law in this book. Instead, I will merely refer to the fact that practice and experience are also relevant for knowledge and skill acquisition for controlling complex technical systems and my concern will be with working out the type of experience and practice that is necessary for this. In this regard, I refer to the instance-based learning theory (IBLT, Gonzalez et al. 2003), the instance theory of attention and memory (ITAM, Logan 2002) and the dual-architecture model by Sun et al. (2001, 2005) and Sun (2002).

Power law of forgetting: "With the passage of time and the lack of opportunity to rehearse or refresh acquired knowledge and skill, performance declines and reflects failure to retain information" (Bourne and Healy 2012, p. 4). The skill degradation expresses itself in an increased response time or decreased accuracy and has been known of since Ebbinghaus (1885). The power law of forgetting (Wixted and Carpenter 2007) can be thought of as the inverse of the power law of practice (Bourne and Healy 2012), although Rubin and Wenzel (1996) debate which function fits best. Here too, Roediger (2008) points out that there are exceptions. For the purpose of this book and referring back to Chap. 2 and to the requirements of handling non-routine situations, it is interesting to think about the power law of forgetting and its relevance for controlling complex technical systems and skill retention. To my knowledge, and also that of Sonnentag et al. (2004), there have not yet been any investigations on how forgetting on-the-job and in process control are expressed, as even if certain non-routine/normal events are temporally separated from one another by retention intervals, the operator does not merely do nothing in the meantime, but continues to be busy with controlling the plant. In terms of the theme of forgetting in this book, I refer above all to the theoretical and empirical works of Bjork and Bjork (1992, 2006) and Bjork (2011).

Transfer: Laws relating to similarity: Transfer describes the process of acquisition of one task that affects the performance of another task (Bourne and Healy 2012; Proctor and Dutta 1995). Transfer is relevant for non-routine abnormal situations which require problem-solving (see Chap. 2). The major variable that determines the extent and direction of transfer is similarity between two tasks (Bourne and Healy 2012) or the number of identical elements (Thorndike and Woodworth 1901; Proctor and Dutta 1995), respectively. Similarity is important across many areas of cognition (Gentner and Markman 1997). Experiences are stored in categories in memory largely on the basis of their similarity to a category or to stored exemplars (Gentner and Markman 1997). Similarities are used in order to generate a set of options. Especially in naturalistic decision contexts, people rely on their previous experience to determine a set of considerations (Markman and Medin 2002). An operator may see a new situation as similar to a prior episode, which suggests potential options. In the following chapter, the concern is therefore with the importance of awareness of similarity for the learning, retention and transfer process.

This chapter is oriented towards these three fundamental components. In this chapter, I begin with learning theories which explain learning processes and sub-processes for controlling complex systems. Skill retention and skill decay, respectively, will then be addressed. Finally, transfer conditions and their similarity to the learning contexts as introduced in Chaps. 2 and 3 are considered.

At the end of each subchapter, propositions are stated concerning the theoretically derived fundamental learning processes which are taken up for suggesting principles of training design in Chap. 5 integrated in the Staged Process Control Readiness Training (SPCRT).

4.2 The Learning Objective: Becoming an Expert with "Lots of Experience"

As outlined in Chap. 3, according to Hollnagel (2007) and Hollnagel and Woods (2005), the control task is a cyclical one. In their contextual control model (COCOM, Hollnagel 2007; Hollnagel and Woods 2005), controlling and adjusting a system encompasses a cyclical relationship linking events followed by the assessment of the situations, intentions followed by choosing what to do, and actions taken. In this respect, it has already been expressed on multiple occasions that, for example, mental models and expertise are formed through *experience*. In the following, the initial concern is therefore with the interplay between practice and experience in relation to the knowledge and skills relevant for process control.

"Novices" who prepare for a job in the control room usually have some years of field experience (see Chap. 3) and are not completely without any prior knowledge.

Table 4.2 Definition of Novice and Expert (Chi 2006; Hoffman 1998; Kolodner 1983)

	Definition
Novice	Someone who is new and has had some minimal exposure to the domain
Expert	Someone whose judgments are uncommonly accurate and reliable, whose performance shows consummate skill and economy of effort, and who can manage effectively with rare and difficult cases and has special skills or knowledge derived from extensive work experience also with sub-domains

The novice is inexperienced in a particular job, and can be perceived as the counterpart of the "expert" in a certain domain (Chi 2006; Hoffman 1998; Kolodner 1983, Table 4.2).

Kolodner (1983) assumes that knowledge for becoming an expert is built up incrementally on the basis of work experience. In this respect, the difference between "experience" and "practice" should be described at the outset. First, I define experience as *work* experience. Work experience and practice have in common that they include the accumulation of instances (Table 4.3). As Osman (2010) outlines, the acquisition of instance-based knowledge is pivotal to the development of skill learning in complex systems in order to map the task demands to previously experienced situations. Instances are sets of environmental cues, called "the situation" (S), of a set of actions applicable to the situation, called "decision" (D), and the evaluation of the goodness of a decision in that particular situation, called "utility" (U) (Gonzalez et al. 2003), as described below. The main difference between experience and practice lies in the fact that work experience means the accumulation of instances in informal settings on-the-job with ongoing task exposure, while practice takes place in deliberately and purposely designed instructional settings near-the-job (Table 4.3).

The term "experience" is further used by the authors of the cited studies in a broad sense, including "a number of learning trials", "discovery learning" or "repeated task execution". "Experience" in these cited studies therefore stands rather for uncontrolled "learning-by-doing" results in knowledge and skill acquisition in experimental, more artificial settings, as opposed to job and work experiences in natural settings.

Informal learning is characterised as unstructured, experiential and non-institutional (Marsick and Volpe 1999) and involves a process that is not determined or designed by the organisation and results from the natural opportunities that occur in a person's working life (Ellinger 2005; Tannenbaum et al. 2010). It is proposed that:

Proposition 1: The overall learning requirements include the development from a novice to an expert.

Proposition 2: The learning process implies the accumulation of instances through work experience and practice.

Table 4.3 Defining and differentiating experience and practice

	Definition and Differentiation
Work experience	Accumulation of instances in informal settings on-the-job through ongoing task exposure
Practice	Accumulation of instances in deliberately and purposely designed instructional formal settings near-the-job, e.g. simulator training through repeated task exposure

4.3 Work Experience and Practice for Instance-Based Learning

A learning theory that is helpful in understanding learning processes to acquire the required skills for controlling a complex system is the instance-based learning theory (IBLT) by Gonzalez et al. (2003), which was developed to explain and predict learning processes for dynamic decision making (see Chap. 3). Referring back to Chap. 3, dynamic decision making means that a series and sequence of decisions is required to reach the goal, these decisions are not independent and the state of the decision problem changes, both autonomously and as a consequence of the operator's action (Brehmer 1992; Edwards 1962; Gonzalez et al. 2003). Dynamic decision making also includes the characteristics that were already described in the COCOM (see above), with the aspects of aging of information, time needed to chose a course of action, windows of opportunity and feedback delay (Hollnagel 2007). Instance-based learning theory (IBLT, Gonzalez et al. 2003) integrates learning processes such as accumulation of examples in memory through training and task repetition, the recognition of patterns and selective search for alternative solutions, similarity-based memory retrieval, gradual withdrawal of attention while increasing memory retrieval, and the transition from rule-based to exemplar-based performance (Gonzalez et al. 2003; Osman 2010).

In Fig. 4.1, the IBLT process is integrated into the COCOM in order to show the links between the two models. The main steps proposed by the IBLT in the dynamic decision making process are recognition (comparable to assessing the situation in COCOM), judgment (comparable to the forming of an intention in COCOM), a choice (choosing what to do in COCOM) and feedback (which is also feedback in COCOM, see Chap. 3).

Based on the IBLT, a control task which is routine, non-routine/normal or non-routine/abnormal can be described as a set of environmental cues named as the situation (S), for example indicators on the screen, alarms, warnings, of a set of actions applicable to the situation, which is named decision (D), for example a number of SOPs required, and the evaluation of the goodness of a decision in that particular situation (U) (Gonzalez et al. 2003), for example with respect to the extent to which organisational goals such as productivity and safety are met.

When assessing the situation, the operator tries to classify the situation as typical or atypical as the IBLT would state, or as routine, non-routine/normal or

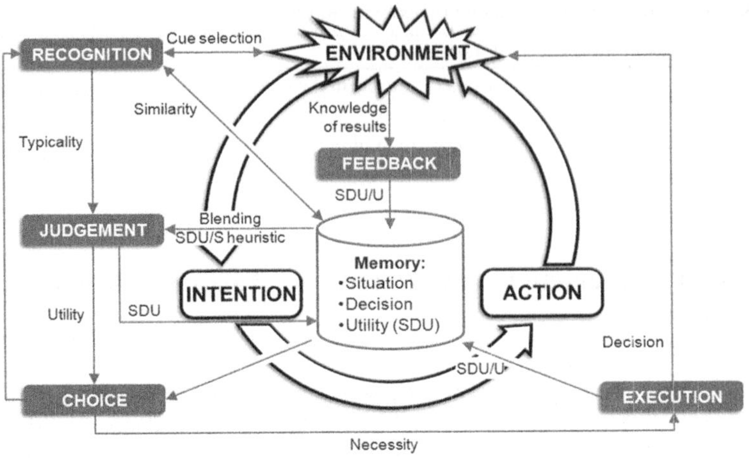

Fig. 4.1 The IBLT integrated into the COCOM

non-routine/abnormal, as introduced as control situation in Chap. 2. A cue is an aspect of the immediate situation, and experienced decision makers know what other elements are found in a situation when a particular cue is present (Ross et al. 2005). The sense of typicality is connected to typical goals, typical actions and typical sequences of activities (Ross et al. 2005).

Facts become integrated through occurrence in the same episode, stored in episodic memory (see Table 4.4). Episodic memory (also called autobiographical recollection) involves re-experiencing a past event that is specific in time and place (Conway 2008; Kolodner 1983; Ryan et al. 2008; Tulving 2002, see Chap. 3). Semantic recollection, in contrast, involves facts and general knowledge about the world (Ryan et al. 2008). According to Conway (2008), episodic memory represents "short time slices of experience" which are either actively constructed into contextualising autobiographical knowledge structures or embedded into these structures in their representation in long-term memory (Conway 2008, p. 21). The content of episodic memory is close to experience, predominantly represented in the form of images, has an observer's perspective and contains sensory-perceptual-conceptual-affective summary features of that experience (Conway 2008). Episodic memory is essential for learning (Conway 2008), in particular for the abstraction and schematisation of knowledge. *Two or more contiguous episodic memory entries provide the structure and process to abstract knowledge from instances for that abstraction* (Conway 2008). This provides a basis for schema and concept formation and the development of autobiographical knowledge and therefore becomes integrated in long-term memory as knowledge of the world (or the technical system to be controlled) or as knowledge of an individual life or job biography (Conway 2008).

Episodic memory provides a detailed record of changes in short-term goal processing and intention implementation, and together with conceptual knowledge,

Table 4.4 Characteristics of episodic memory

	Characteristics
Episodic memory…	…involves re-experiencing a past event that is specific in time and place
	…represents "short time slices of experience"
	…is close to experience, predominantly represented in the form of images, has an observer's perspective and contains sensory-perceptual-conceptual-affective summary features of that experience
	…is essential for learning (Conway 2008), in particular for the abstraction and schematisation of knowledge
	Two or more contiguous episodic memory entries provide the structure and process to abstract knowledge from instances for that abstraction
	…is also necessary for "mental simulation" of future events
	Mentally reconstructing past episodes and mentally constructing future episodes are two sides of a coin of mental time travel
	Generalised episodes serve as an organising point for storing similar episodes

to which episodic memory can give rise, provides the ability to form and achieve long-term goals. Once formed, conceptual knowledge supports the generation and pursuit of goals that extend beyond the range of episodic consciousness (Conway 2008). Episodic memory is also necessary for "mental simulation" of future events as attributed to the supportive characteristics of mental models (see Chap. 3). Episodic memory as memories of past events matters to the extent that such memories inform present and future action (Suddendorf and Corballis 2008). Mentally reconstructing past episodes and mentally constructing future episodes are two sides of a coin of mental time travel (Suddendorf and Corballis 2008) to predict future events or outcomes. Kolodner (1983) assumes that once a generalised episode is formed, full details of individual episodes do not need to be stored. Only the features of each which differentiate it from the generalised episode need to be encoded. The generalised episodes serve as an organising point for storing similar episodes, so that if memory is well organised in this way, retrieval can be directed to only the most relevant items (Kolodner 1983).

Returning to the assumptions of the IBLT (Fig. 4.1), a situation is judged as routine and non-routine/normal if there are (episodic) memories of similar situations ("S"), for example disturbances such as cold or hot weather or planned maintenance work as well as memories about which SOP to apply and implement, and of the "D" part, i.e. knowing that the SOP will lead to the desired result. Operators assess the situation as typical when previous similar situations closely match the cues of the current situation (Gonzalez et al. 2003). In episodic memory, experienced operators' knowledge is "indexed" (Ross et al. 2005), and facts and activities are linked in terms of

- Cues: If I see this, it means this larger pattern probably exists in the situation…
- Expectancies: In a pattern like this, I've usually seen things unfold in this way…
- Goals: It is important in this type of situation to do this....

- Typical Actions: I have seen this goal achieved by doing the following... (Ross et al. 2005)

In the case of an atypical or non-routine/abnormal situation, there is no learned SDU instance (or SOPs) already available which can be retrieved from memory, for example when operators are new in the control room. Therefore, available non-contextual SDUs will be searched for, for example by aggregating a utility value from past experiences if similar situations have ever occurred before. In atypical or non-routine/abnormal situations novice operators perform more disorganized and "random search of alternatives" (Gonzalez et al. 2003) and use heuristics to evaluate a decision's potential success (Gonzalez et al. 2003).

This means that decisions in general are based on similar cases in the past (Gilboa and Schmeidler 2000), whereas a case has three components: the decision problem, the act that was chosen and the outcome experienced (Gilboa and Schmeidler 2000). Courses of action as a decision making result are evaluated by a similarity-weighted sum of the utility they yielded in past cases. This kind of situation assessment is then called "recognition-primed" and based on comparisons with past work experiences and "cases" retrieved from memory. Klein et al. (1986; Klein 2000) formulated the Recognition-Primed Decision Model (RPDM) of how people make decisions in naturalistic settings (Naturalistic Decision Making, NDM) based on their past work experiences and without comparing all possible options in the problem space that can be generally thought of. Similar to the IBLT, the focus of NDM is on the process of decision making in ill-defined situations, in dynamic environments, with competing goals under time pressure, with multiple players in an organisational context and with high personal stakes (Ross et al. 2006). The NDM concept has been applied to process control, for example by Carvallo et al. (2005) and by Greitzer et al. (2008).

Situation assessment as pattern matching

Pattern matching is involved in both the IBLT and the RPDM (Osman 2010). Recognition consists of four constructs: expectancies, relevant cues, plausible goals and typical actions, which lead to a course of action (Klein 2000). In a "simple match" situation, the situation is perceived as typical in terms of being a prototype of the situation or being analogous to something that has been experienced before.

In cases when a situation is not perceived as typical, alternative interpretations of the nature of the situation exist. It will be necessary to analyse the evidence for whether one hypothesis is supported more than others (Klein 2000). This may be realised by constructing a story to check whether each of the alternative explanations or assessments is consistent with the evidence (Klein 2000). Harvey and Fischer (2005) distinguish between a fast recognition-primed loop and a slow cognitive loop for hypothesis testing as proposed in the RPD and NDM.

The IBLT proposes that skills for recognition (situation assessment) develop over time from a heuristic-based procedure applied by novices to a direct retrieval of a solution triggered by the current situational cues (see also Bjork 2011). Inexperienced controllers may search in a disorganised manner for cues in order to classify the situation, whereas more experienced operators have learned the value (or diagnosticity; Tversky 1977, see below) of certain indicators in comparison to others. Experts in that respect spend more time than novices understanding the cues and their dynamics in the situation, whereas novices tend to spend more time considering courses of action (Ross et al. 2006). As was described in Chap. 3, situation assessment is supported by monitoring activities, such as confirming expectations about plant state, pursuing unexpected findings, checking the likelihood of problems, validating initial indication, and determining an appropriate referent for a specific indication (Vicente et al. 2004). For assessing the situation, Vicente et al. (2004) consider knowledge about the set of indicators available (declarative), the location of indicators (declarative), how to read indicators, how they work and how they fail (procedural) as well as how to assess and configure displays (procedural) as important. Finally, the operator also holds knowledge about priorities and frequencies with which relevant indicators should be monitored (Vicente et al. 2004). The IBLT assumes that novices engage in a more thorough search to determine the principles that are applicable to the current situation (Gonzalez et al. 2003). When operators are new in the control room, it might be difficult to know which cues are important, so due to the lack of "cases" and instances in such cases, non-contextual knowledge and heuristics may guide the focus of attention and monitoring. The novice operator is unfamiliar with the salience and diagnosticity (Tversky 1977, described below) of cues.

For operators with greater work experience, cues that have emerged as important stand out in the recognition process because they resemble cues in previous instances. As Vicente et al. (2004) also point out, this experience guides attention and produces selective behaviour (Gonzalez et al. 2003). Recognition is based on attention, guided by previous knowledge and determined by instance similarity (Gonzalez et al. 2003, p. 598; Osman 2010). In the Instance Theory of Attention and Memory (ITAM, Logan 2002), Logan assumes that "*attention and categorization are both choice processes and that both are instantiated as races between competing alternatives. Attention involves choice between competing objects in the display, whereas categorization involves choice between competing classifications of display objects. ITAM assumes that the races underlying these choices run simultaneously and in fact are one and the same. An object is selected and a classification of that object is selected in the same act of cognition. The choice processes are driven by similarities between display objects and memory representations of the alternative categories. Categories are represented as collections of instances, and learning occurs through the accumulation of instances over practice. The output of object selection and category selection is input to a random-walk response selection process*" (Logan 2002, p. 377).

As Logan (2002) proposes that learning occurs through the accumulation of instance over practice, also in NDM theory, through work experience, experts have acquired advanced perceptual skills to make fine discriminations between instances. Experts see more in a situation than novices (Ross et al. 2006). Experts have also acquired a larger repertoire of complex patterns to recognise what is typical, what is missing or is unexpected to be labelled an anomaly (Ross et al. 2006).

Choosing a course of action - evaluating a decision's potential success under time pressure

After assessing the situation as typical (normal) or atypical (abnormal), operators search for a course of action and evaluate the accuracy of a possible action regarding the organisational goals.

The IBLT as well as the NDM and also Kerstholt and Raaijmakers (1997) assume that as, in dynamic decision making, time is limited (e.g. limited by the window of opportunity), the duration of the search for courses of action based on past experiences and stored SDUs in memory is limited and determines the time remaining to take an action. If there is little time left, the decision maker executes the current best (most similar) alternative retrieved from memory (Gonzalez et al. 2003). By practising a task, operators learn from experiences in terms of acquiring more and more SDU instances, which become increasingly differentiated through experiences of several similar and dissimilar situations (Gonzalez et al. 2003; Kolodner 1983; Osman 2010). The IBLT proposes that operators who experience a non-routine/abnormal situation will determine the utility of a course of action by using heuristics and by combining the utility from similar instances generated in the past (Gonzalez et al. 2003). Accordingly, in the RPD (Klein 2000), a course of action is not evaluated by comparing it to all other courses of action stored in memory but is mentally simulated to see whether it will work or whether it needs to be modified (e.g. as described in Chap. 3 in the section on mental models). This is possible through mental time travel based on episodic memory processes (Conway 2008). When a considered course of action is rejected because mental simulation led to the conclusion that the desired outcome is not achieved, the operator considers and simulates the next most similar option from the response repertoire for that situation (Klein 2000). According to Ross et al. (2006), experts have acquired richer internal representations of how things work in their work domain and their mental models allow them to learn and to understand situations more rapidly (Kolodner 1983; Ross et al. 2006).

Under time pressure, the moment of intervention is adjusted to the time left (Kersthold and Raaijmakers 1997), and when choosing a course of action, operators will apply a combination of an optimising and a satisfactory strategy (Simon 1957; Gonzalez et al. 2003). The combination includes the fact that several alternative courses of action deduced from the most similar cases stored in memory are mentally simulated (see Chap. 3, mental models) and after each simulation, the operator decides whether to search further for better-fitting alternatives or whether to execute the currently best alternative. The more time there is left, the more mental simulations might be run because there is no direct need to act fast (Gonzalez et al. 2003; Kerstholt and Raaijmakers 1997). Also in this respect, experience and practice lead to the acquisition of instances and cases which incorporate knowledge about the dynamics and dynamic changes as well as about windows of opportunity and the aging of information (Hollnagel 2007; Hollnagel and Woods 2005). Novices might perceive all or most atypical situations as urgent and react too early. With practice and further work experience, operators should learn the temporal relationship between events and results and react more closely to the moment that would produce the best performance (Gonzalez et al. 2003). The recognition judgment and mental simulation process continues until an appropriate course of action can be identified.

Action implementation

After choosing a course of action, at this point in the COCOM, part-task integration to perform a complex task begins, as introduced in Chap. 2, which is guided in most process industries by SOPs which need to be executed. Work experience and practice in action execution help experts to know how to get things implemented with a wide repertoire of tactics (Ross et al. 2006). As the execution of SOPs is subject to procedural errors as introduced in Chap. 3, it is important to pay attention to automaticity in skill execution. Logan (1988) construes automaticity as a memory phenomenon, governed by the principles that govern memory processes. Automaticity is based on a learning mechanism in terms of the accumulation of separate episodic traces with experience, which is produced as a gradual transition from algorithmic, procedural processing to memory-based processing. Logan (1988) relates the instance theory of automation to existing theories of episodic memory (e.g. Conway 2008; Tulving 2002, see Chap. 3) and skill acquisition (Anderson 1983, 1993; Schneider 1985). The IBLT does not say much about action implementation, for example executing an SOP. Gonzalez et al. (2003) write that the task of the participants in the dynamic decision task Water Purification Plant was to distribute water by opening and closing pumps in a chain of tanks. The Water Purification Plant can be explained in less than one hour and a trial is completed within a few minutes (Gonzalez et al. 2003, p. 601). Although it is not described in more detail, I assume that the actions required in this dynamic decision task used for validating the IBLT were not as comprehensive and did not comprise as many steps to form a sequence as is the case in process control, in which, for example, up to 60 steps must be executed to start up a plant.

As the IBLT does not propose specific learning processes for acquiring skills to execute a course of action, at this point, the theoretical assumption of Sun et al. (2001, 2005) is capitalised on in order to explain the acquisition of skills which are required, for example, in action implementation and SOP execution. Sun et al. (2001, 2005; Sun 2002) assume, in contrast to other theories of skill acquisition, that human learning is gradual, ongoing and concurrent with task performance, one-directional rather than "top-down", starting from a declarative phase and proceeding to a procedural phase, for example as in Anderson's Theory of Skill Acquisition (Anderson 1983, 1993). According to Sun et al. (2001), the individual acquires both procedural and declarative knowledge from ongoing experience in the world and while performing a task, which they call bottom-up learning.

Bottom-up learning is contrasted with top-down learning, which proposes the acquisition of declarative knowledge before procedural knowledge (Table 4.1). Most skill learning theories are built on the distinction between declarative and procedural knowledge and assume a top-down approach from declarative to procedural knowledge (Sun et al. 2005), for example as in Fitts' proposition. According to Fitts' model (1962/1990), skill acquisition starts with a cognitive phase (knowledge-based behaviour, Rasmussen 1983), which includes heavy involvement of conscious cognitive processes in order to understand the nature of the task and how it should be performed (Proctor and Dutta 1995; Johnson in press). After the cognitive phase, skill acquisition proceeds to an associative phase. In the associative phase, situational cues and inputs are more directly linked to appropriate actions (rule-based behaviour, Rasmussen 1983). Error rates and performance time decrease. The transition from the associative phase to the autonomous phase is marked by reduced interference from outside demands and a lessening of attentional requirements (Proctor and Dutta 1995, p. 15). The autonomous phase of skill acquisition performance is automatic, no longer requiring conscious control. But automaticity may take months or even years to develop (Fitts 1962/1990). Rasmussen's framework, which distinguishes between three modes of performance (knowledge-based, rule-based and skill-based performance) refers to Fitts' phases of skill acquisition (Proctor and Dutta 1995), in which knowledge-based behaviour corresponds to the cognitive phase, rule-based performance is guided by rules and production in line with the associative phase, while skill-based behaviour is characterised by "smooth, automated, and highly integrated patterns of behavior" (Rasmussen 1983, p. 258). The major difference between Fitts' and Rasmussen's assumptions lies in Rasmussen's emphasis that, for example, the trained operator can move between modes of behaviour as dictated by task demands, whereas Fitts assumes skill acquisition as a progression through the stages of learning (Proctor and Dutta 1995, p. 17). The basic idea in the models by Fitts and Rasmussen is that novices first acquire a great amount of explicit knowledge in a domain, which is consciously processed in early phases of skill acquisition, which then, through practice, turns into a procedural form, which leads to skilled performance (Sun et al. 2001). According to Anderson (1993), this is accomplished by acquiring explicit memory instances which are utilised in performance through analogical processes and by creating production rules from these instances after repeated use (Sun et al. 2001).

Alternatively, Sun et al. (2001) argue that based on their evidence, a bottom-up process can also be observed the "other way around", in which *after a longer period of practice and ongoing experience a process of generalising specific knowledge sets in, to form generic schemas in forms of declarative knowledge and rules.* Sun (2002) concerns himself with everyday human activities. He assumes that humans constantly interact with the world in a direct, immediate, non-deliberative, "mindless" and non-reflective way. Reactive coping with situational affordances in the world as well as explicit deliberative thinking forms the backdrop of everyday activities (Dreyfus 1992; Sun 2002). Human Thinking is implicitly embodied, for example, in human activities that have become very routine in nature, and in habitual sequences of behavioural responses (Sun 2002). In this respect, the learning of reactive routines is mostly a trial-and-error adaptation process (Sun 2002). Sun (2002) raises the criticism that although explicit knowledge used in explicit thinking does occur, it is not as crucial as is believed in other cognitive theories, such as those described above, for example by Anderson (1983, 1993) or which focused less on everyday activities. Everyday activities are an interwoven set of habitual domains. Acquired skills and routines are used in their respective domains, i.e. in situations for which the skills and routines were learned or similar situations. Skill learning in the everyday world means the continuous process of forming and changing habitual routines with respect to goals and needs.

For this reason, in their assumption on human learning in everyday activities, Sun et al. (2001) and Sun (2002) assume a "two-level" cognitive architecture, which consists of two main components: The top level (declarative level) encodes explicit declarative knowledge and the bottom level encodes implicit procedural knowledge. At each level of the model, there are action-centred and non-action-centred modules (Sun 2002).

In addition to the two levels, Sun et al. (2001) also include instances or episodic memory in the architecture, which stores recent experiences in the form of "input, output and result". This is equivalent to the SDU terminology used by Gonzalez et al. (2003). The episodic memory (see above) is used for learning and is assumed to be a part of the declarative knowledge.

The model that Sun et al. (2005) present incorporates bottom-up (from procedural to declarative) and top-down learning (from declarative to procedural) in skill learning. Based on remarks by Mathews et al. (1989) and Stanley et al. (1989), Sun et al. (2005) argue that novices are guided by two sources in their behaviour in complex cognitive tasks. One source is based on their explicit conceptual representation in terms of declarative knowledge (such as mental models of the target systems, system-based knowledge as suggested by Kluwe 1997 and Vicente et al. 2004, see Chap. 3) and the other an independent source derived from memory-based processing, which abstracts patterns of similar instances based on individual experience (Mathews et al. 1989; Sun et al. 2005). Especially for control tasks, Stanley et al. (1989) argue that operators use interacting knowledge structures, which consist of a memory for past experiences (close analogies) and a current mental model of the task. According to these remarks, it can be derived that also skill acquisition (and not only instances as declarative knowledge) is accomplished through the acquisition of instances, from which, with increasing task exposure and execution, general rules on declarative knowledge are extracted.

Applied to the COCOM (Hollnagel 2007; Hollnagel and Woods 2005), the architecture proposed by Sun et al. (2001) resembles that displayed in Fig. 4.2.

The central hypotheses of Sun et al.'s (2005) model are as follows:

When there is no sufficient a priori knowledge available, learning is bottom-up, which means that it starts with procedural action-centred knowledge. It is assumed that the acquisition of declarative knowledge may be triggered by procedural knowledge. The process is perceived as delayed explication of procedural learning, so that explicit/declarative knowledge is extracted from procedural skills (Stanley et al. 1989; Sun et al. 2005). Moreover, it is assumed that at the bottom level, implicit skills are acquired, whereas the top level extracts explicit rules (Sun et al. 2005). Sun et al. (2005) further assume that procedural knowledge is used

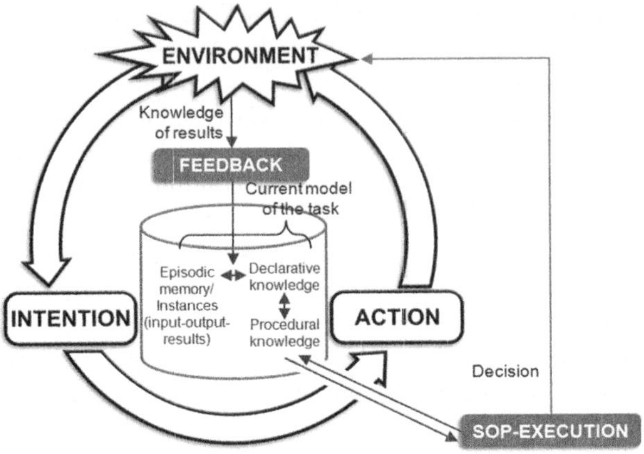

Fig. 4.2 The link between the two-level architecture by Sun et al. (2001) and the COCOM

in declarative learning. It supports declarative learning processes by providing them with relevant information, for example in terms of statistical information and information about relations in time that have to be considered and for which procedural learning is more predestined.

There is a division of labour between the two structures in simple and complex tasks. As Sun et al. (2005) describe, there a division of labour between the two structures. If the knowledge to be acquired is simple and input dimensions are small and salient to the operator, learning is declarative. In cases in which more complex relations and a larger number of input dimensions are involved, procedural learning gains importance (Sun et al. 2005). Procedural learning seems to be "structurally more sophisticated and more able to handle complex situations" (Sun et al. 2005, pp. 166–167). Sun et al. (2005) conclude that when complex relations and high dimensionality are involved and the top level (explicit/declarative) fails to learn or is too slow, then we can expect a reliance on implicit learning on the bottom level. When the involved stimulus material is simple, the top level is able to handle it and is therefore more utilised. In summary, both types of learning are involved, each with varying contributions (Sun et al. 2005, p. 167). In Table 4.5, the top and the bottom level of the cognitive architecture are contrasted.

Declarative and procedural knowledge interact. Declarative knowledge seems to help novices to learn *when it directs subjects to focus on relevant features or when it heightens subjects' sensitivity to relevant information* (Sun et al. 2005), as required, for example, in monitoring (Vicente et al. 2004). Declarative knowledge also helps in dealing with higher-order relations (Sun et al. 2005). The synergies between the two structures become apparent by speeding up learning, improving performance and facilitating transfer of skills (Sun et al. 2005). The learning of complex tasks can be speeded up when subjects are requested to generate explicit knowledge, for example when asked to generate verbal instructions for other subjects during learning. A better performance can be achieved if a proper mix of

Table 4.5 Comparison of the top and the bottom level (Sun 2002) of the dual architecture

Dimensions	Bottom-up	Top-down
Cognitive phenomena	Implicit learning	Explicit learning
	Implicit memory	Explicit memory
	Automatic processing	Controlled processing
	Intuition	Explicit reasoning
Source of knowledge	Trial-and-error	External sources
	Assimilation	Extraction
Representation	Distributed features	Localist conceptual units
Operation	Similarity-based	Symbol-based
Characteristics	More context-sensitive	Less context-sensitive
	Fuzzier	More crisp
	Less selective	More selective
	More complex	Simpler

implicit and explicit processes are used, for example first by implicit processes and later encouraging explicit learning (Sun et al. 2005).

Finally, there is evidence that subjects who also acquired explicit knowledge in a training task reacted faster in a transfer task, when the transfer task was similar to the learned task.

Feedback interpretation and integration to refine instances

Returning to the IBLT and COCOM, the operator detects the results after carrying out the SOP in relation to the desired organisational goals. The feedback is used to refine the SDU instances (Gonzalez et al. 2003; Kolodner 1983). The feedback updating process makes correct and useful instances more likely to be retrieved in the future, so that while becoming more experienced by using feedback of results, the process distinguishes more accurate from less accurate instances, leading to improved decisions (Gonzalez et al. 2003). Therefore, according to the IBLT, expertise is acquired by the refinement of SDU instances. With increasing expertise, over time and in similar situations, a larger number of SDU instances are generated by the accumulation and recombination of previous SDU instances (Gonzalez et al. 2003). However, in process control, a danger inherent in learning from feedback is misperception of feedback, which lies in the fact that feedback might be delayed, and the operator might ignore time delays or simply forget to take the delays into account (Kerstholt and Raaijmakers 1997).

In summary, the relationship between work experience, practice and instance acquisition to control complex technical systems is assumed to be as follows:

- Learning to control a complex system takes place by the accumulation of knowledge about SDUs in the form of instances (Gilboa and Schmeidler 2000; Gonzalez et al. 2003; Gonzalez and Brunstein 2009; Gonzalez 2012; Logan 2002). Knowledge in the form of instances accumulates with practice and instances capture the selected courses of action and the accuracy of the results in achieving organisational goals.

- Situation assessment is based on memory retrieval of SDUs according to the similarity between the perceived situational cues and instances stored in memory (Gonzalez et al. 2003; Harvey and Fischer 2005; Klein 2000). With increased practice and work experience, the operator will use a recognition-based application of the instance-based knowledge. The perception of similarity between two situations increases with practice on the task (Gonzalez et al. 2003), which supports attention management for relevant task cues (Kolodner 1983; Vicente et al. 2004).
- Learning of dynamic decision making in terms of practice in the dynamic control task starts from heuristic-based decision making and develops into instance-based decision making (Gonzalez et al. 2003), or as Rasmussen would put it, from knowledge-based to rule-based performance. With practice in the same task context, operators will proceed to using instance-based knowledge instead of heuristics.
- The duration of a search for a course of action depends on the time left available (Gonzalez et al. 2003). Learning processes based on work experience and practice need to include knowledge about dynamics, for example about windows of opportunity that might close, time needed to assess the situation, aging of information, time needed to choose a course of action, rates of change of the process controlled etc. (Hollnagel 2007; Kerstholt and Raaijmakers 1997).
- Skill acquisition for execution of actions, for example in terms of SOPs, is a dual process (Sun et al. 2001), and takes place through the interaction of bottom-up and top-down processes. e.g. by extracting declarative knowledge after a longer period of practice and ongoing work experience. After extensive practice, a process of generalising specific knowledge sets in to form generic schemas in forms of declarative knowledge and rules (Mathews et al. 1989; Stanley et al. 1989; Sun et al. 2001). Skill learning takes place through the interaction of implicit and explicit processes, which mostly take a bottom-up (implicit to explicit) direction, which is also compatible with issues of automaticity (automatic/procedural versus controlled/declarative processes).
- With increased work experience and practice, feedback of results is used to update the utility of SDUs (Gonzalez et al. 2003). When the SDUs have been modified based on the feedback of the utility, the new utility of the SDUs provides a better representation of the goodness of an action (Gonzalez et al. 2003).

If one transfers the presented theoretical assumptions on the learning processes to knowledge and skill acquisition for controlling complex technical systems, one comes to the following propositions:

Proposition 3: Work experience and practice for becoming an expert in process control for situation assessment and action implementation means the acquisition of episodes.

Proposition 4: Instances are saved in episodic memory.

Proposition 5: Learning occurs through the accumulation of instances over repeated task exposure and execution.

Proposition 6: Episodic memory forms, together with declarative knowledge, the foundation for the representation and use of mental models.

Proposition 7: The instances enable a situation to be assessed in a recognition-primed manner.

Proposition 8: In the acquisition of instances for situation assessment, value must be placed on the learning of the diagnosticity of cues (classification of routine/non-routine/normal and abnormal), on the discovery of similarity, and on the acquisition of perceptual skills for both processes.

Proposition 9: The instances additionally enable mental time travel into the future in order to estimate the effects of decisions.

Proposition 10: With regard to action implementation, learning processes also take place in bottom-up manner from which with increasing practice, rule-based knowledge is extracted.

Proposition 11: In the acquisition of instances for action implementation, value must be placed on the dual bottom-up and top-down approach to acquiring automaticity and attention sharing.

Proposition 12: The assessment and prediction of precision are improved through the acquisition of further episodes.

4.4 Learning Mechanisms Which Support Instance-Based Learning for Novices

The following learning mechanisms are primarily conceived for *novices* (Table 4.2), with no or limited exposure to the task. As introduced in Chap. 2, complex systems impose high cognitive load on the novice due to intrinsic load and due to *element interactivity* while learning. At this point, the theoretical works of Sun (2002) and Logan (2002) again become relevant. As introduced above, human learning is gradual, ongoing and concurrent with task performance. According to Sun et al. (2001), the individual acquires both procedural and declarative knowledge from ongoing experience in the world and while performing tasks, which Sun et al. (2001; Sun 2002) call bottom-up learning. In short, bottom-up learning includes reactive coping with situational affordances in the "world", in which procedural learning is structurally more sophisticated and more able to handle complex situations (Sun et al. 2005, pp. 166–167). When complex relations are involved, the top level (explicit/declarative) is too slow, meaning that one can rely on implicit learning at the bottom level. In that sense, the following learning mechanisms intentionally draw on the strengths of the bottom-up learning processes.

Table 4.6 Central constructs in cognitive load theory (Wickens et al. 2012a, b; Sweller 2006)

Load type	Description
Intrinsic load	Element interactivity inherent to the task elements to be understood or learned simultaneously and its working memory demands
Extraneous load	Imposed by sources of demand unrelated to intrinsic load, but not supportive of learning (e.g. due to badly designed learning material), sources of distraction that arise from suboptimal instructional materials
Germane load	Resources of effort requirements that are part of the learning process. Resources that are invested into the understanding of element interactivity, e.g. relating the material to one's own experiences, rehearsing procedures, using strategies for coding the learning material in long-term memory

Task fractionation – distributing cognitive resources in knowledge and skill acquisition for complex tasks

As Wickens et al. (2012a) propose, it is necessary to attend to the task elements to be learned in order to learn effectively. But what happens if attentional resources do not suffice for the resources demanded by element interactivity or other attentional affordances? With reference to cognitive load theory (Sweller 1988, 2006), which is briefly introduced in Table 4.6, the ideal learning strategy will take whatever resources are available after those related to intrinsic load are expended and deploy them in such a way as to maximise the ratio of germane load to extrinsic load (Wickens et al. 2012a, p. 68).

The balance between attentional resource supply and demand from the task may be disturbed due to three possible reasons: (1) resource competition from the task regarding high intrinsic load and high element interactivity for learning, (2) resource competition from extraneous load (badly designed learning material or tasks), and (3) loss of motivation so that fewer resources or less effort are supplied (Wickens et al. 2012a, b).

Learning to control a complex system can be supported in two ways: By increasing the investment of attentional resources or by reducing resource demands (Schneider 1985; Wickens et al. 2012a, b).

Increasing the attentional resource investment: Wickens et al. (2012a) report several examples showing that the investment of attentional resources into learning can be supported by learning tasks which require *active choices*, e.g. in controlling a complex system, and the associated cognitive processes, rather than merely watching or observing. The so-called "generation effect" (Slamecka and Graf 1978) is also held responsible for the advantage of "active learning" and discovery learning, when designed appropriately according to the learner's skill and competence level. It is not supportive in cases when active choices lead to serious errors and "trashing" (Wickens et al. 2012a). In "trashing", learners' resources are redirected from germane load to simply struggling with the now out-of-control situation and trying to recover from a performance catastrophe.

Reducing resource demands: A second option to support learning other than increasing the investment of resources into learning is to reduce resource demands. Wickens et al. (2012a) propose three strategies for reducing resource demands: (1) gradual increase in difficulty, (2) error prevention and (3) part-task training (Table 4.7).

Table 4.7 Strategies for reducing intrinsic resource demands for novice learners (Wickens et al. 2012a)

Strategy	Description
The gradual increase in difficulty	What: start with a simple version of the task and gradually increase its difficulty as learning progresses Why: in parallel to the increasing task difficulty, skill develops over time, leading to resource demands (intrinsic load) that remain relatively stable over time, leaving enough resources for germane load Challenge: find out which aspects of a task increase difficulty
Error prevention: training wheels	What: approach locks out certain actions that can have serious unintended consequences Why: lower the resource demands of performing, preventing thrashing, and guide resources toward the mastery of mental models or skills to be acquired Challenge: designing a schedule for release
Part-task training: fractionating	What: parts of a task are performed concurrently as time-shared tasks, between which attention must be divided Why: the development of time-sharing skills is an emergent property of the tasks Challenge: making available more part-task practice time for the part-tasks. For this, automaticity should be developed, due to its consistent mappings, and less time should be given to those parts with little consistency

The gradual increase of difficulty: For process control tasks too, it is apparent, as for many other complex tasks, that it is not useful to start training at the full complexity level of the transfer tasks (Wickens et al. 2011, 2012a) according to "sink or swim" principles. The danger of trashing is high and full resources are required to recover from errors, meaning that no more resources are left for learning (germane load). Therefore, an important strategy is to start with a simple version of the task and gradually increase its difficulty as learning progresses (Wickens et al. 2012a), also called "simplification" (Wightman and Lintern 1985). In parallel to the increasing task difficulty, skill develops over time, leading to resource demands (intrinsic load) that remain relatively stable over time, leaving enough resources for germane load (Wickens et al. 2012a). The challenge for the training designer here is to find out the aspects of the task that need to be changed to increase difficulty. A study by Mané et al. (1989), for example, proposed that an effective means of imposing increased difficulty is to *increase time pressure* gradually. *Increasing time pressure* alters the requirements to invest more attentional resources or deploy those resources more efficiently (Wickens et al. 2012a; Schneider 1985). Gonzalez and Brunstein (2009) also found that in a dynamic resource allocation task, learning under time pressure was less supportive of skill acquisition than using a slow pace before exposing learners to realistic time-constrained conditions. Similarly, in the studies cited by Gonzalez and Brunstein (2009), low workload was best during training for fast and high-workload tasks.

What does this mean with respect to the accumulation of instances and decision execution? There is no "one-size-fits-all" solution. Rather, the answer to this question is "it depends" (see introduction and Roediger 2008). Difficulty in process control industries, as outlined in Chap. 2, may have several facets, for example temporal dynamics and time pressure can play a role in some process industries, while in others, the number of alarms an operator has to deal with is important; further difficulties may also be delayed feedback or non-transparency. From a training point of view, this might also mean that operators should acquire a solid cadre of instances (see Chap. 5, the Staged Process Control Readiness Training) which allow them to extract explicit rules and rule knowledge and with increasing difficulty by making it harder to discriminate between instances by raising their similarity. What the relevant difficulties are in a particular process control industry therefore needs to be derived from techniques such as error analysis or another appropriate task analysis method (see Chap. 5).

Error prevention: In error prevention, the task characteristics remain constant, but additional techniques, for example the "training wheels" technique (Carroll 1990) or scaffolding (Pea 2004), are applied in the early stages of skill acquisition, which lower the resource demands of performance, prevent thrashing, and guide resources toward the mastery of mental models or skills to be acquired (Wickens et al. 2012a, b). A training wheel approach locks out certain actions that can have serious unintended consequences. To be effective, the key element in applying training wheels is the schedule for release, which means removing the error prevention lockouts or dismantling the scaffold (Wickens et al. 2012a, b). A meta-analysis by Wickens et al. (2011) demonstrated an overall transfer gain for training wheels and scaffolding compared to control conditions. A challenging aspect for training designers is ensuring that learners do not come to rely on training wheels or scaffolding and learn strategies to depend on them (Wickens et al. 2012a). A technique to overcome this challenge was developed by Lintern and Roscoe (1980), who developed an artificial guidance (in their case, information was provided in a head-up display), which was only displayed adaptively when the operator was beyond a certain criterion. As long as the learner was performing well, he/she was forced to rely on world cues to maintain performance, and the training wheel head-up display information was only provided when a large error began to emerge (Wickens et al. 2012a).

Applied to the process control training setting, different forms of adaptive and error-preventive displays can be conceived of, for example displays that support the learner in identifying relevant cues with high diagnosticity in order to identify similarity on a surface or on a structural level or in supporting the implementation of an SOP. This can be achieved, for example, by preventing the operators from executing actions with severe consequences (e.g. in a simulator), which would lead to restarting and interrupting the learning process in a way that is not helpful for the learning process.

Task Fractionation: As a particular form of part-task training, fractionation is introduced for the purpose of this book. In fractionation, the parts of a task are performed together but with different priorities to later combine them into a time-shared tasks between which attention must be divided (Wickens et al. 2012a). In this respect, one has to make sure that those part-tasks receive more part-task practice time, for which automaticity should be developed. Additionally, it should be considered that especially for cognitive tasks, the development of time-sharing skills to integrate part-tasks is an emergent property of the task (Schneider 1985). *Time-sharing skill (also called attention allocation skill) is the ability to fluently and optimally allocate and reallocate resources between tasks* (Gopher 2007; Wickens et al. 2012a). An important characteristic of the attention allocation skill is visual scanning because experts show qualitatively different scanning patterns in complex multitasking skills (Belenkes 1999). Part-task training that addresses dynamic attention allocation skills transfer very effectively to a whole-task (dual-task) performance (Wickens et al. 2012a, b). Gopher (2007) and Gopher et al. (1989) developed a technique named variable priority or emphasis shift training, in which the task is practised as a whole, but in parallel, sub-parts of the task are treated separately in that one or another subtask is emphasised during training. In order to develop the required skills, the operator must perceive and deal with whole-task situations consistently, for example by using analogies, mock-ups, cases, and low- to high-fidelity simulations. Practising must reinstate the conditions of the "field", including primary and secondary tasks (Healy et al. 2012).

In process control, the time-sharing and attention allocation skills play some role in situation assessment, for example when monitoring several screens and displays in parallel, but are even more important when executing an SOP while monitoring the plant (in non-routine/normal situations). This occurs in parallel or in the phase of team interaction in order to jointly collect and restructure data, combine, sort and filter cues, search for patterns, exchange hypotheses, develop a joint problem space, resolve opposing interpretations, negotiate team consensus and orchestrate actions (see below).

Variants of part-task training: Emphasis change

Gopher (2007) describes emphasis change as a training method that requires the learner to systematically change their emphasis, effort, and attention allocation, respectively, on major subcomponents of the task during skill acquisition (Gopher 2007). Emphasis levels are varied between practice trials lasting for a few minutes or among pre-specified short durations of task performance. Gopher (2007) distinguishes four major variants of the emphasis change training approach (Table 4.8).

In *variable priorities training*, on a display/screen on which two concurrent subtasks are executed, learners are shown with which priority they should work on which of the two concurrent subtasks, for example with a priority level of .75, .65, .50, or .25: Priority changes are proportional and add up to 1.0. The desired performance priority is indicated by a vertical line in the upper part of the display. Moving the desired performance line to the left or right of the centre changes the priority level of the two tasks (Gopher 2007).

In *emphasis change training*, to learn a complex task with subtasks (e.g. dynamic and discrete manual control, visual scanning, short- and long-term memory performed under time constraints and attention load), which should be attended to concurrently and is generally difficult to learn for beginners, the emphasis shift training maintains the rhythm of the complete task. During the

Table 4.8 Variants of the emphasis change protocol as part-task training techniques

Emphasis-change variant	Applied instructional technique
Variable priorities	Manipulation of attention allocation in concurrent task performance
Emphasis change	Change of emphasis on components of a complex task through instruction and augmented feedback
Introduction to a secondary task	Change of primary task performance strategies by adding a secondary task
Task switching	Training under task-switching requirements

different subsequent training sessions, the emphasis on components is changed by instruction and augmented feedback. Under emphasis change training conditions, learners are exposed and respond to the whole task throughout training. However, the emphasised element is brought to the fore and is made "a figure" while all of the other elements become "ground", with the whole task being active at all times (Gopher 2007). For example, subjects are instructed during a specific training trial to pay special attention to one of the several task subcomponents. The emphasis is changed through instructions and by adding counters dedicated to specific aspects of performance relevant to the emphasised element. Emphasised elements are changed between practice trials.

The *introduction to a secondary task* has been used as a training tool to force learners to change their response and coping strategies with primary task demands (Gopher 2007). Usually, as introduced in Chap. 3, the secondary task method is used to assess the difficulty and demands of the concurrently performed primary task. In this respect, in the instructional design, care needs to be taken that the secondary task is also designed in such a way as to foster the primary task. In process control, this could be, for instance, a secondary task which fosters the monitoring and targeted search for indicators and cue configurations. Alternatively, it could be a secondary task which fosters the accurate working through of SOPs as a primary task, or fosters the development of strategies even when the sequence of input is interrupted, through looking up and observing the values on the display at the point at which the values on the display which were previously interrupted are reinstated. For example, for certain, very important SOPs which have to be known by heart, a secondary task can be introduced which gently and indirectly "punishes" the operator for looking at the paper templates rather than at the screen. This is achieved through a symbol randomly appearing on the screen, which has to be confirmed with a key combination or otherwise the screen will turn black. In other words, the concern is not with "any old" secondary task, but rather, it has to be designed in such a way that it also fosters the desired strategy, for example the working through of the procedure by memory.

Finally, training in *task switching* originates from the experimental paradigm in which subjects are asked, with a block of trials, to switch from the performance of one task to the performance of another. Imagine a task with the following sequences of numbers: 5555, 777, 33333, 8888. In a first trial, the operator is required to name the number (e.g. "5555"; the correct answer is 5); in the second trial, the operator is required to count the number of figures presented (e.g. "5555"; the correct answer is 4). Switching between the task requirements is an act of conscious control and the costs of switching reflect the adaptation required for the ignition of the new task and the inhibition of the old demand. This training method is useful if operators need to perform rapid transitions between task components or alternative computations in which the richness of the situational demands is introduced from the start.

Gopher (2007) summarises his and others' research and concludes that emphasis change and variable priorities training showed slower progress in the early stages of training but that learners excelled at advanced stages of training and subsequent task transfer and in terms of adaptation to changed conditions. In contrast to a more self-directed learning within a whole task without emphasis shift training variants, when performing multi-element, high-demand tasks, uninstructed practice and equal opportunity training are likely to lead most learners to focus on a single suboptimal performance strategy. In contrast, emphasis change training guides learners through a well-constructed exploration of the intact task (Gopher 2007). It requires the learner to perform the task from different perspectives in order to evaluate the outcome of different strategies and to learn to adapt their behaviour, use different attention management strategies and cope with different demands (Gopher 2007).

All of these techniques should reduce the extraneous load for the novice in order to acquire knowledge and skill to handle the element interactivity of the complex system's elements. On the whole, as Barshi and Loukopoulos (2012) conclude, learning to handle "multitasking" requires a focus on dual-task combinations. The demands of the task are gradually increased and the priorities of the task altered, and the need for focused attention to execute it is reduced. This allows the development of time-sharing skills, which are crucial for handling tasks in the control room (Barshi and Loukopoulos 2012). Gradually, increasing time pressure can teach learners to optimally deploy attentional resources and to acquire scan patterns for attention allocation and monitoring as well as methods for selecting salient cues, and to set up artificial and team cross-checking (Barshi and Loukopoulos 2012).

Ongoing learning for experts through deliberate practice

As outlined at the beginning of this chapter, experts can be distinguished from novices through their extensive work experience. Additionally, as introduced above, Sun et al. (2005) assume that human learning is gradual, ongoing and concurrent with task performance, and that from ongoing experience in the world, the individual learns both procedural and declarative knowledge. However, Ericsson (2006) raises the concern that there are "many types of experiences and that these different types have qualitatively and quantitatively different effects on the continued acquisition and maintenance of an individual's performance" (p. 683). Ericsson (2006) further states that merely executing proficiently during routine work may not lead to further improvement, and that further improvement depends on deliberate efforts to change particular aspects of performance (Fig. 4.3). With reference to Fitts' model of skill acquisition (see above), which proceeds from

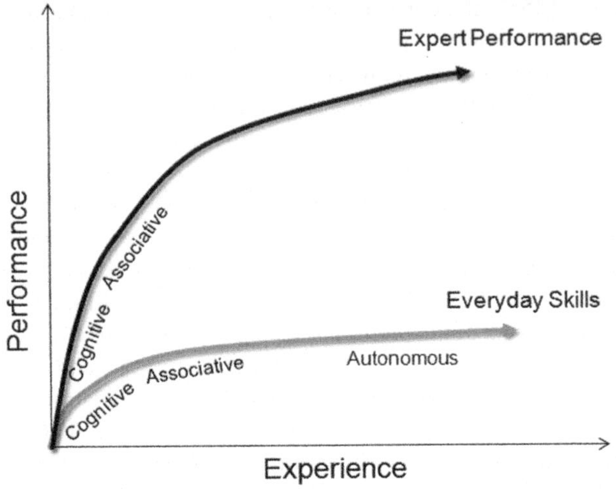

Fig. 4.3 Illustration of qualitative difference deliberate practice to achieve expert performance and everyday skills (Adapted from Ericsson 2006)

a cognitive to an associative to an autonomous level of performance, Ericsson (2006) claims that *expert performance counteracts automaticity by developing increasingly complex mental representations to attain higher levels of control of their performance and will therefore remain within the cognitive and associative phase*. Whereas the goal of "everyday activities" is often to reach a satisfactory level of performance as soon as possible and to perform tasks with a minimum of cognitive effort (in the autonomous phase), deliberate practice by experts incorporates exercises to still control the execution of these highly automated skills, but making intentional modifications and adjustments (Ericsson 2006).

The key challenge for continuous improvement is to acquire the cognitive skills to preserve the advantages of the associative phase and to overcome the detrimental effects of automaticity by actively acquiring and refining cognitive mechanisms (Ericsson 2006). Practice is therefore not only mere repetition but provides the learner with exercises that gradually refine performance, thus supporting learners to acquire mechanisms that increase their ability to control, self-monitor and evaluate performance in representative situations (Ericsson 2006, p. 694). "*Skill acquisition is viewed as an extended series of gradual changes of the physiological and cognitive mechanisms that allow the observable performance to show associated improvements. The acquisition of expert performance can thus be described as a series of relatively stable states, where each state has a set of mechanisms that mediate the execution of the associated performance*" (Ericsson 2006, p. 694).

In that respect, the length of work experience alone has been frequently found to be a weak correlate of job performance beyond the first two years (McDaniel et al. 1988; Tesluk and Jacobs 1998). Not all practice is equivalent in terms of effectiveness (Healy et al. 2012; Schneider 1985). The key challenge of designing practice for continuous improvement is to acquire the cognitive skills to preserve the advantages of the associative phase and to overcome the detrimental effects of automaticity by actively acquiring and refining cognitive mechanisms (Ericsson 2006).

Further cognitive development and skill acquisition (as is the prerequisite in the IBLT) requires the opportunity to find suitable training tasks that operators master sequentially. The operator must be confronted with tasks that are initially outside the current scope of reliable performance, yet can be mastered within hours of practice by concentrating on critical aspects and gradually refining performance through repetitions after feedback (Ericsson 2006, p. 692). Important is the notion of concentration on critical aspects that differentiates deliberate practice from mindless and routine as well as from playful engagement. Deliberate practice aims at modifying cognitive processes rather that strengthening them (such as by mere repetition). Through deliberate practice, learners continually assess and improve their own strategy and performance through iterative feedback cycles including goal-setting, performance, self-observation and self-reflection (Darabi et al. 2009).

Unfortunately, so far, we know little about learning through experience and deliberate practice in the organisational context. Empirical and longitudinal studies are lacking in both cases (Sonnentag et al. 2004). Nevertheless, the following proposition appears plausible:

Proposition 13: Becoming an expert requires ongoing learning that counteracts automaticity through the development of increasingly complex mental representations to attain higher levels of control of their performance.

4.5 Instance-Based Learning for Learning Teamwork Skills

As elaborated in Chap. 3, the task of an operator is embedded in a team task, which is not always the essential part of the task but becomes increasingly important and essential when more tasks turn from routine to non-routine/abnormal situations, thus requiring collaborative dynamic decision making. In non-routine/abnormal situations, teamwork consists of coordinated effort and coordinated task management to make sense of a large amount of information in order to develop a shared understanding of the situation to gain back control over the situation. For example, as outlined in Chap. 3, team members voice their suspicions and assumptions, reflect on and discuss hypotheses and assumptions, resolve opposing interpretations, and negotiate shared interpretations (see Chap. 3, Fig. 3.16).

In collaborative problem-solving, the linkage between individual and team performance is not additive (Kozlowski and Salas 1997) but interdependent. The action of each team member, for example detecting deviances, information collection and interpretation, passing on information, providing periodic situation updates and resolving opposing interpretations as well as critical thinking (see Chap. 3), may have crucial impacts on overall team performance.

Taskwork and teamwork as dual-task performance

As introduced in Chap. 3, in non-routine/abnormal situations, team members not only need to perform the taskwork, but also need to coordinate team members' actions toward the collaborative dynamic problem-solving task. In this respect, coordination in teams involves integrating the operations of the team members in a timely manner to form a composition of operations (Eccles and Tenenbaum 2004) which achieves the desired collaborative dynamic problem-solving results.

The distinction made between taskwork and teamwork can be found in Salas et al. (1992), Shuffler et al. (2011), Entin and Serfaty (1999) or Eccles and Tenenbaum (2004). Concerning the scope of this book, *taskwork involves performing the technical components of the task based on mental models of the target system, and knowing and executing SOPs, whereas teamwork requires the application of non-technical skills in order to integrate team members' individual contributions into a coordinated team performance.*

Teamwork skills are supposed to enhance team performance by reducing process losses (Steiner 1972) and coordination decrements (Fiore et al. 2001; Eccles and Tenenbaum 2004), which affect central teamwork aspects such as retrieving and communicating information (Wilson et al. 2007) during situation assessment, conflict negotiation and deciding what to do in abnormal situations. In order to counteract process losses, teamwork requires successful processes of coordination through communication beyond the skills required by the individual team member (Hodges et al. 2006). With cumulative experience and learning, team performance is assumed to be enhanced through the reduction of process losses (Steiner 1972) and coordination decrements (Fiore et al. 2001). Coordination in control room teams is achieved by intra-team communication, which means that communication pertains to team *in-process coordination* directly. Fiore et al. (2001) distinguish between pre-, in- and post-process coordination, in which pre-process coordination comprises preparatory behaviour such as setting goals, and planning and allocating role responsibilities. With reference to Chap. 3, pre-process coordination might take place during shift handover or in the preparation for a non-routine/normal task, for example a scheduled repair task. Because non-routine/abnormal situations occur by surprise, pre-process coordination is difficult to preplan. Post-process coordination includes after-action reviews (e.g. Ellis 2012), reflections and discussing lessons learned (Schmith-Jentsch et al. 2008). *Pre-process and post-process coordination are assumed to be valuable and supportive for the creation, learning and activation of task-related, team-related, process-related, and goal-related team knowledge* (Wickens et al. 2012a, b, see Chap. 3).

Both taskwork and teamwork require cognitive resources which place cognitive demands on team members in terms of coordinating the teamwork process which are not imposed on individual operators (Eccles and Tenenbaum 2004). Carron and Hausenblas (1998) provide a valuable formula to demonstrate the coordination requirements of a given team size, which argues for an exponential relationship between group size and coordination demands. The coordination between two members is considered as a coordination link (Carron and Hausenblas 1998).

The number of coordination links, which affects the additional demands on cognitive resources, is determined by the formula:

$$\text{Coordination Links} = N(N-1)\Big/2$$

In a group of six control room team members ($N = 6$), this means that there are $6 \times 5/2 = 30/2 = 15$ coordination links to be managed.

Through experience and practice, teams acquire refined and shared knowledge and skills for an extensive repertoire of team scripts and routines across a range of specificity and contingent on a range of situation assessments (Eccles and Tenenbaum 2004; Gersick and Hackman 1990).

On the whole, in-process coordination is demanding "because the time and cognitive resources required for coordination, and the communication required for coordination are scarce, owing to concurrent taskwork demands" (Eccles and Tenenbaum 2004, p. 552). Translated into process control situations, especially in non-routine/normal and abnormal situations, coordination-related communication places additional cognitive demands, with higher requirements of cognitive resources and a higher cognitive workload on the operators due to concurrent taskwork demands. In that sense, integrating taskwork and teamwork skills is likewise a complex task, in which several sequences of actions such as information exchange, interpretation and integration, need to be interleaved by several operators. The communication sequences required for the collaborative situation assessment, choosing what to do, critical thinking and action implementation as in COCOM (Hollnagel 2007; Hollnagel and Woods 2005) need to be orchestrated by the team members. Collaborative dynamic problem-solving is characterised as a *multi-step* activity (see Chap. 3) in which team members need to orchestrate collaborative "thinking and reasoning" steps. These steps are taken and executed while the situation may be dynamically changing, due to aging information or feedback delays. This means that the taskwork/teamwork integration consists of part-tasks, which include a sequence of steps that need to be integrated, which in turn require coordination based on attentional processes (see definition of a complex task in Chap. 2).

Thus, from the perspective of learning theory and human factors, the challenging and interesting issues are as follows:

- First, these coordination requirements introduce additional cognitive resource demands to the team members (Eccles and Tenenbaum 2004) and lead to a higher mental workload.
- Second, particularly in non-routine/abnormal situations, technical taskwork and non-technical teamwork skills as concurrent task demands need to be integrated and thereby share elements with a dual task that requires time-sharing and attention allocation.

Let us recall here that in the study by Patrick et al. (2006), for example, it was shown above all that operators and supervisors become fixated on SOPs and do not apply sufficient monitoring activities while they are absorbed by the SOP execution. Both types of learning, technical and non-technical, need to be provided at the same time during skill acquisition in order to enhance real-time coordination of individual technical skills into a well-coordinated team activity (Kozlowski and Salas 1997). Salas et al. (1992) also support the argument for teamwork as a dual-task environment, in which team members integrate taskwork performance with the teamwork behaviours. Thus, within a task environment such as in a control room crew, team members must coordinate the performance of two separate types of behaviour (Salas et al. 1992). Back in 1992, Salas et al. concluded that at that time, it was not clear how team members should be trained to integrate taskwork and teamwork. They proposed the creation of training programs to train these strategies as important research issues. Since then, the issue has not been very well investigated, although several team training methods (outlined and explained in Chap. 5) show promising results. Nevertheless, in this book, I propose that the dual task of taskwork and teamwork integration can be learned in a similar way to that described above by Wickens et al. (2012a, b) and Gopher (2007).

Based on the assumption that the integration of taskwork and teamwork share many elements with a dual task, learning mechanisms as described by Wickens et al. (2012a, b) or Gopher (2007) can be applied, by increasing difficulty, for example increasing the number or team members from learning trial to learning trial or increasing time pressure (if applicable; this depends on the process industry in question, see Chap. 2). However, variants of the emphasis shift can also be applied, such as the variable priorities training, emphasis change, introduction of a secondary task, or task switching (Table 4.8).

Proposition 14: The integration of taskwork and teamwork skills is a concurrent task demand. It shares elements of a dual task, which requires time-sharing and attention allocation.

Proposition 15: The in-process integration of teamwork and taskwork skills can best be learned according to the learning mechanism which is also effective for dual-task performance.

Proposition 16: Pre-process and post-process coordination activities are assumed to be valuable and supportive for the creation, learning and activation of task-related, team-related, process-related, and goal-related team knowledge.

The role of experience and practice in intact teams for instance-based learning of teamwork skills

I assume that like the learning of taskwork skills, learning teamwork skills includes a cognitive component (knowledge), such as a schema concerning teamwork characteristics, as well as a behavioural component in which specific concrete behaviours, for example scripts and skills, need to be acquired and applied. With respect to teamwork, the link between cognition and behaviour proposed here is the team knowledge (Wickens et al. 2012a, b) introduced in Chap. 3. Team knowledge includes task-related team knowledge (task and duties of the team), team-related team knowledge (characteristics and qualities of teammates), process-related team knowledge (team and interaction process) and goal-related team knowledge (goals and how to achieve them, see Chap. 3) for task mastery (Edmondson et al. 2008).

As yet, there is no theory of the learning processes for the acquisition of team skills. A great deal of literature exists concerning group learning (Wilson et al. 2007), team training and training outcomes, for example shared mental models, transactive memory (e.g. Cannon-Bowers and Bowers 2011; Edmondson et al. 2008; Entin and Serfaty 1999; Shuffler et al. 2011), and shared situation awareness (e.g. Prince and Salas 2000; Endsley and Robertson 2000), but not with respect to the team skill learning process itself. Currently, little is known about the teamwork skill learning process, but taking into account all of the theoretical considerations of the IBLT (Gonzalez et al. 2003) and NDM (Klein 2000) introduced above, it can be assumed *that teamwork is also learned through the accumulation of instances of teamwork episodes*. This means that for teamwork too (in addition to taskwork), SDUs are acquired and differentiated through work experience and practice.

Additionally, in line with Sun (2002) and Sun et al. (2001, 2005), it is *assumed that most of the things one knows about teamwork are procedural and implicitly stored, and with everyday experience and increasing job experience, explicit and rule-based knowledge is extracted.* By "doing" teamwork, it can be assumed that team knowledge (Wildman et al. 2012) also develops, in a similar way to the system knowledge proposed, for example, by Kluwe (1997). This occurs through individuals interacting with the target system, but this time, the target system is a social system. This proposition is supported by the work of Rentsch et al. (1994), who showed that similarly to the development of domain-related expertise, highly experienced teams perform more effectively than less experienced teams (see also Dyer 1984). Rentsch et al. (1994) assume, and indeed demonstrate, that team performance will be advanced if team members possess expert-like teamwork knowledge structures, which are abstract, multilevel and well articulated. Rentsch et al. (1994) assume that core teamwork knowledge provides individual team members with an understanding of working as a team. The more experienced they are in teamwork, the more team members develop abstract, multilevel, well-articulated expert-like knowledge structures, in contrast to team members with lower experience levels. *As experience increases, individuals are likely to generalise their teamwork episodes to similar team tasks and experiences.* This assumption is in accordance with the dual-process model by Sun (2002) and Sun et al. (2001).

Edmondson et al. (2008) also argue that teams improve with cumulative experience, and Reagans et al. (2005) showed that increased experience in working together in a team promoted better coordination. Cumulated experience in terms of "learning by doing" is supported by team stability, which is more of a given for control room crews than for other teams (e.g. military ad hoc teams) and by sustained coordination requirements at the team level. Although these findings by Edmondson et al. (2008) and Reagans et al. (2005) mainly focused on investigating team performance improvements in repetitive team tasks, the fact that cumulative experience in stable teams supports teamwork later becomes relevant for designing deliberate practice opportunities.

Representative design for learning in intact teams

In order to translate team knowledge into concrete behaviour, Kozlowski and Salas (1997) as well as Mathieu et al. (2008) point out that skills required for interdependent team tasks require the training to be delivered to the team as an intact group. Teamwork skills, focused on the behaviours necessary for effective team functioning, are believed to be best delivered to intact teams as opposed to individual members (e.g. Cannon-Bowers et al. 1995; Moreland et al. 1998; Swezey and Salas 1992). The underlying logic is that the training of intact teams provides opportunities for members to integrate their teamwork skills and to jointly practice complex coordinated actions (Kozlowski 1998; Kozlowski et al. 2000; Mathieu et al. 2008; Reagans et al. 2005). In short, in-process coordination can be only learned in an in-process manner.

Due to this proposition, teamwork skills are assumed to be most effectively acquired by a representative learning design (Pinder et al. 2011) in which the organism-environmental relations need to be considered comprehensively ("representative design", Brunswick 1956). Representative design emphasises the need to ensure that, for example, (experimental) task conditions should represent the transfer task conditions of the performance environment, in which the acquired skill should be applied. Representative design is the arrangement of conditions in an experimental design in such a way that they represent the behavioural setting to which the results are intended to apply (Pinder et al. 2011). In research, one has become very aware how strongly contextual factors influence and interact with the novice (Cooke and Fiore 2010). When the design of learning task conditions results in the careless removal of, for instance, critical information sources that an operator in a team uses to coordinate action into a team performance, different undesired patterns of action emerge (Travassos et al. 2012). Therefore, "action fidelity" is required (Stoffregen et al. 2003) for teamwork skill acquisition, which describes the degree of correspondence between the behaviour in a learning setting and the target setting, for example a control room crew collaborative problem-solving task.

Proposition 17: Equivalently to learning taskwork skills, learning teamwork skills includes a cognitive component (knowledge), such as a schema concerning teamwork characteristics, as well as a behavioural component, in which specific concrete behaviours, e.g. scripts and skills, need to be acquired and applied.

Proposition 18: Teamwork is learned through the accumulation of instances of teamwork episodes.

Proposition 19: Assuming that most of the things one knows about teamwork are procedural and implicitly stored, with everyday experience and increasing job experience, explicit and rule-based knowledge is extracted.

Proposition 20: Teamwork skills, focused on the behaviours necessary for effective team functioning, are believed to be best learned in intact teams rather than individually.

Proposition 21: Teamwork skills are acquired most effectively with a high level of action fidelity.

Finally, we turn to issues which arise in planning and developing deliberately designed practice sessions for acquiring teamwork skills and teamwork instances. *It is assumed that the acquisition of teamwork skills proceeds most effectively and efficiently when individual team members develop individual taskwork skills before learning coordination and communication skills* (Salas et al. 1992; Swezey and Salas 1992). This means that the learning of team coordination should proceed after individual members have mastered their own duties (Swezey and Salas 1992). Before team members are trained in developing teamwork skills, they must have reached some threshold level of competence in their individual knowledge and skill, because differences in team performance can often be directly related to the inadequately developed proficiency level of the individual team members (Swezey and Salas 1992). In this respect, novice team workers should be aware of the relationships between individual preparation and team performance.

Proposition 21: Before team members are trained in developing teamwork skills, they must have reached some threshold level of competence in their individual knowledge and skill.

Now that the main points regarding processes of acquisition of instances for taskwork and teamwork have been described, in the following, we will turn to skill retention.

4.6 "Power Law of Forgetting" – Skill Decay due to Periods of Non-use

As outlined in Chaps. 2 and 3 and described in the context of non-routine situations, due to highly automated systems, many skills are required only infrequently and only after long periods of non-use during daily operations. In terms of skill acquisition when trained skills are needed after a long period of non-use, it is important to consider skill retention (Arthur et al. 2010; Farr 1987; Kim, Ritter and Koubek 2013; Kluge and Frank 2014). According to Arthur et al., this is "particularly salient and critical in situations where individuals receive initial training on skills and knowledge that they may not be required to use or may not have the opportunity to perform for extended periods of time" (Arthur et al. 2010, pp. 428/9). In particular, complex procedural tasks are highly liable to forgetting (Farr 1987).

Which processes play a role in forgetting? According to Bjork (2009, 2011) and Bjork and Bjork (1992), human memory is characterised by an essentially unlimited storage capacity. Forgetting therefore arises not due to the storage capacity but because retrieval capacity is severely limited. Bjork (2011) and Bjork and Bjork (1992) argue that although memories might be not accessible without continued use and access, they remain in memory. Bjork and Bjork's (1992) new theory of disuse distinguishes between

- *retrieval strength* of a memory representation, e.g. the accessibility at a given point in time, and
- *storage strength* of that representation, which is an indicator of how entrenched or inter-associated that representation is with related representations in memory (Bjork 2011; Bjork and Bjork 2006).

Similarly, Anderson (1995) argues that speed and probability of accessing an element from memory is determined by its level of activation which in turn is determined by how frequently and how recently one has used that element. Memory traces become active when associated concepts are presented but will become less available if not used or rehearsed (Anderson 1995)

The original law of disuse by Thorndike (1914) assumed that with continued disuse, memories decay or fade from memory. In contrast, the new theory of disuse assumes that memories, once acquired, remain in long-term memory, and difficulties in recalling knowledge and skill are entirely determined by the current retrieval strength (Bjork 2011). Losing access is the problem, not the "loss" of knowledge and skill. Losing access to information is caused by inference from competing information and altered stimulus conditions such as recency and current cues. The retrieval of knowledge and skills becomes inhibited with continuous disuse due to the acquisition of new knowledge. As one learns new information, procedures and skills, there is potential for competition with related information, procedures and skills that already exist in memory (Bjork 2011). In contrast to a computer or MP3 player, where retrieving the stored information leaves the stored representation unchanged, the act of retrieving information from human memory modifies the system (Bjork and Bjork 2006). Retrieved information becomes more accessible in the future and other information becomes less accessible (Bjork and Bjork 1992), which means that the act of retrieval is itself a potent learning event. Several studies (e.g. Roediger and Karpicke 2006) demonstrated that the act of retrieving an item from memory, for example by means of taking a test, is considerably more potent in terms of facilitating than additional practice trials on that item (Bjork and Bjork 2006).

As a person is using his/her memories, for example instances, memories which the person uses often are made more accessible (higher retrieval strength), and by using these instances, other instances are made less accessible due to competing information, procedures and skills (Bjork 2011). The competition results from the phenomenon that the act of recalling information from memory requires not only the information searched for to be selected and produced, but also the other information associated with the cues to be deliberately not selected or produced, or inhibited (Bjork 2011; Bjork and Bjork 1992). Cues may be environmental, interpersonal, emotional or physical, such as body states (Bjork and Bjork 1992, 2006).

The limited retrieval capacity is assumed to be caused by the cue-dependent nature of retrieval. For an item to be recalled in response to a given cue, this representation must be discriminated from the other representations or memory items associated with that cue (Bjork and Bjork 1992). Discriminating an item is assumed to be a function of retrieval strength *relative* to the strength of other items in the cue set. Reconstructing the item for a response is presumed to be a direct function of its absolute retrieval strength. The net effect of these assumptions is that a limit is placed on the number of items that can be accessible in memory at a given time. As new items are learned and added to memory, or as the retrieval strength of certain items are increased, for example by more frequent recall, other items become less retrievable (Bjork and Bjork 1992).

The competition between information for retrieval is bidirectional: Earlier learned information can block or inhibit access to more recently learned information, and more currently used information inhibits access to earlier learned and not often used information. This peculiarity of human memory shows that over time, the accessibility of memory representation constructed earlier tends to increase relative to the accessibility of related memory representation constructed later (Bjork and Bjork 1992), explained by a sort of regression process. When a person learns new information, it is the new representation that is most accessible at the end of the learning process. With disuse of both representations (older and newer), the pattern changes from recency to primacy: There is a loss of access to the more recent presentation and a recovery in retrieval of the earlier (older) representation (Bjork and Bjork 1992).

In summary and displayed in Fig. 4.4, "forgetting" means that increasing the retrieval strength of certain items (e.g. by further practice or test events) makes other items less retrievable (Bjork and Bjork 1992). The underlying competitive effects will tend to be governed by similarity or category relationships defined semantically or episodically (Bjork and Bjork 1992).

With respect to this book and longer periods of non-use due to high automaticity in process control, it is apparent that knowledge and skills, however well they are learned, become inaccessible if not periodically retrieved. The gradual loss of retrieval access is not a consequence of the mere passage of time, but rather a consequence of learning and practising other items (Bjork and Bjork 1992).

The new theory of disuse proposes the following (see Bjork and Bjork 1992, p. 42):

- No matter how accessible and over-learned a piece of information, concept or skill is at some point in time, it eventually becomes non-recallable with disuse
- An item, piece of information, or skill in memory has two "strengths": a storage strength (how well an item is learned) and a retrieval strength (probability that an item can be recalled in response to a given cue)
- The storage strength of a given item grows as a pure accumulation of study and recall opportunities. Once accumulated, storage strength is never lost
- Retrieval capacity is limited concerning the total number of items that are retrievable at one point in time
- Retrieval strength decreases as a function of non-use (e.g. studying or testing)
- The act of retrieval is itself a potent learning event

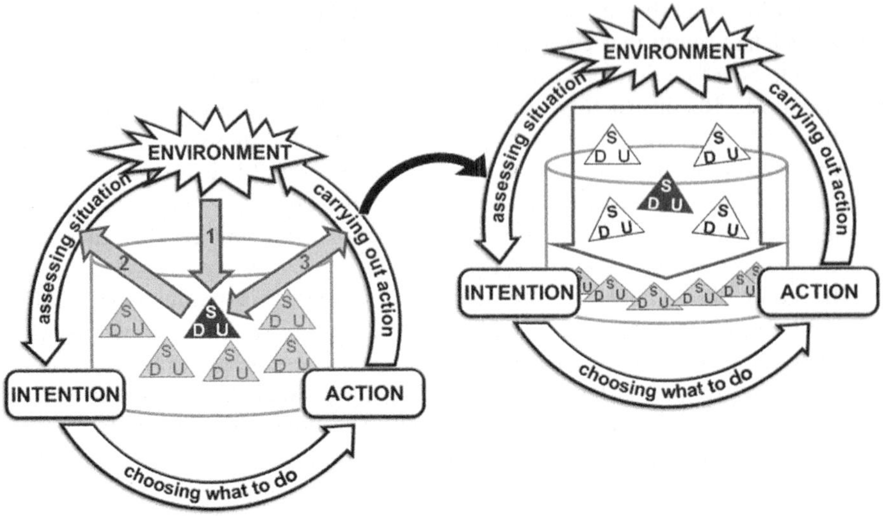

Fig. 4.4 The new theory of disuse applied to the COCOM. With work experience or practice, instances (SDUs) that are not used frequently have a lower retrieval strength than SDUs that are used frequently or are currently being acquired. Increasing the retrieval strength of certain items (e.g. by further practice or test events) makes other items less retrievable

- Memories one uses often are made more accessible (higher retrieval strength)
- As new items are learned and added to memory, or as the retrieval strength of certain items are increased, e.g. by more frequent recall, other items become less retrievable (Bjork and Bjork 1992)
- Gain and loss of retrieval strength are both negatively accelerated, and storage strength enhances the gain and delays the loss of retrieval strength

In the IBLT as well as the RPDM, processes of forgetting have not yet been addressed explicitly, although it can be inferred that the retrieval strength of instances depends on frequency and recency of instance retrievals. Unfortunately, the new theory of disuse has so far not primarily investigated the control of complex technical systems. It has been used above all in the context of everyday phenomena of memory and in the rather classical school learning context. For the area of complex tasks as considered in this book, the implications of the new theory of disuse can only be transferred on a theoretical level.

With regard to the remarks on accumulation of instances and their use, it can be assumed that:

Proposition 22: Instances that are very well entrenched and inter-associated with other instances show a high storage strength.

Proposition 23 Instances that are retrieved less frequently have a lower retrieval strength than instances that are retrieved more frequently and regularly, e.g. SOPs of non-routine/normal tasks.

However, there is still a clear need for research. What, for example, is not yet clear is the extent to which continuous work experiences of routine tasks can foster the retrieval strength of at least overlapping elements of other instances which are not routine. Indeed, as was described and defined in Chap. 2, a complex task can be decomposed into part-tasks that include sequences of steps which need to be integrated and coordinated based on attentional processes (Table 1.4). And thus, on the one hand it can be assumed that, for example, SOPs that are used more frequently possess a higher retrieval strength than SOPs that are used less. On the other hand, the sequences within the SOPs are not all fundamentally different, but share part-sequences. As yet, it has not been empirically investigated, for example, to what extent the performance of routine tasks transfers the retrieval strength of part-sequences to other SOPs. Therefore, there is a clear need for research here concerning processes of forgetting in everyday working life.

4.7 Learning Mechanism to Support Storage and Retrieval Strength

In practice, to counterbalance skill decay, so-called refresher or recurrent training is used. Kluge et al. (2012) define refresher training as follows: "*Refresher training aims to re-establish a specific skill level that was acquired at the end of an initial training, which should be re-established after a certain time interval during which the skill was not required to be recalled*" (p. 2437). Refresher training is especially *important for task elements which are not continuous constituents of the routine tasks* during normal operations (Kluge et al. 2012; Kluge and Frank 2014). The distinction between distributed practice and refreshing seems fluent. Bjork and Bjork (2006) propose that effects of spacing and distributed practice on learning and retention are complex. The temporal spacing of practice trials on episodes has shown to be a function of the length of the final retention interval, which means the length of the interval between the last presentation of the to-be-remembered material and the testing of it, and the interval over which it must be maintained (Bjork and Bjork 2006). When the retention interval is short, closely spaced massed learning episodes produce a better test performance compared to distributed practice. In the case of long retention intervals, distributed practice produces better retention (Bjork and Bjork 2006). Distributed practice enhances long-term retention and performance. The explanation provided by the new theory of disuse is that the advantage of massed practice at short retention intervals arises because massed study episodes lead to a more rapid growth in retrieval than do distributed learning episodes, owing to the greater loss of retrieval strength between subsequent distributed learning trials. When retention is tested at a short interval, retrieval strength – which determines current performance – is higher in the case of massed practice.

On the other hand, distributed practice produces a greater increase in storage strength than massed practice because according to the new theory of disuse, increments in storage strength are a negatively accelerated function of current retrieval strength (Bjork and Bjork 2006). With distributed practice, there is more forgetting or loss of retrieval strength between the learning episodes, which creates better conditions for new learning, meaning greater increments in storage strength (Bjork and Bjork 2006). In turn, *the greater accumulation of storage strength with distributed practice slows the loss of retrieval strength with disuse* (Bjork and Bjork 2006), which leads to a better performance after a delay. These conditions of distributed practice are also called *desirable difficulties* (Bjork and Bjork 1992, 2006; Bjork et al. 2013).

In addition to distributed practice, other difficulties include

- interleaving instead of blocking of part-tasks,
- varying rather than keeping learning conditions constant,
- reducing rather than increasing feedback to the learner, and
- using tests rather than studying trials as learning events (Bjork and Bjork 2006; Bjork et al. 2013).

They are called difficulties because they slow the apparent rate of knowledge and skill acquisition but enhance long-term retention and transfer. The demand for varying rather than keeping learning conditions constant is also supported by Gonzalez and Brunstein (2009). According to the IBLT, heterogeneity of practice implies a larger diversity of instances in the problem space that defines the instances (Gonzalez and Brunstein 2009).

However, for relearning, a somewhat different effect was shown (Bjork and Fritz 1994). In relearning, for example in the form of refresher training, massing relearning trials are as effective as distributed relearning. Massed relearning produces more rapid reacquisition during refresher training than does distributed relearning (Bjork and Fritz 1994). The new theory of disuse provides the following explanation for this: Because storage strength, once accumulated, is assumed to be permanent, the storage strength that results from original learning carries over to relearning. The disadvantage exerted by massed practice during initial learning (a limited accumulation of storage strength) is mitigated (Bjork and Bjork 2006).

A second proposed way of optimising the scheduling of learning episodes across the acquisition phase is called *expanding retrieval practice* (Landauer and Bjork 1978). In this method of scheduling practice, the first attempt is scheduled shortly after the first learning episode, the next retrieval attempt is scheduled after a slightly longer retention interval and the third after a longer interval still, and so on (Bjork and Bjork 2006). Ideally, each retrieval attempt should occur at the point when retrieval would be maximally difficult (see desirable difficulties) but still possible given the present level of retrieval strength Bjork and Bjork (2006).

Another benefit for long-term retention is the *introduction of variations into the learning of a new task*. The benefits of variation are that retrieval is made more difficult because the cues available from the just prior learning episode will be somehow changed from those of the current learning episode, which produced greater increments to storage strength as well as retrieval strength. Secondly, each time the new episode occurs in a slightly different manner, it becomes associated with different retrieval cues and contexts, thus improving the generalisability of the newly learned knowledge and skill. Third, the variation of the task is assumed to force the learner to engage in higher-order learning to overcome the interference of the task, for example by discovering similarities and differences between the episodes (see differentiation between instances, above) (Bjork and Bjork 2006).

Proposition 25: The greater accumulation of storage and retrieval strength is achieved by desirable difficulties during learning.
Proposition 26: The greater accumulation of storage and retrieval strength is achieved by expanding retrieval practice.
Proposition 27: The greater accumulation of storage and retrieval strength is achieved by variations introduced into a learning task.

Finally, after looking in the first parts of the chapter at the acquisition of instances and retention, we now turn to "similarity", the final fundamental component of learning (acquisition, retention and transfer) which is deemed as important by Bourne and Healy (2012).

4.8 Transfer: Laws Relating to Similarity

Transfer describes the process of acquisition of one task that affects the performance of another task (Bourne and Healy 2012; Proctor and Dutta 1995). The major variable that determines the extent and direction of transfer is similarity between two tasks (Bourne and Healy 2012). Similarity has already been mentioned frequently in the previous sections; for example in the IBLT and RPDM, recognition is based on instance similarity. A situation is judged as routine or non-routine if there are memories of similar situations. For this reason, similarity plays a special role here, which will specifically be addressed again.

According to Tversky (1977), similarity plays a crucial role in theories of knowledge and behaviour. Similarity serves as an organising principle used by persons to classify objects, form concepts and make generalisations (Tversky 1977).

Similarity is demonstrably important across many areas of cognition (Gentner and Markman 1997). Experiences are stored in categories in memory largely on the basis of their similarity to a category or to stored exemplars (Gentner and Markman 1997). As cited above, Gilboa and Schmeidler (2000) assume that utilities of possible decision alternatives are computed from similar past experiences and decisions are based on similar cases in the past. The RPDM and IBLT both presume pattern matching (Osman 2010) and recognition is based on attention guided by previous experiences determined by instance similarity (Gonzalez et al. 2003). Transfer based on similarity principles is therefore an inherent characteristic of case-based reasoning, the IBLT, RPDM and the model by Sun (2002). In transfer, new problems are solved using procedures taken from prior similar problems (Gentner and Markman 1997; Holyoak and Koh 1987).

Similarities are used in order to generate a set of options, especially in naturalistic decision contexts, in which people rely on their previous experience to determine a set of considerations (Markman and Medin 2002). An operator may see a new situation as similar to a prior episode, which suggests potential options.

Research on similarities suggests that mental representations contain information about objects and features of those objects as well as structural information relations among features and objects (Markman and Medin 2002). The process involved in similarity comparisons is one of structural alignment and mapping between mental representations (Gentner and Markman 1997). Structural alignment means that a decision maker sees the commonalities and differences of items (Markman and Medin 2002).

It is assumed that the comparison process operates over a person's current representations, however they are derived. In order to predict the outcome of a comparison, one needs to know a person's current construal of the things being compared (Gentner and Markman 1997). Comparisons based on literal similarity are made with respect to relational predicates and object attributes, whereas comparisons based on analogy are made with respect to relational predicates only (Gentner and Markman 1997).

The judgment of similarity depends on context and frame of reference as well as on the salience of a feature, which is determined by two types: Intensity and diagnosticity (Tversky 1977). *Intensity refers, for example, to brightness of light, loudness of a tone, saturation of colour, the frequency of an item. Diagnosticity refers to the classificatory significance of features, which means the importance of the classifications that are based on these features.* The diagnosticity of features is determined by the classifications that are based on them, which can change with the context. In contrast, intensity of a feature is determined by perceptual and cognitive factors that are relatively stable across contexts (Tversky 1977).

Similarity is a process of structural alignment and mapping over articulated representations. In this respect, similarity-based retrieval from long-term memory is based on overall similarity, with surface similarity strongly weighted, rather than by the structural alignment which would support decision making best (Gentner and Markman 1997; Holyoak and Koh 1987). This is because retrieval likelihood is sensitive to surface similarity, but successful problem-solving is sensitive to structural similarity (Gentner and Markman 1997). This is also the case in the RPDM, in which it was shown that if somebody needs to decide on the course of action quickly and under time pressure, surface similarity is considered first. In contrast, if there is no time pressure, structural similarity is considered in more detail (Gonzalez et al. 2003; Klein 2000).

In addition to the situation assessment in the operator's current work situation, similarity also plays a fundamental role in transfer of training (Proctor and Dutta 1995). Based on the theory of identical elements (Thorndike and Woodworth 1901), it is proposed that transfer of knowledge and skills is supported only when two tasks have particular elements in common (Proctor and Dutta 1995). Identical elements include aims, methods, and approaches and also stimuli and responses (Goldstein 1993). Transfer in an organisational setting aims at using the acquired knowledge and skills that result from a training experience on-the-job in order to lead to meaningful changes in work performance (Baldwin et al. 2009). In the training literature, there is a high level of consensus that the acquisition of knowledge, skills and attitudes is of little value if the new characteristics are not generalised to the job setting or are not maintained over time. Transfer is the core issue with respect to linking individual changes to requirements of the organisational system (Kozlowski and Salas 1997).

Propositions:

Proposition 28: Becoming an expert in controlling a complex technical system includes knowledge and skills for discovering the surface and structural similarity between situational cues, which is particularly important for situation assessment.

Proposition 29: Becoming an expert in controlling a complex technical system includes the acquisition of knowledge concerning the diagnosticity of cues, which is particularly important for situation assessment.

Proposition 30: Becoming an expert in controlling a complex technical system includes acquired knowledge and skills being generalised to an organisational context that shares elements with the learning context.

This chapter aimed to facilitate the understanding of the fundamental learning process of how novices become experts in dealing with routine, non-routine/normal and non-routine/abnormal situations. These underlying principles and learning mechanisms are used in the following to derive the Staged Process Control Readiness Training.

Here is a summary of all of the propositions:

Proposition 1: The overall learning requirements include the development from a novice to an expert.

Proposition 2: The learning process implies the accumulation of instances through work experience and practice.

Proposition 3: Work experience and practice for becoming an expert in process control for situation assessment and action implementation means the acquisition of episodes.

Proposition 4: Instances are stored in episodic memory.

Proposition 5: Learning occurs through the accumulation of instances over repeated task exposure and execution.

Proposition 6: Episodic memory forms, together with declarative knowledge, the foundation for the representation and use of mental models.

Proposition 7: The instances enable a situation to be assessed in a recognition-primed manner.

Proposition 8: In the acquisition of instances for situation assessment, value must be placed on the learning of the diagnosticity of cues (classification of routine/ non-routine/normal and abnormal), on the discovery of similarity, and on the acquisition of perceptual skills for both processes.

Proposition 9: The instances additionally enable mental time travel into the future in order to estimate the effects of decisions.

Proposition 10: With regard to action implementation, learning processes also take place in a bottom-up manner, i.e. through the acquisition of instances from which, with increasing practice, rule-based knowledge is extracted.

Proposition 11: In the acquisition of instances for action implementation, value must be placed on the dual bottom-up and top-down approach to acquiring automaticity and attention sharing.

Proposition 12: The assessment and the prediction of precision are improved through the acquisition of further episodes.

Proposition 13: Becoming an expert requires ongoing learning that counteracts automaticity through the development of increasingly complex mental representations to attain higher levels of control of their performance.

Proposition 14: The integration of taskwork and teamwork skills is a concurrent task demand. It shares elements of a dual task, which requires time-sharing and attention allocation.

Proposition 15: The in-process integration of teamwork and taskwork skills can best be learned according to the learning mechanism which is also effective for dual-task performance.

Proposition 16: Pre-process and post-process coordination activities are assumed to be valuable and supportive for the creation, learning and activation of task-related, team-related, process-related, and goal-related team knowledge.

Proposition 17: Equivalently to learning taskwork skills, learning teamwork skills includes a cognitive component (knowledge), such as a schema concerning teamwork characteristics, as well as a behavioural component, in which specific concrete behaviours, e.g. scripts and skills, need to be acquired and applied.

Proposition 18: Teamwork is learned through the accumulation of instances of teamwork episodes.

Proposition 19: Assuming that most of the things one knows about teamwork are procedural and implicitly stored, with everyday experience and increasing job experience, explicit and rule-based knowledge is extracted.

Proposition 20: Teamwork skills, focused on the behaviours necessary for effective team functioning, are believed to be best learned in intact teams rather than individually.

Proposition 21: Teamwork skills are acquired most effectively with a high level of action fidelity

Proposition 22: Before team members are trained in developing teamwork skills, they must have reached some threshold level of competence in their individual knowledge and skill.

Proposition 23: Instances that are very well entrenched and inter-associated with other instances show a very high storage strength.

Proposition 24: Instances that are retrieved less frequently have a lower retrieval strength than instances that are retrieved more frequently and regularly, e.g. SOPs of non-routine/normal tasks.

Proposition 25: The greater accumulation of storage and retrieval strength is achieved by desirable difficulties during learning.

Proposition 26: The greater accumulation of storage and retrieval strength is achieved by expanding retrieval practice.

Proposition 27: The greater accumulation of storage and retrieval strength is achieved by variations introduced into a learning task.

Proposition 28: Becoming an expert in controlling a complex technical system includes knowledge and skills for discovering the surface and structural similarity between situational cues, which is particularly important for situation assessment.

Proposition 29: Becoming an expert in controlling a complex technical system includes the acquisition of knowledge concerning the diagnosticity of cues, which is particularly important for situation assessment.

Proposition 30: Becoming an expert in controlling a complex technical system includes acquired knowledge and skills being generalised to an organisational context that shares elements with the learning context.

References

Anderson, J. R. (1983). *The architecture of cognition*. Cambridge, MA: Harvard University Press.

Anderson, J. R. (1993). *Rules of the mind*. Hillsdale: Erlbaum.

Anderson, J. R. (1995). *Cognitive psychology and its implications*. New York: Freeman & Company.

Arthur, W., Jr., Day, E. A., Villado, A. J., Boatman, P. R., Kowollik, V., Bennett, W., Jr., & Bhupatkar, A. (2010). The effect of distributed practice on immediate posttraining, and long-term performance on a complex command-and-control simulation task. *Human Performance, 23*, 428–445.

Baldwin, T. T., Ford, J. K., & Blume, B. D. (2009). Transfer of training 1988–2008. An updated review and agenda for future research. *International Review of Industrial and Organizational Psychology, 24*, 41–70.

Barshi, I., & Loukopoulos, L. (2012). Training for real world job performance. In A. F. Healy & L. E. Bourne Jr. (Eds.), *Training cognition. Optimizing efficiency, durability, and generalizability* (pp. 287–306). New York: Psychology Press.

Belenkes, A. (1999). *The use of pilot performance models to facilitate cockpit visual scanning*. Unpublished Doctoral Dissertation. University of Illinois, Urbana-Champaign.

Bjork, R. A., & Bjork, E. L. (1992). A new theory of disuse and an old theory of stimulus fluctuation. In A. Healy, S. Kosslynm, & R. Shiffrin (Eds.), *From learning processes to cognitive processes: Essays in honor of William K. Estes* (pp. 35–67). Hillsdale: Erlbaum.

Bjork, R. A. (2009). Structuring the conditions of training to achieve elite performance: Reflections on elite training programs and related themes in Chapters 10–13. In K. A. Ericsson (Ed.), *Development of professional expertise. Toward measurement of expert performance and design of optimal learning environments* (pp. 312–332). Cambridge: Cambridge University Press.

Bjork, R. A. (2011). On the symbiosis of learning, remembering, and forgetting. In A. S. Benjamin (Ed.), *Successful remembering and successful forgetting: A Festschrift in honour of Robert A. Bjork* (pp. 1–22). London, UK: Psychology Press.

Bjork, R. A., & Bjork, E. L. (2006). Optimizing treatment and instruction: Implications of the new theory of disuse. In L. G. Nilsson & N. Ohta (Eds.), *Memory and society. Psychological perspectives* (pp. 109–134). Hove: Psychology Press.

Bjork, R. A., & Fritz, C. O. (1994). Reinforcing and competitive dynamics in the maintenance of knowledge. In H. Bahrick (Chair), *The maintenance of knowledge. Symposium. practical aspects of memory conference*, College Park, MD.

Bjork, R. A., Dunlosky, J., & Kornell, N. (2013). Self-regulated learning: Beliefs, techniques, and illusions. *Annual Review of Psychology, 64*, 417–444.

Bourne, L. E., & Healy, A. F. (2012). Introduction. Training and its cognitive underpinnings. In A. F. Healy & L. E. Bourne Jr. (Eds.), *Training cognition. Optimizing efficiency, durability, and generalizability* (pp. 1–12). New York: Psychology Press.

Brehmer, B. (1992). Dynamic decision making: Human control of complex systems. *Acta Psychologica, 81*, 211–241.

Brunswick, E. (1956). *Perception and representative design of psychological experiments*. Berkeley: University of California.

Cannon-Bowers, J. A., Tannenbaum, S. I., Salas, E., & Volpe, C. E. (1995). Defining competencies and establishing team training requirements. In R. Guzzo & E. Salas (Eds.), *Team effectiveness and decision making in organizations* (pp. 333–80). San Francisco: Jossey-Bass.

Cannon-Bowers, J. A., & Bowers, C. A. (2011). Team development and functioning. In S. Zehdeck (Ed.), *APA handbook of industrial and organizational psychology* (Building and developing the organization, Vol. 1, pp. 597–650). Washington, DC: American Psychological Association.

Carroll, J. M. (1990). *The Nurnberg funnel: Designing minimalist instruction for practical computer skills*. Cambridge, MA: MIT Press.

Carron, A. V., & Hausenblas, H. A. (1998). *Group dynamics in sport*. Morgantown: Fitness Information Technology.

Carvallo, P. V. R., dos Santos, I. L., & Vidal, M. C. R. (2005). Nuclear power plant shift supervisors' decision making during microincidents. *International Journal of Industrial Ergonomics, 35*, 619–644.

Chi, M. T. H. (2006). Two approaches to the study of experts' characteristics. In K. A. Ericsson, N. Charness, P. J. Feltovich, & R. R. Hoffman (Eds.), *The Cambridge handbook of expertise and expert performance* (pp. 21–30). Cambridge: Cambridge University Press.

Cooke, N. J., & Fiore, S. M. (2010). Cognitive science-based principles for the design and delivery of training. In S. W. J. Kozlowski & E. Salas (Eds.), *Learning, training and development in organizations* (pp. 169–202). New York: Routledge.

Conway, M. A. (2008). Exploring episodic memory. In E. Dere, A. Easton, L. Nadel, & J. P. Huston (Eds.), *Handbook of episodic memory* (pp. 19–29). Amsterdam: Elsevier.

Darabi, A. A., Nelson, D. W., & Seel, N. M. (2009). Progression of mental models throughout phases of a computer-based instructional simulation: Supportive information, practice and performance. *Computers in Human Behavior, 25*, 723–730. doi:10.1177/0149206308316061.

Dreyfus, H. (1992). *Being-in-the-world*. Cambridge, MA: MIT Press.

Dyer, J. L. (1984). Team research and team training: A state-of-the-art review. In F. A. Muckler (Ed.), *Human factors review* (pp. 285–323). Santa Monica: Human Factors Society.

Ebbinghaus, H. E. R. M. (1885). *Uber das Gediichtnis. Untersuchungen zur experimentellen Psychologie*. Leipzig: JA Barth.

Eccles, D. W., & Tenenbaum, G. (2004). Why an expert team is more than a team of experts: A social-cognitive conceptualization of team coordination and communication in sport. *Journal of Sport & Exercise Psychology, 26*, 542–560.

Edmondson, A. C., Dillon, J. R., & Roloff, K. S. (2008). Three perspectives on team learning. Outcome improvement, task mastery, and group process. *The Academy of Management Annals, 1*, 269–314.

Edwards, W. (1962). Dynamic decision theory and probabilistic information processing. *Human Factors, 4*, 59–73.

Ellinger, A. D. (2005). Contextual factors influencing informal learning in a workplace setting: The case of "reinventing itself company". *Human Resource Development Quarterly, 16*, 389–415.

Ellis, S. (2012). Learning from errors: The role of after event reviews. In J. Bauer & C. Harteis (Eds.), *Human fallibility. The ambiguity of errors for work and learning* (pp. 215–232). Dordrecht: Springer.

Endsley, M. R., & Robertson, M. M. (2000). Training for situation awareness in individuals and teams. In M. R. Endsley & D. J. Garland (Eds.), *Situation awareness analysis and measurement* (pp. 349–366). Boca Raton: CRC Press.

Entin, E. E., & Serfaty, D. (1999). Adaptive team coordination. *Human Factors, 41*, 312–325.

Ericsson, K. A. (2006). The influence of experience and deliberate practice on the development of superior expert performance. In K. A. Ericsson, N. Charness, P. J. Feltovich, & R. R. Hoffman (Eds.), *The Cambridge handbook of expertise and expert performance* (pp. 683–703). Cambridge: Cambridge University Press.

Farr, M. J. (1987). *The long-term retention of knowledge and skills. A cognitive and instructional perspective*. New York: Springer.

Fiore, S. M., Salas, E., & Cannon-Bowers, J. A. (2001). Group dynamics and shared mental model development. In M. London (Ed.), *How people evaluate others in organizations: Person perception and interpersonal judgement in I/O psychology* (pp. 309–336). Mahwah: Erlbaum.

Fitts, P. M. (1962/1990). Factors of complex skill training. In M. Venturino (Ed.), *Selected readings in human factors* (pp. 275–295). Santa Monica: Human Factors Society (Original work by Fitts published in 1962).

Gentner, D., & Markman, A. B. (1997). Structure mapping in analogy and similarity. *American Psychologist, 52*, 45–56.

Gersick, C. J., & Hackman, R. (1990). Habitual routines in task performing groups. *Organizational Behavior and Human Decision Process, 47*, 65–97.

Gilboa, I., & Schmeidler, D. (2000). Case-based knowledge and induction. *IEEE Transactions on Systems, Man, and Cybernetics–Part A: Systems and Humans, 30*, 85–95.

Goldstein, I. L. (1993). *Training in organisations. Needs assessment, development and evaluation*. Monterey: Brooks/Cole.

Gonzalez, C. (2012). Cognitive models of training principles and the instance based learning tool. In A. F. Healy & L. E. Bourne Jr. (Eds.), *Training cognition. Optimizing efficiency, durability, and generalizability* (pp. 181–200). New York: Psychology Press.

Gonzalez, C., & Brunstein, A. (2009). Training for emergencies. *Journal of Trauma Injury, Infection, and Critical Care, 67*, 100–105.

Gonzalez, C., Lerch, J. F., & Lebiere, C. (2003). Instance-based learning in dynamic decision making. *Cognitive Science, 27*, 591–635.

Gopher, D. (2007). Emphasis change as a training protocol for high-demand tasks. In A. Kramer, D. Wiegmann, & A. Kirlik (Eds.), *Attention: From theory to practice*. Oxford: Oxford University Press.

Gopher, D., Weil, M., & Siegel, D. (1989). Practice under changing priorities: An approach to the training of complex skills. *Acta Psychologica, 71*, 147–197.

Greitzer, F. L., Podmore, R., Robinson, M., & Ey, P. (2008). Naturalistic decision making for power system operators. In *Proceedings of the NDM9, the 9th international conference on naturalistic decision making*, London. Also available online: http://www.bcs.org/upload/pdf/ewic_ndm09_s1paper2.pdf

Harvey, N., & Fischer, I. (2005). Development of experience-based judgment and decision-making: the role of outcome feedback. In T. Betsch & S. Haberstroh (Eds.), *The routines of decision-making* (pp. 119–138). New York: Erlbaum.

Healy, A. F., Schneider, V. I., & Bourne, L. E., Jr. (2012). Empirically valid principles of training. In A. F. Healy & L. E. Bourne Jr. (Eds.), *Training cognition. Optimizing efficiency, durability, and generalizability* (pp. 13–39). New York: Psychology Press.

Heathcote, A., Brown, S., & Mewhort, D. J. K. (2000). The power law repealed: The case for an exponential law of practice. *Psychonomic Bulletin & Review, 7*, 185–207.

Hodges, N. J., Starkes, J. L., & MacMahon, C. (2006). Expert performance in sport: A cognitive perspective. In K. A. Ericsson, N. Charness, P. J. Feltovich, & R. R. Hoffman (Eds.),

The Cambridge handbook of expertise and expert performance (pp. 471–488). Cambridge: Cambridge University Press.

Hoffman, R. R. (1998). How can expertise be defined? Implications of research from cognitive psychology. In R. Williams, W. Faulkner, & J. Fleck (Eds.), *Exploring expertise* (pp. 81–100). New York: Macmillan.

Hollnagel, E. (2007). Decision about "what" and decisions about "how". In M. Cook, J. Noyes, & Y. Masakowski (Eds.), *Decision making in complex environments* (pp. 3–13). Aldershot: Ashgate.

Hollnagel, E., & Woods, D. D. (2005). *Joint cognitive systems. Foundations of cognitive systems engineering*. Boca Raton: Taylor & Francis.

Holyoak, K. J., & Koh, K. (1987). Surface and structural similarity in analogical transfer. *Memory & Cognition, 15*, 332–340.

Jenkins, J. J. (1979). Four points to remember: A tetrahedral model of memory experiments. In L. S. Cermak & F. I. M. Craik (Eds.), *Levels of processing in human memory* (pp. 429–446). Hillsdale: Erlbaum.

Johnson, A. (in press). Procedural memory and skill acquisition. In A. F. Healy, & R. W. Proctor (Vol. Eds.), & I. B. Weiner (Ed.-in-Chief), *Handbook of psychology* (Experimental psychology, 2nd edn., Vol. 4). Hoboken: Wiley.

Kerstholt, J. H., & Raaijmakers, J. G. W. (1997). Decision making in dynamic task environments. In R. Ranyard, R. W. Crozier, & O. Svenson (Eds.), *Decision making: Cognitive models and explanations* (pp. 205–217). New York: Routledge.

Kim, J. W., Ritter, F. E., & Koubek, R. J. (2013). An integrated theory of skill acquisition and retention in the three stages of learning. *Theoretical Issues in Ergonomics Science, 14*, 22–37.

Klein, G. A. (2000). Analysis for situation awareness from critical incident reports. In M. R. Endsley & D. J. Garland (Eds.), *Situation awareness analysis and measurement* (pp. 51–72). Boca Raton: CRC Press.

Klein, G. A., Calderwood, R., & Clinton-Cirocco, A. (1986). Rapid decision making on the fire ground. In *Proceedings of the Human Factors Society 30th annual meeting* (pp. 576–580). Santa Monica: Human Factors Society.

Kluge, A., Burkolter, D., & Frank, B. (2012, September). "Being prepared for the infrequent": A comparative study of two refresher training approaches and their effects on temporal and adaptive transfer in a process control task. *Proceedings of the Human Factors and Ergonomics Society Annual Meeting, 56*, 2437–2441.

Kluge, A., & Frank, B. (2014). Counteracting skill decay: Four refresher interventions and their effect on skill retention in a simulated process control task. *Ergonomics*. doi:10.1080/00140139.2013.869357.

Kluwe, R. H. (1997). Acquisition of knowledge in the control of a simulated technical system. *Le Travail Human, 60*, 61–85.

Kolodner, J. L. (1983). Towards an understanding of the role of experience in the evolution from novice to expert. *International Journal of Man-Machine Studies, 19*, 497–518.

Kozlowski, S. W. J. (1998). Training and development in adaptive teams: Theory, principles, and research. In J. A. Cannon-Bowers & E. Salas (Eds.), *Making decisions under stress: Implications for individual and team training* (pp. 247–270). Washington, DC: American Psychological Association.

Kozlowski, S. W. J., & Salas, E. (1997). A multilevel organizational system approach for the implementation and transfer of training. In J. K. Ford, S. W. J. Kozlowski, K. Kraiger, E. Salas, & M. S. Teachout (Eds.), *Improving training effectiveness in work organizations* (pp. 247–287). Mahwah: Lawrence Erlbaum.

Kozlowski, S. W. J., Brown, K., Weisbein, D., Cannon-Bowers, J., & Salas, E. (2000). A multilevel approach to training effectiveness: Enhancing horizontal and vertical transfer. In K. Klein & S. W. J. Kozlowski (Eds.), *Multilevel theory, research, and methods in organizations*. San Francisco: Jossey-Bass.

Landauer, T. K., & Bjork, R. A. (1978). Optimal rehearsal patterns and name learning. In M. N. Gruneberg, P. E. Morris, & R. N. Sykes (Eds.), *Practical aspects of memory* (pp. 625–632). London: Academic.

Lintern, G., & Roscoe, S. (1980). Visual cue augmentation in contact flight and simulation. In S. N. Roscoe (Ed.), *Aviation psychology* (pp. 227–238). Ames: Iowa State University.

Logan, G. D. (1988). Toward an instance theory of automatization. *Psychological Review, 95*, 492–527.

Logan, G. D. (2002). An instance theory of attention and memory. *Psychological Review, 109*, 376–400.

Mané, A. M., Adams, J. A., & Donchin, E. (1989). Adaptive and part-whole training in the acquisition of a complex perceptual-motor skill. *Acta Psychologica, 71*(1–3), 179–196.

Markman, A. B., & Medin, D. L. (2002). Decision making. In *Stevens' handbook of experimental psychology*. Wiley. Retrieved January 23, 2013, from http://dx.doi.org/10.1002/0471214426.pas0210

Marsick, V. J., & Volpe, M. (1999). The nature and need for informal learning. *Advances in Developing Human Resources, 3*, 1–9.

Mathews, R., Buss, R., Stanley, W., Blanchard-Fields, F., Cho, J., & Druhan, B. (1989). Role of implicit and explicit processes in learning from examples: A synergistic effect. *Journal of Experimental Psychology. Learning, Memory, and Cognition, 15*, 1083–1100.

Mathieu, J., Maynard, M. T., Rapp, T., & Gilson, L. (2008). Team effectiveness 1997–2007: A review of recent advancements and a glimpse into the future. *Journal of Management, 34*, 410–476.

McDaniel, M. A., Schmidt, F. L., & Hunter, J. E. (1988). Job experience correlates of job performance. *Journal of Applied Psychology, 73*, 327–330.

Moreland, R. L., Argote, L., & Krishnan, R. (1998). Training people to work in groups. In G. M. Wittenbaum, S. I. Vaughan, G. Stasser, & R. S. Tindale (Eds.), *Theory and research on small groups* (pp. 37–61). New York: Plenum.

Newell, A., & Rosenbloom, P. S. (1981). Mechanisms of skill acquisition and the law of practice. In J. R. Anderson (Ed.), *Cognitive skills and their acquisition* (pp. 1–55). Hillsdale: Lawrence Erlbaum.

Osman, M. (2010). Controlling uncertainty – A review of human behavior in complex dynamic environments. *Psychological Bulletin, 136*(1), 65–87.

Patrick, J., James, N., & Ahmed, A. (2006). Human processes of control: Tracing the goals and strategies of control room teams. *Ergonomics, 49*, 1395–1414.

Pea, R. D. (2004). The social and technological dimensions of scaffolding and related theoretical concepts for learning, education, and human activity. *The Journal of the Learning Sciences, 13*, 423–452.

Pinder, R. A., Davids, K., Renshaw, I., & Araujo, D. (2011). Representative learning design and functionality research in practice in sport. *Journal of Sport & Exercise Psychology, 33*, 146–156.

Prince, C., & Salas, E. (2000). Team situation awareness, errors and crew resource management: Research integration for training guidance. In M. R. Endsley & D. J. Garland (Eds.), *Situation awareness analysis and measurement* (pp. 325–349). Boca Raton: CRC Press.

Proctor, R. W., & Dutta, A. (1995). *Skill acquisition and human performance*. Thousand Oaks: Sage.

Rasmussen, J. (1983). Skills, rules, and knowledge: Signals, signs, and symbols, and other distinctions in human performance models. *IEEE Transaction on System, Man, and Cybernetics, SMC-13*(3), 257–266.

Reagans, R., Argote, L., & Brooks, D. (2005). Individual experience and experiencing working together: Predicting learning rates from knowing what and knowing how to work together. *Management Science, 51*, 869–881.

Rentsch, J. R., Heffner, T. S., & Duffy, L. T. (1994). What you know is what you get from experience. Team experience related to teamwork schemas. *Group and Organization Management, 19*, 450–474.
Rickard, T. C. (1997). Bending the power law: A CMPL theory of strategy shifts and automatization of cognitive skills. *Journal of Experimental Psychology: General, 126*, 288–311.
Roediger, H. L., & Karpicke, J. D. (2006). The power of testing memory. Basic research and implications for educational practice. *Perspectives on Psychological Science, 1*, 181–210.
Roediger, H. L., III. (2008). Relativity of remembering: Why laws of memory vanished. *Annual Review of Psychology, 59*, 225–254.
Ross, K. G., Lussier, J. W., & Klein, G. (2005). From recognition primed decision model to training. In T. Bentsch & S. Haberstoh (Eds.), *The routines of decision making* (pp. 327–341). Mahwah: Lawrence Erlbaum.
Ross, K. G., Shafer, J. L., & Klein, G. (2006). Professional judgements and "naturalistic decision making". In K. A. Ericsson, N. Charness, P. J. Feltovich, & R. R. Hoffman (Eds.), *The Cambridge handbook of expertise and expert performance* (pp. 403–419). Cambridge: Cambridge University Press.
Rubin, D. C., & Wenzel, A. E. (1996). One hundred years of forgetting: a quantitative description of repetition. *Psychological Review, 103*, 734–760.
Ryan, L., Hoscheidt, S., & Nadel, L. (2008). Perspectives on episodic and semantic memory retrieval. In E. Dere, A. Easton, L. Nadel, & J. P. Huston (Eds.), *Handbook of episodic memory* (pp. 5–18). Amsterdam: Elsevier.
Salas, E., Dickinson, T. L., Converse, S. A., & Tannenbaum, S. I. (1992). Toward and understanding of team performance and training. In R. W. Swezey & E. Salas (Eds.), *Teams: Their training and performance* (pp. 3–29). Norwood: Ablex.
Schneider, W. (1985). Training high – Performance skills: Fallacies and guidelines. *Human Factors, 27*, 285–300.
Shuffler, M. L., DiazGranados, D., & Salas, E. (2011). There's A science for that: Team development interventions in organizations. *Current Directions in Psychological Science, 20*, 365–372.
Simon, H. A. (1957). *Models of man: Social and rational*. New York: Wiley.
Slamecka, N. J., & Graf, P. (1978). The generation effect: Delineation of a phenomenon. *Journal of Experimental Psychology: Human Learning and Memory, 4*, 592–604.
Schmith-Jentsch, K. A., Cannon-Bowers, J. A., Tannenbaum, S. I., & Salas, E. (2008). Guided team self-correction: Impacts on team mental models, processes, and effectiveness. *Small Group Research, 39*, 303–327.
Snoddy, G. S. (1926). Learning and stability: A psychophysiological analysis of a case of motor learning with clinical applications. *Journal of Applied Psychology, 10*, 1–36.
Sonnentag, S., Niessen, C., & Ohly, S. (2004). Learning at work: Training and development. *International Review of Industrial and Organizational Psychology, 19*, 249–289.
Stanley, W., Mathews, R., Buss, R., & Kotler-Cope, S. (1989). Insight without awareness: On the interaction of verbalization, instruction and practice in a simulated process control task. *Quarterly Journal of Experimental Psychology: Human Experimental Psychology, 41*, 553–577.
Steiner, I. D. (1972). *Group process and productivity*. New York: Academic.
Stoffregen, T. A., Bardy, B. G., Smart, L. J., & Pagulayan, R. J. (2003). On the nature and evaluation of fidelity in virtual environments. In L. J. Hettinger & M. Haas (Eds.), *Virtual and adaptive environments: Applications, implications, and human performance issues* (pp. 111–128). Mahwah: Lawrence Erlbaum.
Suddendorf, T., & Corballis, M. C. (2008). Episodic memory and mental time travel. In E. Dere, A. Easton, L. Nadel, & J. P. Huston (Eds.), *Handbook of episodic memory* (pp. 31–56). Amsterdam: Elsevier.
Sun, R. (2002). *Duality of the mind. A bottom-up approach toward cognition*. Mahwah: Erlbaum.

Sun, R., Merrill, E., & Peterson, T. (2001). From implicit skills to explicit knowledge: A bottom-up model of skill learning. *Cognitive Science, 25*, 203–244.

Sun, R., Slusarz, P., & Terry, C. (2005). The interaction of the explicit and the implicit in skill learning: A dual-process approach. *Psychological Review, 112*, 159–192.

Sweller, J. (1988). Cognitive load during problem solving: Effects on learning. *Cognitive Science: A Multidisciplinary Journal, 12*, 257–285.

Sweller, J. (2006). How the human cognitive system deals with complexity. In J. Elen & R. E. Clark (Eds.), *Handling complexity in learning environments. Theory and research* (pp. 13–27). Amsterdam: Elsevier.

Swezey, R. W., & Salas, E. (1992). Guidelines for use in team-training development. In R. W. Swezey & E. Salas (Eds.), *Teams: Their training and performance* (pp. 219–246). Norwood: Ablex.

Tannenbaum, S. I., Beard, R. L., McNall, L. A., & Salas, E. (2010). Informal learning and development in organizations. In S. W. J. Kozlowski & E. Sales (Eds.), *Learning, training, and development in organizations* (pp. 303–332). New York: Routledge.

Teigen, K. H. (2002). One hundred years of laws in psychology. *American Journal of Psychology, 115*, 103–118.

Tesluk, P. E., & Jacobs, R. R. (1998). Toward an integrated model of work experience. *Personnel Psychology, 51*, 321–355.

Thorndike, E. L. (1914). *The psychology of learning*. New York: Teachers College.

Thorndike, E. L., & Woodworth, R. S. (1901). The influence of improvement in one mental function upon the efficiency of other functions I–III. *Psychological Review, 8*, 247–261, 384–395, 553–564.

Travassos, B., Duarte, R., Vilar, L., Davids, K., & Araujo, D. (2012). Practice task design in team sports: Representativeness enhanced by increasing opportunities for action. *Journal of Sports Science, 30*, 1447–1454.

Tulving, E. (2002). Episodic memory: From mind to brain. *Annual Review of Psychology, 2002* (53), 1–25.

Tversky, A. (1977). Features of similarity. *Psychological Review, 84*, 327–352.

VanLehn, K. (1996). Cognitive skill acquisition. *Annual Review of Psychology, 47*(1), 513–539.

Vicente, K. J., Mumaw, R. J., & Roth, E. M. (2004). Operator monitoring in a complex dynamic work environment: A qualitative cognitive model based on field observations. *Theoretical Issues in Ergonomic Science, 5*, 359–384.

Wickens, C. D., Hutchins, S., Carolan, T., & Cumming, J. (2011). Investigating the impact of training on transfer: A meta-analytic approach. In *Proceedings of the Humans Factors and Ergonomics Society 55th annual meeting* (pp. 2138–2142). Thousand Oaks: Sage.

Wickens, C., Hutchins, S., Carolan, T., & Cumming, J. D. (2012a). Attention and cognitive resources load in training strategies. In A. F. Healy & L. E. Bourne Jr. (Eds.), *Training cognition. Optimizing efficiency, durability, and generalizability* (pp. 67–88). New York: Psychology Press.

Wickens, C. D., Hutchins, S., Carolan, T., & Cumming, J. (2012b). Effectiveness of part-task training and increasing-difficulty training strategies: A meta analysis approach. *Human Factors*. Published online ahead of print July 20, 2012. doi: 10.1177/0018720812451994 (Online first).

Wightman, D. C., & Lintern, G. (1985). Part-task training for tracking and manual control. *Human Factors, 27*, 267–283.

Wilson, J. M., Goodman, P. S., & Cronin, M. A. (2007). Group learning. *Academy of Management Review, 32*, 1041–1059.

Wildman, J. L., Thayer, A. L., Pavlas, D., Steward, J. E., & Howse, W. R. (2012). Team knowledge research: Emerging trends and critical needs. *Human Factors, 54*, 84–111.

Wixted, J. T., & Carpenter, S. K. (2007). The Wickelgren power law and the Ebbinghaus savings function. *Psychological Science, 18*, 133–134.

Chapter 5
Training Design for Instance-Based Learning – The "Staged Process Control Readiness Training" (SPCRT)

Chapter 4 ended with a number of propositions regarding how learning processes support the knowledge and skill acquisition and the retention for controlling complex systems. In this chapter, these basic learning processes are translated into training designs which provide a framework for activating these learning processes in order to achieve the training objectives formulated in Chap. 3.

Knowledge and skill acquisition within the work and organisational context aims at building and/or changing motivational, cognitive or behavioural prerequisites for the job (Sonnentag et al. 2004). Noe et al. (1997) define training as "a planned effort by a company to facilitate the learning of specific knowledge, skills, or behaviors that employees need to be successful in their current job" (Sonnentag et al. 2004, p. 154).

The training design proposed is named "Staged Process Control Readiness Training" (SPCRT). It is *staged* in terms of having a first stage in which novice operators accumulate instances during the training session designed for them, and a second stage in which more expert operators are supported in terms of skill retention, deliberate practice and teamwork skills through instance-based training specifically designed for this group. It is called "readiness training" because it prepares operators for the tasks described as training objectives. As a large proportion of the training objectives and performance are not routinely called upon every day, the training should foster the readiness for controlling complex systems and also prepare for non-routine situations. *Readiness* is defined as possessing the taskwork and teamwork knowledge and skills an operator needs to establish and sustain competent performance in order to be in control in routine, non-routine/normal and non-routine/abnormal situations. The readiness concept is borrowed from Bolstad et al. (2008), and adapted from Morrison and Fletcher (2002) in Kluge and Burkolter (2013).

At its core, the SPCRT includes practice-based training (Salas and Cannon-Bowers 1997), which corresponds to and matches the propositions formulated in the previous chapter. The practice-based training can be supplemented with information-based methods and demonstration-based methods (Salas and

A. Kluge, *The Acquisition of Knowledge and Skills for Taskwork and Teamwork to Control Complex Technical Systems*, DOI 10.1007/978-94-007-5049-4_5,

Cannon-Bowers 1997), but practice as accumulating instances is central to the endeavour.

5.1 Issues for Training Design Preparation

Issues for training design preparation include

(a) The analysis of the organisational and production context in order to design instances which are presented to novice operators to support the accumulation of instances, and
(b) A cognitive task analysis in order to guide and debrief operators for improving their Recognition Primed Decision Making (RPDM, see Chap. 4).

Both issues are explained in the following sections.

Analysing and understanding the organisational and production context

As was outlined in Chap. 2, the process industries diverge with respect to the number of productions, number of product steps, product variety, routings of products, production speed and throughput time (Fransoo and Rutten 1994), number and particularities of raw materials, equipment flexibility, formulation multiplicity (Dennis and Meredith 2000), the use of computer control and automation and the structure of the control room crew. Therefore, the first step which the training designer needs to take for training design is to understand the particularities of the specific process control target job. This can be derived from the technical aspects of the process to be controlled but needs to be more precisely specified, for example by means of observations, interviews, questionnaires, key consultation, print and multimedia analysis, group discussion, records and reports (e.g. Goldstein 1993; Salas et al. 1996; Steadham 1980). A description of methods relevant for control room operators is outlined in Table 5.1. Methods are differentiated into methods based on the analysis of documents and their content (unobtrusive, text-based methods, "desk research") and methods requiring interaction with operators and subject matter experts (interactive, obtrusive methods).

The preparation includes selecting and gathering essential materials for the job performance such as the SOPs, rules and regulations and other equipment needed to complete the job, for example which SOPs exist.

Some of the methods, which require more explanation, will be described in more detail in the following. The logic of Critical Incident Analysis (Flanagan 1954) can be applied as event-based analysis techniques (Flin et al. 2008) for selecting a number of instances for training. HROs in particular have systems for recording safety incidents, accidents and also near-misses. At times, confidential reporting systems (Chappell 1994) are also essential for extracting relevant instances (Flin et al. 2008; Ritzmann 2012). These reports can be used to analyse the underlying instance and to provide data from actual events to derive training needs, for example in terms of a correction of a mental model or learned instance for both

Table 5.1 Sources for the specification of training design (in line with Goldstein 1993, pp. 48/49; Steadham 1980, p. 59; Buckley and Caple 1990)

Technique	Examples
Documents and content analysis methods	
Print and multimedia analysis (Goldstein 1993; Steadham 1980)	Can include professional journals, legislative news, notes, industry rags, trade magazines, in-house publications, accident analysis reports and multimedia material, provided e.g. on the CSB or IAEA website, and scientific publications such as those reviewed in Chap. 3 for deriving evaluation possibilities.
Record and report analysis (Goldstein 1993; Steadham 1980)	Organisational charts, planning documents, policy manuals, audit reports, accident reports, e.g. the analyses based on the HFACS Human Factors Analysis and Classification System by Wiegmann and Shappell (2001).
Critical incident analysis (Flanagan 1954)/ event-based analysis (Flin et al. 2008)	Includes collecting information about incidents which have proven to be critical to the effective performance of the job, incidents that have contributed to success or failure. Analysis of safety incidents, accidents and near-misses.
Additional methods for in-depth understanding	
SOP analysis	Based on the print and multimedia analysis, analysing SOPs to derive the required mental model and skills to execute a procedure.
Key point analysis, e.g. for the development of SOPs (Buckley and Caple 1990)	Based on the incident reports, this method focuses on three main aspects of a task: the sequence or stages in which it is performed, instructions which describe how the task is to be done and the key points which have to be emphasised so that the operator avoids errors, e.g. by means of a job aid/SOPs for the job holder.
Fault analysis (Buckley and Caple 1990)	Based on the incident analysis, analysis of where problem areas are likely to occur, what are the consequences of errors and how errors can be prevented, e.g. by the CREAM method (Hollnagel 1998, see Chap. 3).
DIF (difficulty, importance, frequency) analysis (Buckley and Caple 1990)	Helps to decide between the "need to know" and "nice to know" content of training, as well as to estimate the retention interval to be bridged (Fig. 5.1).
Interactive methods	
Questionnaires (Goldstein 1993; Steadham 1980)	Surveys, pre-designed or self-generated, e.g. to find out about the frequency and importance of certain job elements.
Observation (Goldstein 1993; Steadham 1980)	Unstructured or structured, can be technically specific, such as video analysis, or functionally or behaviourally specific.
Interviews (Goldstein 1993; Steadham 1980)	Can be formal or informal, structured or unstructured, used with a sample of a particular group or

(continued)

Table 5.1 (continued)

Technique	Examples
	with the whole group, can be done in person, by phone, at the work site.
Group discussion (Goldstein 1993; Steadham 1980)	Resembles face-to-face interview technique, structured and unstructured, formal or informal, focused on job roles, group problem analysis, group coordination themes.
Key consultation (Goldstein 1993; Steadham 1980)	Secures information from those persons, e.g. trainers, safety managers, who by virtue of their formal or informal standing are in a good position to know the particularities of the job and organisation, e.g. by means of interviews, questionnaires, group discussion.

technical and non-technical skills. This means that event-based analysis is essential for developing instances to acquire teamwork skills.

Based on print, media, document and incident and event analysis, subsequent further deeper analysis of the underlying cognitive processes, for example the causes of errors, should be investigated. For the industries addressed in this book, an SOP analysis, a key point analysis, a fault analysis, and a difficulty-importance-frequency analysis (Buckley and Caple 1990), also described in Table 5.1, are suggested.

Especially for the execution of SOPs, which are written as a series of rules and actions and for which each action may be conditional on a particular state of the plant ("if x, then do y", Wickens and Hollands 2000), a fault or error analysis is a valuable supplement. This is the case because too often, the "if x" part is merely assumed by the operator, who does y, forgetting to carefully evaluate whether condition x actually exists and thus producing a rule-based error (Wickens and Hollands 2000). Additionally, one could also conceive of an SOP analysis in terms of importance and frequency, or an analysis of everything one has to know to execute the SOPs.

Fault analysis is supposed to supplement incident analysis and its results can be built into job aids, training guides used as indicators which will give advance warning to the trainees of possible problems, the symptom of problems and appropriate actions to take or to apply in order to prevent problems from happening. In one of our own studies, we analysed log data in order to understand the errors made by operators in their fault-finding and diagnosis process with the aim of optimising training and training materials (Kluge et al. 2013b).

I would also like to emphasise the usefulness of the DIF Analysis (see also Chap. 2), which is displayed in Fig. 5.1. As can be seen in Fig. 5.1, there are three criteria according to which the decision how to train is made: the level of difficulty, the importance which is placed on it and the frequency with which it is performed, which is in turn relevant for skill retention. I marginally extended the DIF described by Buckley and Caple (1990) in the upper part in order to demonstrate how several aspects introduced and outlined in Chap. 4 can be integrated, such as the

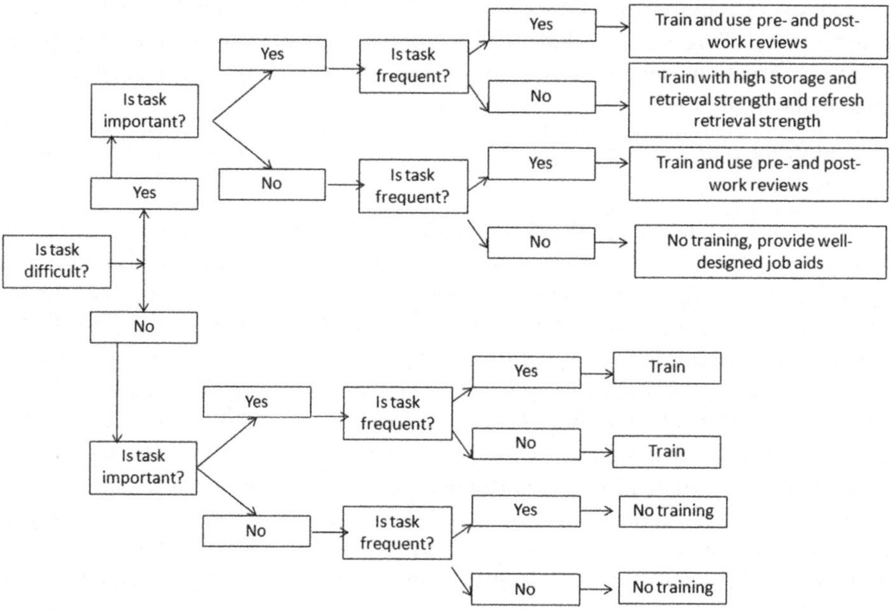

Fig. 5.1 DIF analysis, partially applied to monitoring and controlling tasks

prepositions concerning storage and retrieval strength (Bjork and Bjork 1992, 2006) as well as pre- and post-work reviews as suggested above, for example for the creation, learning and activation of task-related, team-related, process-related and goal-related individual and team knowledge.

The DIF analysis is related to the distinction between routine and non-routine/normal tasks and can be enhanced by defining different degrees of difficulty (e.g. not difficult, difficult, very difficult), importance (not important, moderately important, very important) and frequency (infrequent, moderately frequent, very frequent, Buckley and Caple 1990), which give indications of the priority of training and the performance and retention level to be achieved (Stammers 1981). The result of such an extended DIF analysis might be that a skill that is difficult, moderate or very important and performed infrequently has a very high priority in training to a standard which will ensure a high level of skill retention without the job being done frequently (Buckley and Caple 1990). In process control, task difficulty can be derived, for example, by means of a sequence analysis (Kluge and Burkolter 2013) based on the sub-goal template method by Ormerod and Shepherd (2004) and Ormerod et al. (1998) to distinguish between fixed sequences, which are most likely to error-prone (Farr 1987), contingent, parallel and free sequences (see Chap. 3 non-routine/normal situations).

To give an example concerning teamwork skills and the use of a questionnaire, in one of our own studies, we used a Teamwork Analysis Inventory (TAKAI, Hagemann 2011; Hagemann et al. 2012) to analyse the specific requirements of the teamwork requirement, for example with respect to relational complexity and adaptiveness. This was combined with interviews with subject matter experts, direct observations and the analysis of records and reports (Hagemann 2011; Hagemann et al. 2012).

Analysing and understanding the cognitive processes required by Cognitive Task Analysis

For each particular control room job, a cognitive task analysis is also essential. Cognitive task analysis methods supplement traditional task analysis techniques to detect the knowledge and information-processing aspects that underlie task performance in a more fine-grained manner (Roth 2008; Schraagen et al. 2000). "*A cognitive task analysis allows training designers to gain insight into the cognitive processes and requirements for job performance of subject matter experts by the use of knowledge elicitation techniques*" (Salas et al. 2006, p. 477; Schraagen et al. 2000) in order to uncover experts' relevant but tacit knowledge and knowledge structures (van den Bosch and Riemersma 2004). Cognitive task analysis aims at determining the cognitive processes and skills required to perform, for example, the task of a control room operator at high proficiency levels and the changes that occur while skills develop (O'Hare et al. 1998). Cognitive task analysis methods are used to anticipate contributors to errors (e.g. lack of information or inaccurate understanding) and to specify how to improve individual and team performance, for example through training (Roth 2008). In order to develop training programs, the cognitive task analysis is based on the analysis of the actual user activity in an already functioning system (O'Hare et al. 1998).

Cognitive task analysis refers to a series of methods such as verbal protocols with experts thinking aloud while performing a simulated task, observations, interviews about concepts and cues experts use as well as conceptual methods (van den Bosch and Riemersma 2004), or critical incident analysis techniques such as the critical decision method (Klein et al. 1989; Roth 2008).

A useful list and description of CTA techniques can be found in Crandall et al. (2006). Cognitive task analysis results can then be used for expert mental model development, cues for guiding visual search and monitoring, and cues promoting complex decision-making skills (Salas et al. 2006). Cognitive task analysis links the constructs and basic psychological theory (e.g. regarding information processing, planning, monitoring, decision making) to a real-world task (Kozlowski and DeShon 2004). These results can also be used for the design of training evaluation instruments and feedback and for the design of simulation and scenario-based training (Salas et al. 2006) with high action and cognitive fidelity (Kozlowski and DeShon 2004).

According to Roth (2008), one of the most widely used cognitive task analysis methods is the critical decision method (CDM) by Klein et al. (1989). CDM was designed to address the basis of expert decision-making performance (goals-cues-expectancies-courses of action) as described in the RPDM (see Chaps. 3 and 4), to be applicable under field conditions, and to have applied value in training or system design (Klein et al. 1989; O'Hare et al. 1998). In the CDM, a series of structured probing questions (Table 5.2) are used to elicit retrospective descriptions of actual past incidents (Roth 2008). The probing questions require the expert to reflect on their own strategies and bases for decisions (Klein et al. 1989). The CDM (also) builds on the critical incident technique (Flanagan 1954, see above) "by using a set of cognitive probes to determine the bases for situation assessment and decision making during non-routine incidents" (Klein et al. 1989, p. 462), because non-routine situations are the richest source of data about the capabilities of skilled personnel (Klein et al. 1989). Participants are requested to bring to mind an incident in which their expertise made a difference to the outcome, which is then recalled in detail and a time line is constructed to trace the sequence of events (O'Hare et al. 1998). Once the incident is selected, the interviewer asks for a brief description (Klein et al. 1989). The recalled incidents can themselves also be useful for the design of training scenarios and episodes with a high psychological fidelity (Kozlowski and DeShon 2004).

Table 5.2 demonstrates that the probes can vary with respect to the context and task for which they are used and that probes should be adapted to the particularities of the RPDM processes one wishes to understand in order to subsequently design instances that provide the relevant cues and which involve the required cognitive processes.

The basic procedure of the CDM consists of five steps (Klein et al. 1989): Select incident; Obtain unstructured incident account; Construct incident technique; Decision point identification; Decision point probing (e.g. using the probes in Table 5.2). A current description of the CDM by Crandall et al. (2006) proposes four phases:

- Selecting an incident: For example routine, non-routine, challenging events.
- Time line verification: Gaining a clear, refined and verified overview of the incident structure, identifying key events and segments.
- Deepening: Discovering the story behind the story. Finding out, for example, what the operator knew, when he/she knew, how he/she knew, what he/she did with this knowledge.
- Application of "What-if" queries as proposed in Table 5.3.

As a result of the CDM, it might be found, for example, that novices in a control room should be trained to develop the perceptual differentiations and monitoring activities used by experts. In order to develop such perceptual skills, practice needs to take place under conditions in which the relevant cues are consistently associated with certain responses (O'Hare et al. 1998), for example in a simulator environment (see below).

With regard to the proposition in Chap. 4, the CDM is helpful for designing learning instances that support the acquisition of diagnosticity of cues (proposition 8) and their salience as well as for learning surface and structural similarity between situational cues (propositions 28 and 29), for example in order to enhance situation assessment and accurate pattern recognition. In that respect, CTA can be helpful for developing simulations and materials for scenarios by using the stories gathered during CDM to address cognitive requirements (Crandall et al. 2006). Additionally, CTA can be used for feedback and debriefing. CTA can be used to find out how the

Table 5.2 Critical decision interview probes by Klein et al. (1989, p. 466), Crandall et al. (2006) and extracts of the CDM probes used by O'Hare et al. (1998, p. 1717–1718)

Probe type	Probe content (Klein et al. 1989)	Probes used by O'Hare et al. (1998)
Cues	What were you seeing, hearing, smelling, ...	What features were you looking at when you formulated your decision? How did you know when to make the decision?
Information	What information did you use in making this decision, and how was it obtained?	Conceptual model: Are there any situations in which your decision would have turned out differently? Information integration: What were the most important pieces of information which you used to formulate the decision?
Analogies	Were you reminded of any previous experience?	Were you at any time reminded of previous experiences in which a *similar* decision was made? Were you at any time reminded of previous experiences in which a *different* decision was made?
Goals	What were your specific goals at that time?	What were your specific goals at the various decision points?
Options	What other courses of action were considered by or available to you?	Were there any other alternatives available to you other than the decision you made? Why were these alternatives considered inappropriate?
Basis	How was this option selected/how were other options rejected? What rule was being followed?	Do you think that you could develop a rule, based on your experience, which could assist another person to make the same decision successfully? Do you think that anyone else would be able to use the rule successfully? Why? Why not?
SOPs	Does this case fit a standard or typical scenario?	
Experience	What specific training or experience was necessary or helpful in making this decision?	
Time Pressure	How much time pressure was involved in making this decision?	
Assessment	Imagine that you are asked to describe the situation to a relief officer at this point; how would you summarise the situation?	

Table 5.3 What-if queries according to Crandall et al. (2006)

Issues	What-if query
Expert-novice contrasts	If a novice had been in charge at this particular point in the incident, what type of error might he/she have made and why? Would he/she have noticed what you noticed? Would he/she have known to do x?
Experience	What specific training or experience was necessary or helpful in making this decision?
	"What-if" query: What training might have offered an advantage in this situation?
Aiding	"What-if" query: If the decision was not the best, what training, tools, knowledge, or information could have helped?
Hypotheticals	"What-if" query: If a key feature of the situation had been different, what difference would it have made in your decision?

operator made sense of the scenario and to spot ways in which an operator may be confused (Crandall et al. 2006).

What is the relevance for training design?

Conducting analysis of the organisational and production context as well as the cognitive task analysis serves the purpose of selecting and compiling instances for the training of novice operators. The analysis should lead to an assembly of routine, non-routine/normal and non-routine/abnormal situations (at least those that had no SOP) which are put into a meaningful sequence. This should enable an adequate mental model of the target system to be built up through the accumulation of instances and allow the learning of cues of the situation, decisions and utilities. The instances should then be organised according to their cues and the pattern behind them – not according to the underlying knowledge, i.e. not as is the case, for example, with ontology or knowledge taxonomy. Indeed, as described in Chap. 4, knowledge is *not* represented in this way in the operator.

An event-based analysis should additionally be used to work out the shared elements of the instances on the surface and structural level. In this respect, it is suitable for novices to first of all practise the instances which have a high surface similarity so that the SDUs can be acquired, differentiated and assimilated. With increased practice and on the foundation of a basis of instances, variety should be brought into the training scenarios, which also allow shared elements and similarities to be discovered on the structural level. Instances for acquiring teamwork skills must also be carefully selected and compiled, for which the event-based analysis method can be used. I will make further remarks on this below.

5.2 The First Stage of the Process Control Readiness Training – Making the Most of Practice – Training Design for Novices

As was proposed in Chap. 4, the learning process implies the accumulation of instances through work experience and practice (propositions 3 and 5). Work experience was defined as the accumulation of instances in informal settings on-the-job through ongoing task exposure. Practice was defined as the accumulation of instances in deliberately and purposely designed formal settings near-the-job.

What needs to be considered concerning the operators being novices? As novices in part have no job experience, it is important to bear in mind the particularities of learning with high element activity here (see Chaps. 2 and 4). For novices, the complexity of the system is linked to a high intrinsic load. When the concern is with acquiring mental models, if elements that need to be understood and learned, for example the process in a refinery unit, interact greatly with each other, they have to be processed and considered simultaneously. Therefore, in cases of high element interactivity, they exceed the limits of the human working memory capacity (Sweller 2006). Working memory holds only the most recently activated, or conscious, proportion of long-term memory, and it moves these activated elements in and out of brief, temporary memory storage (Dosher 2003; Sternberg 2009).

Element interactivity refers, in the definition by Sweller (2006), not to the task per se, but to the content to be learned. As the complex task of the operator consists of operating a complex system, knowledge is, of course, also required about the operation of the plant and the process which is being controlled. The understanding of the plant requires the simultaneous processing of interconnected variables because, as described above, interconnectivity constitutes a feature of a complex system and places a strong burden on working memory during learning. In the acquisition of knowledge, it is therefore important to consider that such instructional techniques are selected that optimally support rather than overtax working memory during the process of learning information.

Possibly, the control room operators, who have already been field operators, have a mental model of the plant which can be built on. In other words, one does not have to explain the foundations of the chemical or physical processes of the technical plant to be operated. However, it will be uncertain whether this mental model is accurate. Therefore, even for novices in the control room who have field experience, it should be ensured through the training that the mental model of the target system also depicts the actual connectivity and dynamics. In the following, the outlines for a training design are based on the assumption that the control room operators bring with them prior knowledge about the plant (but not prior knowledge about the control room activity). This training concept is targeted at the *individual skill acquisition*. The training should lead to the individual operator becoming so proficient that he will later be in a position to add the teamwork skills for non-routine/abnormal situations on top of this (proposition 22).

Training components

In the first stage of the process control readiness training, propositions 2 and 18 are built on: The learning process implies the accumulation of instances through work experience and practice. To convert this proposition into a training design for novice control room operators, the training needs the following components, which are described below:

- A full-scope simulator
- Instances
- Experiential learning
- Component practice
- Briefing
- Debriefing

The full-scope simulator

Training simulators are systems which provide realistic training by incorporating and replicating a working representation of reality (Cannon-Bowers and Bowers 2010). Based on the remarks of Sun (2002) and Sun et al. (2001, 2005), it emerged (propositions 9 and 10) that particularly in complex tasks, bottom-up learning is relevant and used, and this can be accelerated by explicit top-down learning. Accordingly, it would make sense to first of all allow novice control operators to experience instances in the *full-scope simulator*, enabling them to acquire procedural knowledge about the control room (control knowledge on the interface level, operating knowledge (Kluwe 1997). As Sun et al. (2005) state, when there is no sufficient a priori knowledge available, learning is bottom-up and starts with procedural action-centred knowledge. It is therefore useful in this respect to begin with routine situations in order to meet demand for task fractionation (Wickens et al. 2012) on the basis of increasing difficulty (see Chap. 4, proposition 25).

*Why a full-scope simulato*r? Firstly, the daily routine tasks in many process industries provide the novice with too few possibilities to acquire instances, as due to the high automation, few active learning opportunities are available (see Chap. 2, high automation, also Duncan and Shepherd 1975). Moreover, learning and practising in high-hazard industries is, of course, less indicated due to the associated dangers on-the-job. Therefore, learning should not take place on site (Wexley and Latham 2002). Learning should also not take place in the classroom off-the-job or "off site" (Wexley and Latham 2002), as then, a mental model cannot be acquired. A mental model can only be acquired through the interaction with the target system (Norman 1983; Sun et al. 2001). Norman (1983): The users' mental models are acquired through interaction with the target system. An operator, through interaction with the system, will continue to modify the mental model in order to get to a workable result. *Simulator training therefore combines the advantages of on-the-job and off-the-job training.* On-the-job learning would include training directly conducted in the control room, while off-the-job learning allows for deliberately

Table 5.4 Simulator-relevant definitions

Simulator type	Definition
Full-scope simulator	Incorporates a detailed model of the system with which the operator works in the actual control room. Such simulators also include a replica control-room operating console (Kluge et al. 2009).
Generic simulator	Includes basic-principles and part-task simulators. Basic-principles simulators illustrate general concepts, demonstrating and displaying the fundamental physical process of a plant (Kluge et al. 2009).
Physical fidelity	Degree to which the equipment, interface, procedures replicate the control room (Elliot et al. 2004)
Psychological fidelity	Extent to which the training environment *prompts* the essential underlying psychological processes relevant to key performance characteristics in the real-world setting (Kozlowski and DeShon 2004)
Cognitive fidelity	Degree to which scenario content is similar in *cognitive* demands for underlying cognition and information processing (Elliot et al. 2004).
Acton fidelity	Degree of correspondence between the *behaviour* in a learning setting and the target setting (Stoffregen et al. 2003).

designed instances to be acquired, practice without hazardous consequences for the environment, explicit feedback, correction and component practice of crucial skills guided by the trainer for experiential learning.

The full-scope simulator (Table 5.4) is important, moreover, because only this offers the cognitive fidelity, the relevant cues for the RPDM on the basis of which, with increasing experience, the mental model is differentiated and developed further (see remarks on CDM, Klein et al. 1989; IBLT, Gonzales et al. 2003; Kolodner 1983; Norman 1983).

The usefulness for training in full-scope simulators for acquiring instances is vividly described by Greitzer et al. (2009): "Prior to the blackout of August 14, 2003, only a small fraction of power system operators had ever trained with realistic operator training simulators. Following the blackout, the North American Electric Reliability Council (NERC) Emergency Operations Recommendation No. 6 required that: 'All reliability coordinators, control areas, and transmission operators shall provide at least 5 days per year of training and drills in emergencies, *using realistic simulations*, for each staff person with responsibility for the real-time operation or reliability monitoring of the bulk electric system.'" (Greitzer et al. 2009, pp. 37–38, also Podmore et al. 2008, p. 1).

Through the acquisition of instances in the full-scope simulator, the application of procedures supports bottom-up learning. In this respect, I understand procedures not only as control actions and SOPs but also as monitoring procedures, as described by Vicente et al. (2004), which includes the configuration of display and the priorities and frequencies with which relevant indicators and cues are monitored.

On the whole, the learning theories predict that the instances and the cues contained within them, the decisions derived from them as well as the utilities can only be acquired "in situ" (propositions 1–13). Generic simulators offer too few actual, real decision-critical cues and draw too strongly on the general understanding of associations. Starting from the basic assumption that control room operators were previously field operators, it can be assumed that a general understanding of the chemical and physical processes has already been acquired.

It is deemed as very important that *novices* in particular *begin with bottom-up learning at the full-scope simulator* and that learning is supported in the form of feedback and debriefing through top-down learning processes and declarative knowledge. Unfortunately, a different procedure is frequently found in practice; the full-scope simulators are primarily used for experts, while novices have to work with generic simulations (if at all). Due to the element interactivity, the latter are difficult for learning and must be learned under high cognitive load. Or often, very extensive theoretical training takes place, which attempts to build an abstract mental model. Indeed, a fairly common assumption is that operators need to understand the fundamental principles on which the design and operation of the system is based. The theoretical knowledge of principles and facts includes, for example, fundamentals of thermodynamics, heat transfer, fluid mechanics, solid mechanics, dynamics, electricity and mathematics (Morris and Rouse 1985, p. 36): "Unfortunately, there is little if any evidence that this results in better or more useful mental models". It has been found that knowledge test scores of fundamental understanding did not correlate significantly with process control performance (Morris and Rouse 1985). And this is still the case 30 years later.

With this component, propositions 1–13 can be put into practice.

The instances and their sequencing

As described above, the instances should emerge from event-based analyses and then, as described in Chap. 4, be organised with increasing difficulty and according to their surface and structural similarity.

First of all, two or three familiarisation instances should be run through, in which the operator is familiarised with the control room and the display. In this regard, monitoring priorities and frequencies can be learned, for example in which certain values have to be read off. As described in Chap. 2 (Table 2.2), the operator should learn how to monitor the process, consult SOPs, communicate his/her observations, keep a record of significant events, schedule testing of routine equipment, make changes to the system, for example in order to prevent or compensate for drifts and faults, and introduce long-term changes and adjustments so that it evolves towards a more efficient system. This should be followed by more demanding routine situations, for example with special products or under special weather conditions as well as non-routine/normal situations which are planned or unexpected (see Chap. 3 for non-routine/normal situations).

The demand for increasing difficulty can also be fulfilled by making the instances become gradually more difficult, i.e. it becomes difficult to discriminate between cues or cue configuration, time pressure is increased or the number of part-tasks to be integrated increases (see Chap. 4). Moreover, instances can be designed such that they enable emphasis-shift training variants such as the variable priorities training of SOP execution and plant monitoring, emphasis change or the introduction of a secondary task, for example communication with a second operator in order to acquire time-sharing skills.

In this respect, the selection of instances should be such that, with increased practice, the operator will use a recognition-based application of the instance-based knowledge (proposition 7). The perception of similarity increases with practice, which supports attention management for relevant task cues (see Chap. 4). Situation assessment and accuracy will increase with the accumulation of further instances and learning episodes. In other words, the selection of instances should be such that they are initially very similar to each other to enable general instances and SDU combinations as well as general rules to be extracted. These can then be further differentiated with further instances and refined with a corresponding debriefing. In this way, a mental model that becomes ever more differentiated can develop.

Moreover, with further instances, the difficulty should also increase, as already described above. As Wickens et al. (2012) as well as Merrienboer et al. (2003) describe, in parallel to the increasing task difficulty, skill develops over time, leading to resource demands (intrinsic load due to element interactivity) which remain relatively stable over time. During instance accumulation, the novice is provided with and supported by procedural information, for example SOPs as they would also be used and occur on-the-job. This instance-based training experience can then be viewed as an episode in terms of a series of cumulative stimuli experienced by the learner and the cognitions associated with these experiences (Baldwin and Magjuka 1997; Baldwin et al. 2009). The training episode then represents a "natural slice" of organisational life (Baldwin and Magjuka 1997).

In this way, operators work their way through these different instances until they are in a position to handle the situations professionally and with a high individual proficiency, and are later able to learn teamwork instances.

With this component, propositions 1–13, 22 and 24–27 can be realised.

Experiential Learning

If one wishes to translate this use of instances into a training concept, the experiential learning circle according to Kolb (1984) presents itself as an opportunity. The IBLT (Gonzales et al. 2003) and COCOM model (Hollnagel and Woods 2005) have elements in common and therefore similarity with Kolb's experiential learning circle (Fig. 5.2).

Experiential learning theory defines learning as "the process whereby knowledge is created through the transformation of experience. Knowledge results from the combination of grasping and transforming experience" (Kolb 1984, p. 41; Kolb et al. 2000). The experiential learning approach consists of four elements (Kolb 1984):

- Concrete experience,
- Observation and reflection,
- The formation of abstract concepts, and
- Testing in new situations.

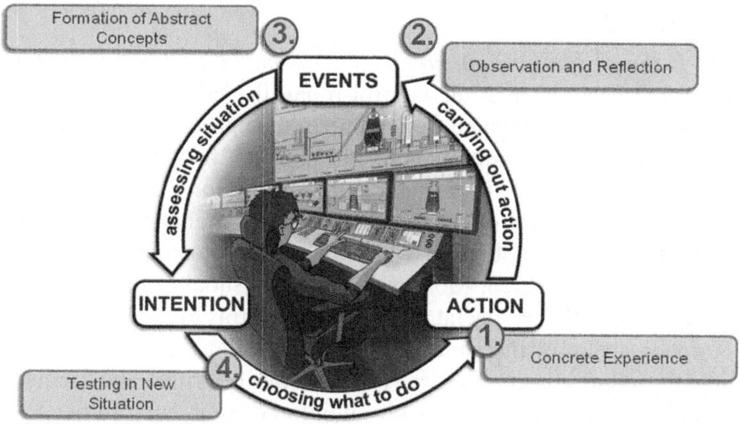

Fig. 5.2 Kolb's experiential learning integrated into the COCOM (Hollnagel 2007)

It is suggested that the learning process often begins with a person carrying out a particular action and then seeing the effect of the action in this situation. Following this, the second step is to understand these effects in the particular instance, so that if the same action were taken in the same circumstances, it would be possible to anticipate what would follow from the action. According to this pattern, the third step would be to understand the general principle under which the particular instance falls. Although is not always taken entirely seriously in psychology as the empirical testing is lacking and it has been criticised, for instance by Miettinen (2000), for not correctly reviewing the literature used as a foundation, several basic learning principles outlined in the previous chapters can be recognised in it. Moreover, the organisational psychology literature does contain references to Kolb, for example in Sonnentag et al. (2004) or Tannenbaum et al. (2010) to name but a few.

Kolb's (1984) approach is conceptualised as a symmetrical cycle which depicts four learning activities, which in the original model are all presented with equal weightings. However, if one considers the previous theoretical remarks, then the learning of control of a complex system must bring with it a clearly higher proportion of experience and practice compared to reflection and forming abstract concepts. According to Sun et al. (2001, 2005) as well as Gonzales et al. (2003), the abstract model results from practice and experience through the process of generalising specific knowledge to form generic schemas, so that later, for example, case-based reasoning becomes possible, or also the RPDM. Therefore, based on these theoretical assumptions, it is useful to practise for approx. 2/3 to 3/4 of the time and to use 1/4 of the time on debriefing, as presented in Fig. 5.2 and explained below.

Experiential learning stands for the implementation of propositions 1–13.

Briefing and Debriefing

Briefing is the verbal introduction to the instance-based learning episode that "sets the scene". Like later in the control room, the briefing should occur in the form of a shift handover in which, for example, the entries in a shift book are read and the "state" of the plant and plans for the shift are talked through. This means that the *briefing* is necessary to introduce the setting, for example what happened previously, what is the state of the plant, is it day or night, summer or winter? In other words, information is briefed which helps the situation to be assessed and relevant cues to be interpreted. Moreover, reference should be made to constraints in the decisions, to SOPs or special regulations. In terms of the IBLT, the operators should be made aware of the situation and given indications of what is expected concerning the monitoring activities, for example priorities and frequency with which relevant indicators should be monitored (e.g. according to Vicente et al. 2004).

Debriefing is defined here as the verbally guided analysis by the trainer of operator experience to extract rules and explicit knowledge, build up or correct mental models. In the debriefing, guidance in the use of knowledge should be provided (Morris and Rouse 1985, p. 39) in order to support bottom-up and top-down learning (Sun et al. 2001, proposition 11).

In order to achieve the training objective for routine situations stated in Chap. 3, Table 3.3, debriefing should include:

- Information concerning the results in terms of the level of achievement of the multiple or contradictory goals (see Chap. 2), for example safety and productivity,
- Information concerning the quality of performance, for example to point out ineffective monitoring strategies (priorities and frequencies), available cues and inappropriate use of displays which made the situation assessment more difficult, feedback referring to diagnosis skills and hypothesis-testing or by correcting errors in an SOP execution, correcting non-technical skills such as wrong prioritisation of tasks, scheduling jobs and allocating tasks,
- Explanation and disclosure of the complex technical processes behind the instance in terms of the explanation and disclosure of the non-transparent aspects of the technical processes as well as the dynamics and interconnectivity, which are difficult to "see" and understand as a novice,
- Summarising the causal relationships and extracted rules of the plant behaviour,
- Summarising the cues relevant in that instance (proposition 6),
- Summarising the courses of action and their utility in that situation (propositions 5 and 11),
- Indicating similarities and shared elements with other instances previously experienced (propositions 28–30).

In addition, the debriefing session should also be used to elucidate why there are regulations for certain technical procedures. For frequently, accidents occur due to infringements of regulations, as described by Reason (1998), Mason (1997), Kluge et al. (2013) or von der Heyde et al. (2012). The less prior knowledge is brought in, also about the plant, the more important the debriefing session mentioned in the following, in which the basic understanding and terminology of the process to be controlled is elucidated.

In the debriefing session, the use of case-based reasoning can also be supported. As introduced in Chap. 4, cased-based reasoning has its traditions in the field of cognitive science and focuses on skill development and situational hypothesis generation based upon knowledge acquired from past experience (Cooke and Fiore 2010). In specially designed case-based reasoning, training solutions from previous cases are integrated, adapted for a solution to the novel problem and retaining the solution if validated. But for this, various cases first have to have been experienced, for example through IBL and simulator sessions.

This component incorporates propositions 6–8 and 11.

Component practice

The accumulation of instances should be supplemented by component practice of task components that require time-sharing and attention allocation skills (Gopher 2007; Wickens et al. 2012, see Chap. 4). Merrienboer et al. (2003) describe that additional component practice can be very effective after learners have been introduced to the whole task and the recurrent aspects in the context of the learning task, so that part-task practice takes place "in a fruitful cognitive context that allows learners to identify the activities that are required to integrate the recurrent aspects in the whole task" (Merrienboer et al. 2003; Carlson et al. 1990). Merrienboer et al. (2003) raise the issue that over-reliance on part-task training is not helpful for complex learning, but in cases in which a high level of automaticity is required (e.g. in executing SOPs) for particular recurrent task sequences, the learning task does not provide enough practice to reach this level because the learning process would require a large number of practice trials, which are not available.

In this respect, component practice serves to automate controlled behaviour processes (Paris et al. 2000). Automating these behaviours makes them more resilient to the effects of stress, thus bolstering performance under stressful conditions because these kinds of complex tasks to be learned (see Chap. 2) are more likely to be undermined by stressors such as cognitive overload than simpler tasks (Keinan and Friedland 1996). The objective of component practice is to achieve durability and automaticity of the skill itself, which has positive side effects of reducing stress. In this sense, skill training can ameliorate the effects of stress by producing over-learned behavior that is not consciously controlled and leaves reserve capacity for information processing of a large amount of data (see Chap. 3). Finally over-learned tasks instil the perception of control and predictability (Keinan and Friedland 1996).

This means that a special component practice is not ruled out from the outset just because one chooses the whole-task approach. However, special component practice is then only effective if the novice is clear about the appropriate cognitive context. Therefore, effective component practice must preserve an appropriate

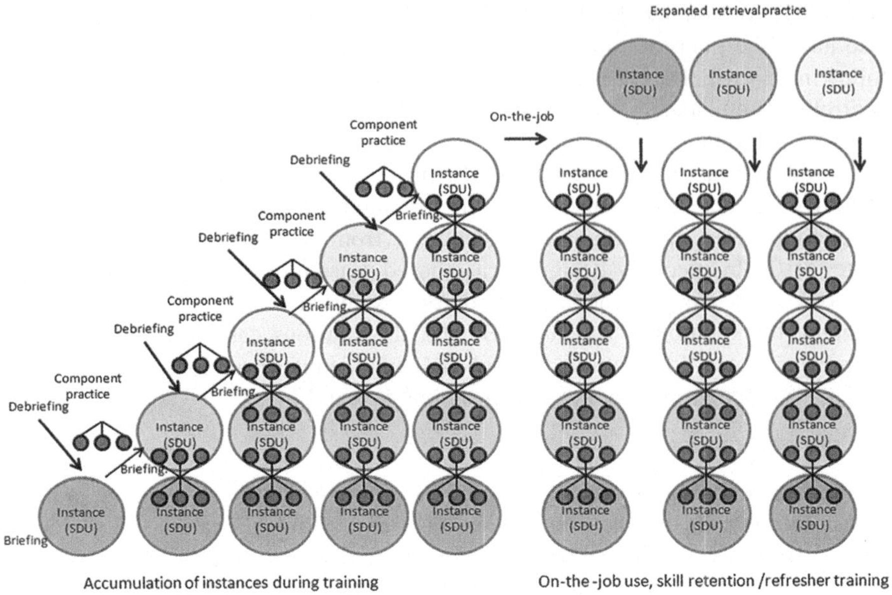

Fig. 5.3 Stage 1 process control readiness training, accumulation of instances for novices with instances sharing elements, and expanded retrieval practice for skill retention

cognitive context (Carlson et al. 1990). Exposure to the target context increases the effectiveness of component practice (Carlson et al. 1990).

Accordingly, there are very sound theoretically and empirically founded reasons for integrating component practice into whole-task training (Kluge et al. 2008).

In this procedure, propositions 11 and 22 are reflected, as illustrated in Fig. 5.3.

What needs to be done if somebody has no previous knowledge and field experience?

First of all, it should be asked why somebody without prior knowledge should be working in a control room. However, generally speaking, even for novices who were not previously field operators, the same principles can be applied, but one should plan more time for this, and even more intensive supportive and procedural knowledge should be provided, as suggested by Merrienboer et al. (2003). This should be presented just-in-time, in a direct, step-by-step manner or with how-to instructions, and should be faded away for subsequent instances (Merrienboer et al. 2003). Of course, instance-based learning for persons without any prior knowledge takes a lot longer. Moreover, for novices without previous field experience, generic simulators could be employed, which enable a mental model to be built up of the chemical and physical processes, as well as of the plant, with its interconnectivity, dynamics and non-transparency.

The responsibilities of the trainer

One important point should be emphasised in particular here: The competence of the *training designer* is called upon for a hugely important task, in which he/she has to design instances and learning episodes which build on one another so that the novices can acquire an accurate mental model of the target system. The main task of the trainer lies in the selection and compiling of the instances in a temporally sequential manner, which a novice works through and experiences in order to extract patterns and derive cues, and from which he/she learns cue configurations, decisions and utilities.

Moreover, he/she has to select the components for which the component practice is to be applied. And the trainer also needs the skills to be able to carry out the feedback and debriefing in such a way that misunderstanding and errors in the mental model can be uncovered and corrected.

After training and to evaluate training success, evaluation possibilities described in Chap. 3 for routine and non-routine/normal situations can be used, such as instruments for assessing mental models, situational judgement tests, the Situation Awareness Control Room Inventory (SACRI, Hogg et al. 1995), observations of performance in trained instances, and error analysis.

5.2.1 Designing Practice to Support Skill Retention

One proposition from Chap. 4 was that instances which are well entrenched and inter-associated with other instances possess a high storage strength. In this respect, a procedure of instance-based learning such as described above can also lead to a high entrenchment with other instances. But what else needs to be given attention?

Bjork and Bjork (2006) suggest in this regard so-called desirable difficulty during the initial training, such as distributed practice, interleaving of part-tasks, varying rather than keeping learning conditions constant, reducing rather than increasing feedback and using tests. Distributed practice supports skill retention, as greater accumulation of storage strength with distributed practice slows the process of retrieval strength with disuse.

It would therefore make sense to not necessarily learn all of the instances in blocks, but rather broken up with a certain retention interval in between. Here, for example, an *expanding retrieval practice* could be arranged. In this method of scheduling practice, the first attempt is scheduled shortly after the first learning episode, the next retrieval attempt is scheduled after a slightly longer retention interval, the third after a longer interval still etc. (see Chap. 4). Each retrieval attempt should occur at the point when retrieval would be maximally difficult. The method of expanding retrieval practice can then be combined with the introduction of variations into the learning of a new task so that retrieval is made more difficult and each time the new episode occurs in a slightly different manner it becomes associated with different retrieval cues and improvement of context. The approach is to provide training in a variety of routine situations (for more than one situation, one or more of which will be unfamiliar). The use of unfamiliar scenarios can "force" operators to utilise general principles such as analogies because it might be the only way in which the task can be solved (Morris and Rouse 1985).

This implements propositions 23–27.

If one considers the demand to expand retrieval practice, the transitions to refresher training are fluid for novices. Indeed, one form of refreshing is retrieval practice, for example in the form of tests or skill demonstrations (Kluge et al. 2012), which also increase the retrieval strength through an increased retrieval effort. Our own investigations (Kluge et al. 2013a) demonstrate that skill demonstration under test conditions represents a very suitable method for this. Moreover, massed relearning is also useful, as massed relearning (in contrast to massed initial learning) enables more rapid reacquisition. This is because storage strength, once accumulated (with distributed practice) is assumed to be permanent, meaning that storage strength carries over to relearning (Bjork and Bjork 2006). Refresher training and relearning sessions become all the more important the less opportunity the operator has to apply instances in the meantime. However, this can differ according to the respective process industry, as described in Chap. 2. Propositions 23 and 24 are reflected here.

A summary of stage 1 of the SPCRT is listed in Table 5.5

Is this worthwhile? Critics may argue with regard to the introduced SPCRT that the instance-based learning takes too long. Long is a relative term. Bakken (2008), for example, assumes that if one chooses the top-down approach over the information-based approach (Salas and Cannon-Bowers 1997), it may initially feel as though it were more efficient, but for it to reach the training goals, such an approach requires 2–3 years in order to form a mental model. Critics may additionally object that instance-based learning requires the experiences of real-time processes so that every instance-based learning training session requires an 8-h shift. This has not yet been empirically proven. However, it can be countered that shorter episodes in terms of component practice (Merrienboer et al. 2003, see above) are also effective if one episode is not defined as a "shift" but rather as an incident (which can occur within a shift).

Unfortunately, no officially accessible values are available on the use of such intensive simulator training. However, the author does have empirical values from organisations which show that intensive simulator training of novices in a refinery is worthwhile. These novices had 6 months of experience in the plant plus an intensive simulator training of special instances. Subsequently, they were able to perform a start-up following a shutdown, react to a top reflux pump malfunction or to a gas compressor malfunction to the same level as control room operators with an average of 20 years of work experience (Kluge and Schüler 2007). This theme in particular, namely "catching up on experiences", will become even more important in the future because the demographic change will make it increasingly important to train experiences in as condensed an instance-based manner as possible, as otherwise the experience will vanish with the retired workers.

Table 5.5 Summary of stage 1 of the SPCRT

Important training design issues for stage 1
1. Select instances, e.g. based on an event-based analysis.
2. Convert instances into training scenarios with a high physical and psychological fidelity, e.g. based on CDM.
3. Sequence instances with increased difficulty, e.g. routine situation, non-routine/normal (planned and unexpected), non-routine/abnormal.
4. Brief to set the scene, e.g. in the form of a shift handover.
5. Debrief with respect to results concerning quality and quantity of goal achievement, disclosure of complex technical processes (see Chap. 2), summarise cues, actions to be taken and similarities between instances.
6. Provide component practice for tasks that need to be automatised after introducing the whole task.
7. Use expanded retrieval practice with retention intervals between instance accumulations.

5.3 The Second Stage of the Process Control Readiness Training

In stage 2, the same components will be implemented as in stage 1, i.e. with instances, experiential learning, briefing and debriefing. However, the focus and content of the instances will lie on the teamwork skill for collaborative dynamic problem-solving.

Making the most of practice – training design for skill retention and deliberate practice for experts

Experts are, by definition, operators whose judgements are uncommonly accurate and reliable, whose performance shows consummate skill and economy of effort, and who can manage effectively with rare and difficult cases and have special skills or knowledge derived from extensive work experience, also with sub-domains (see Chap. 4). As Ericsson (2006) pointed out, expert performance counteracts automaticity through the development of increasingly differentiated mental models in order to control their performance. They will therefore try to maintain an attitude of intentionally remaining in the associative phase (see Chap. 4). Deliberate practice for control room experts should therefore incorporate exercises that require them to still control the execution of highly automated skills by making intentional modifications and adjustments (Ericsson 2006).

For experienced operators, based on proposition 13, derived in Chap. 4, skill retention and deliberate practice can be integrated into one training format. For experienced and expert operators, training should include:

(a) Demanding instances in order to support retrieval strength (Bjork and Bjork 1992/2006), which, for example, challenge the situation assessment through ambiguous cues, conflicting goals, or surface similarity to previous cases and other elements, making situation assessment difficult, and

(b) Which additionally require the expert operator to make intentional modifications and adjustments, for example by training and applying critical thinking skills and stress coping skills.
(c) The training of teamwork skills especially for abnormal situations.

Deliberate practice by means of Decision Skill Training, Critical Thinking Training, Stress Exposure Training and Team Training

In contrast to the individual instance-based learning presented in the first stage, deliberate practice should be *applied in the context of teamwork* situations. This takes into account propositions 16, 17, and 18. Four selected training methods are presented in this chapter: Decision skill training, critical thinking training, stress exposure training and team training. These training methods are chosen in accordance with the training objectives selected for non-routine/abnormal situations derived in Chap. 3, which address collaborative dynamic problem-solving.

Critical thinking skills training or decision skill training belongs to the umbrella term of training thinking skills. Cooke and Fiore (2010) state that situation assessment, decision making, planning, and coordination are all thinking skills. These skills are all very context-sensitive and cannot be learned and then transferred in a general manner (see Chap. 4 on similarity). Both critical thinking skills training and decision skill training are developed based on the approach of naturalistic decision making (Pliske et al. 2001).

Decision Skill Training

In contrast to training efforts that try to improve the operator's decision making strategies or teach generic strategies, decision skill training attempts to facilitate the development of the decision maker's basis of experience within a particular domain, which results in improved recognitional decision-making skills (Pliske et al. 2001).

Decision skill training (DST) addresses domain-specific learning issues to accelerate the transition towards expertise (Pliske et al. 2001; Ross et al. 2006). The DST program was developed based on a survey of literature on expertise in order to deduce principles to facilitate learning Recognition-Primed Decision Making (RPDM, see Chap. 4). These principles include (Klein et al. 1997):

- Engaging in deliberate practice, so that each opportunity for practice has a goal and evaluation criteria.
- Using attentional control exercises to practise flexibility in scanning situations, for example practice seeing and assessing cues and their associated patterns.
- Building their own mental models to envision courses of action.
- Sampling alternative task strategies.
- Compiling an extensive experience bank (of SDUs as in the IBLT).
- Obtaining feedback that is accurate, and diagnostic and reasonably timely.
- Enriching experience (i.e. reviewing prior experience to derive new insights and lessons from mistakes) by receiving feedback on what was not recognised or accounted for in the mental model.
- Obtaining coaching.

The training uses a scenario-based approach with low-fidelity simulation approaches (Ross et al. 2006).

The aim of decision skills training is to enable novices to experience the decision strategies of experts rather than teaching these skills directly. Klein et al. (1997) and Pliske et al. (2001) use six different methods to deliberately enhance experience and to practise decision skills, which are adapted to the control room operators' training in terms of their description:

1. Decision-making exercises (DME) are low-fidelity, paper-and-pencil simulations of incidents that might occur in the plant. They are intended to provide simulated, domain-relevant experiences and allow operators to train their RPD skills. The DME also provide context for the subsequent methods. Operators are presented with a challenging situation in which a decision must be made, and typically some sort of action must be taken. The situation includes uncertainty and participants are only given a few minutes to determine their course of action (Pliske et al. 2001).
2. Decision-making critique supports the thinking about what was difficult in decision making during an exercise, for example cues that might have been seen earlier, assessments that were mistaken, types of uncertainties that were encountered (Pliske et al. 2001).
3. Decision requirement exercises are supposed to help the operators to unpack the challenging decision they faced. The method is combined with the decision-making critique in order to identify difficult decisions and the types of information one needed to consider, as well as why these particular decisions were so difficult to make (Pliske et al. 2001).
4. Premortem exercises aim to identify key vulnerabilities in a plan. After the operators have agreed on a course of action, individual operators are asked to write down reasons why the plan will fail. The trainer then leads a discussion in which he/she asks for reasons until all concerns have been raised. The intention of this process is to support the use of multiple perspectives and for the operators to decentre from their current vision (Pliske et al. 2001) in order to uncover critical flaws and improve the plan.
5. The Operators' Intent exercise, in conjunction with a DME, provides the opportunity for operators to practise their skills for communicating their intent. Operators write down a set of steps of a suggested course of action and also provide a description of their intent. The trainer then identifies a plausible but unexpected event that will interfere with the course of action. The operators are then asked to write down how they would actually react and their interpretations are compared (Pliske et al. 2001).
6. Situation Awareness Calibration Exercises provide insight into how different operators perceive the same environment, and are used in a simulator exercise or also with a DME. The training exercise is stopped at some point and each team member is required to independently answer a brief questionnaire that assesses his/her current SA, for example what was the immediate goal of the team? What are you doing to support the goal? What is your biggest worry? What is the

current problem location? What do you think the situation will look like in _______ minutes? (Pliske et al. 2001, p. 46).

Critical Thinking Skill Training

Critical Thinking Skills are required for abnormal situations, as introduced in Chap. 3 (Fig. 3.16). Critical thinking skills are supposed to support constructive controversy (Johnson and Johnson 2003). Constructive controversy is required when the control room team members have different information, perceptions, opinions, reasoning processes, theories and conclusions on which they must reach a consensus (Johnson and Johnson 2003). Critical Thinking Skill Training (CTST), based on the ideas of Cohen and Thompson (2001) and Cohen, Freeman and Thompson (1998), is about supporting pattern recognition in novel situations, such as abnormal situations. Operators are trained to apply meta-recognitional processes so that operators learn to think critically about their results of recognition, for example by asking "What in the situation conflicts with my expectation? How can I stretch a pattern, i.e. tell a new story to make the pattern fit? What assumptions must I accept in order to believe the story? What information is missing that would clarify the assumption? How plausible is the story? What alternative pattern may apply? What story must I tell to make one of the other patterns fit, and what assumptions does it require? Which story is more plausible?" (Cohen and Thompson 2001, p. 256). In this respect, a fundamental meta-recognitional skill is to distinguish the cues given in a situation from conclusions and interpretations (Cohen and Thompson 2001).

The meta-recognitional process that underlies critical thinking consists of three elements:

1. Quick test, which is a rapid assessment of the value of taking more time for critical thinking versus acting immediately to the current recognitional response,
2. Critiquing the current results of recognition in order to identify problems, for example by looking for uncertainties in the argument composing a present recognitional interpretation. Uncertainties can result from the instance that more than one conclusion seems plausible, due to gaps in knowledge, no conclusion seems entirely plausible owing to conflicting beliefs, or the conclusion is subject to variation over time, and unreliable assumptions over time (Cohen and Thompson 2001, p. 262),
3. Correcting these problems by influencing the operation of the recognition system, by shifting attention from cues in the situations to selected elements of the recognitional interpretation (Cohen and Thompson 2001). This results, for example, in the activation of potentially relevant knowledge in long-term memory which has not been considered so far. The result of attention shifting is to increase the amount of knowledge brought to bear on the situation in order to fill gaps in an argument, through a deeper consideration of the conflicts with goals and intention. Attention shifting also supports the discovery of unreliability through the identification of hidden assumptions by articulating reasons for divergent conclusions and comparing justifications.

Additional training for constructive controversy would also imply the practice of presenting one's own position, or advocating one position, in order to additionally view the issue from all perspectives (Johnson and Johnson 2003).

The CTST can be integrated particularly into emergency exercise simulator training or any other training relevant for skill retention. It requires a trainer who moderates the critical thinking process and provides probes for activating meta-recognitional processes. Operators should be asked to apply critical thinking skills in the non-routine situation, for example by looking for incomplete and missing arguments, looking for conflicts, which means looking for arguments with contradictory conclusions, and looking for unreliability, which means looking for arguments that depend on unconsidered assumptions in order to collect more data. They are also required to shift focus and retrieve knowledge, and add or drop assumptions (Cohen et al. 1996).

Stress Exposure Training

Stress exposure training aims to enable operators to cope and maintain performance under stress (in non-routine/abnormal situations). Stress exposure training includes a combination of training methods:

- Provide preparatory information,
- Training skills for maintaining attentional focus,
- Apply and practise the acquired skills in a simulated stress environment.

One part of the training consists in conveying knowledge of the stressful environment (Driskell and Johnston 1998; Johnston and Cannon-Bowers 1996; Moore et al. 2012) through the provision of *preparatory information*. This procedure is based on several assumptions:

- First, it is assumed that if people are informed and instructed about what symptoms they may experience in stressful situations, the symptoms are less disturbing and less distressing to them because they know what they are. Preparatory information renders the task less novel and unfamiliar, and leads to a positive expectation of self-efficacy when experiencing a "normal" reaction to an abnormal event (Moore et al. 2012).
- Furthermore, it enables the individual to form accurate expectations regarding stress in abnormal situations, thereby increasing predictability (cognized control, Frey and Jonas 2002).
- It also decreases the distraction involved in attending to novel situations and novel sensations and activities in the stress situation (Driskell and Johnston 1998/2006) and supports the increasing attention to task-relevant stimuli.

Individuals under stress tend to over-interpret stress symptoms and judge these "normal" reactions as catastrophic; the novelty or unfamiliarity of these symptoms leads to them being bestowed with a disproportionate amount of attentional capacity, which distracts from task-focused activity (Driskell and Johnston 1998/2006). Under stress, operators may begin to "time-share" cognitive resources between the task and worrying about the stress itself. "Performance suffers as attention is distributed between task-relevant and task-irrelevant cognitions" (Driskell and Johnston 1998/2006, p. 201).

Driskell and Johnston (1998/2006) define three types of preparatory information:

- *Sensory information*, which is information about how the operator is feeling when under stress, including the perception of a number of intrusive physical and emotional sensations, for example increased heart rate, sweating, shallow breathing, muscular tension,
- *Procedural information*, which describes events that are likely to occur in the stress environment and includes descriptions of the setting and types of stressors,
- *Instrumental information*, which describes what to do to counter the undesirable consequences of stress and how to resolve the problems posed by the stressful situation (Driskell and Johnston 1998/2006).

Subsequent to the provision of preparatory information, Driskell and Johnston (1998/2006) suggest *training specific skills to maintain attentional focus* on task-relevant stimuli in the face of external distraction due to stressors. Skill training strategies are listed in Table 5.6. These skill training strategies are equivalent to the component practice introduced in the first stage of the SPCRT for novices.

Following the training and skill acquisition for maintaining performance levels in non-routine/abnormal situations, operators are supposed to *apply and practise the acquired skills in a simulated stress environment* (Driskell and Johnston 1998/2006). This allows operators to apply and adapt the acquired skills and to experience the type of performance problems in abnormal situations. Second, pre-exposure to criteria like stressors reduces uncertainty and anxiety regarding these events, as also explained in conjunction with the effects of providing preparatory information. Third, events that have been experienced during training are less likely to distract operators when they are faced with an abnormal situation (Driskell and Johnston 1998/2006). This kind of training in three phases, including presentation of requisite preparatory knowledge, skill training and skill application in the criterion environment, is called Stress Exposure Training (Driskell and Johnston 1998/2006; Johnston and Cannon-Bowers 1996).

This training design incorporates propositions 13, 14 and 22, which state that becoming an expert requires ongoing learning that counteracts automaticity through the development of increasingly complex mental representations to attain higher levels of control over performance.

Training teamwork skills

It was proposed (proposition 22) that before team members are trained in developing teamwork skills, they must have reached some threshold level of competence in their individual knowledge and skill.

This requirement is fulfilled by stage 1 of the process control readiness training, which should have built up the threshold level of competence of the individual operators. It was additionally proposed that

Table 5.6 Skill training strategies to maintain attentional focus (Driskell and Johnston 1998/2006)

Skill training strategy	Training objective
Cognitive control strategies	Trains cognitive coping strategies to establish or maintain control over distracting or dysfunctional thoughts and emotions.
	Trains operators to recognise task-irrelevant thoughts that degrade performance and to replace them with task-focused cognitions by redirecting attention to task-relevant aspects.
Physiological control strategies	Trains operators to establish and maintain control over dysfunctional physiological reactions to stress in order to teach them to bring their physiological processes under conscious control.
Over-learning, e.g. in terms of component practice	Deliberate overtraining of a performance beyond the level of initial proficiency
	Trains a set of habitual responses with high automaticity (see Chaps. 3/4) that are less vulnerable to stress decrement.
	Given the effect that stress reduces attentional capacity, behaviours with a higher automaticity are more resistant to degradation.
Mental practice	Cognitive rehearsal of a task in the absence of overt physical movement (Richardson 1967).
	Trains by mentally rehearsing a task, offers the opportunity to rehearse behaviors and to code them into easily remembered words to aid recall.
Training time-sharing skills	Trains operators to time-share skills due to an increased task load and time pressure and the need to interleave multiple tasks. Time-sharing is considered a task-specific skill that must be practised in context.
	Trains prioritisation skills in multiple-task environments.
Training team skills	Trains operators to strengthen a team perspective because under stress, team members are narrowing their attention and are likely to adopt a more individualistic perspective on task activity (see Chap. 3, Patrick et al. 2006a, b).

- Teamwork is learned through the accumulation of instances of teamwork episodes (proposition 18),
- Most of the things one knows about teamwork are procedural and implicitly stored, and with everyday experience and increasing job experience, explicit and rule-based knowledge is extracted (proposition 19).
- Teamwork skills, focused on the behaviours necessary for effective team functioning, are believed to be best learned in intact teams rather than individually (proposition 20).
- Teamwork skills are acquired most effectively with a high level of action fidelity (proposition 21).

Taking these propositions into account, training teamwork skills requires the trainer to select and compile full-scope simulator exercises that support the acquisition of teamwork episodes. This can be implemented by the development of simulator exercises that are specifically aimed at improving the similarity and accuracy of team members’ mental models (Uitdewillingen et al. 2010). Furthermore, team feedback and debriefs, which take place after task performance episodes, can positively affect the development of rich and accurate mental models (Ellis and Davidi 2005; Xinwen et al. 2006).

Here too, the teamwork instance experience should be supported by procedural information such as checklists or team skills-related SOPs for collecting and restructuring data, combining and sorting cues, sharing mental models, exchanging hypotheses, resolving opposing interpretations, negotiating team consensus and applying critical thinking (as introduced above). While stage 1 (process control readiness training) included component practice for technical skill aspects of the task, *stage 2 (process control readiness training component practice for teamwork skills) aims at the integration of taskwork and teamwork skills as concurrent task demands and shares elements of a dual task that requires time-sharing and attention allocation.* It was additionally proposed that the in-process integration (proposition 15) of teamwork and taskwork skills is best learned according to the learning mechanisms which are also effective for dual-task performance such as variable priorities, emphasis change or training under task-switching requirements.

Furthermore, it was proposed (proposition 16) that equivalently to the learning of taskwork skills, learning teamwork skills includes a cognitive component (knowledge), such as a schema concerning teamwork characteristics, as well as a behavioural component, in which specific concrete behaviours, for example scripts and skills, need to be acquired and applied. In order to also support the development of the cognitive component, the feedback and debriefing is aimed at the acquisition of team knowledge (Wildman et al. 2012), i.e. task-related knowledge, team-related team knowledge, process-related knowledge and goal-related team knowledge (Wildman et al. 2012).

The concept of guided team self-corrections, during which the team is guided in critically reflecting upon and discussing its own functioning, fosters the construction of accurate (Smith-Jentsch et al. 2008) and similar (Blickensderfer et al. 1997) mental models (Uitdewillingen et al. 2010).

Guided team self-correction develops the team’s skill to diagnose teamwork process losses and coordination decrements within the team and to reach effective solutions on a continuous basis (Smith-Jentsch et al. 1998; Smith-Jentsch et al. 2008). The guided team self-correction (Smith-Jentsch et al. 1998; Shuffler et al. 2011) is applicable for process control room teams of operators.

Guided team self-correction makes use of a trainer or trainers who guide a team in reflecting on their teamwork skills, for example after a simulator exercise. The trainer guides the team to determine what specific topics they should discuss and how they should discuss them. In this respect, the guided team self-correction first of all needs to determine the teamwork skills which make up successful teamwork in the control room. The guided team self-correction (GTSC) is centred on the predefined teamwork skills that are central for successful collaborative problem-solving in abnormal situations. These are, for example, the teamwork skills described in Chap. 3 concerning (a) information exchange (utilising all available resources, passing on information, providing periodic updates), (b) communication (phraseology, completeness of standard reports, brevity), (c) supporting behaviour (monitoring and correcting errors), and (d) team initiative/leadership (providing guidance or suggestions), but need to be specified more precisely for the respective control room.

In designing the instance, the trainer has to embed two to three trigger events into the team exercise, which are expected to strain communication and coordination among specific team members (Smitsch-Jentsch et al. 1998).

As the guide, the trainer is responsible for guiding the team through a process of four steps (Smith-Jentsch et al. 1998) which is already adjusted here to the control room team context:

1. Prebriefing: Before the instance, the operators are informed about the method of the GTSC. Teamwork skills are pointed out to them, and where appropriate they are again reminded of knowledge which should be involved in the upcoming simulator session. This can once again be briefly elucidated to ensure a uniform understanding of the terminology, and where appropriate, previous exercises are also referred to as well as the lessons learned which were previously worked out in this regard (Smith-Jentsch et al. 1998). It is pointed out to the operators that the concern should be with attention to the teamwork process and not with the outcome.
2. Observation of teamwork episode: During the teamwork episode in the simulator, the trainer records positive and negative examples among the pre-briefed teamwork skills. To this aim, he/she has developed an observation sheet in advance, which lists the teamwork skills and has space in which to note positive or negative behaviours of the operators. If several trainers are present, it is appropriate to divide the teamwork skills to be observed among the observers.
3. Support the diagnosis and reflection of performance: Following the exercise, the trainers sit together and discuss which examples of positive and negative courses of action of teamwork skills they wish to select for the debriefing. Strengths and goals for improvement are identified for each teamwork skill.
4. Debriefing: The trainers remind operators of the exercise objectives by again presenting the relevant teamwork skills. Operators are than informed how the debriefing will proceed and that they will be led through a self-critique of their team skill application (Smith-Jentsch et al. 1998). The trainer then briefly summarises the teamwork process into key event outcomes (Smith-Jentsch et al. 1998). Subsequently, the trainer asks for positive examples of the relevant teamwork skills (as defined in the pre-briefing) for collaborative problem-solving, as well as for negative examples. The team is always asked to provide a concrete example of their behaviour that fits a particular category (e.g. communicate hypothesis, provide periodic updates) before the trainer provides his/hers (Smith-Jentsch et al. 1998). Subsequently, the team sets concrete goals for the improvement of teamwork skills they want to work on in future exercises (Smith-Jentsch et al. 1998). Here, the task of the trainer is above all to ensure that all persons can get involved, independent of their hierarchical position or tenure.

The guided team self-correction principles can also be used for and transferred to shift handovers and after specific events for after-action reviews. The guided team self-correction method is a good example of how to implement the proposition that pre-process and post-process coordination activities are valuable (proposition 16) and supportive for the creation, learning and activation of task-related, team-related, process-related, and goal-related team knowledge. The instances which are packaged within the training scenarios purposely depict "slices of organisational life" which should be acquired as instances. As the simulator training sessions should depict learning episodes that refer to routine and non-routine situations, the debriefing techniques applied in the simulator training both in the first stage and the second stage can, of course, also be implemented after each shift, and also after particular incidents, in the sense of an After Event Review (Ellis 2012). Thus, non-routine situations are generally suitable for debriefing, meaning that the skills acquired in guided team self-correction can equally be used for learning opportunities during shift work and transferred to other teams in order to build a shared mental model of the situation as it evolved and developed and was (successfully) solved. As described in the digression in Chap. 3, operators continually update and refine their mental models during their shift work.

A second specific training concept applicable here to the collaborative problem-solving required for non-routine/abnormal situations and the achievement of the defined training goals is the *team adaptation and coordination training* (TACT). This training aims at teaching teams to recognise changes in situational stress levels, a set of adaptive coordination strategies and the most appropriate conditions under which to use each adaptive strategy (Entin and Serfaty 1999; Shuffler et al. 2011). In TACT, the five adaptive strategies of preplanning, use of idle periods, favouring information transmission, anticipation of information needs and dynamic redistribution of workload cited from the literature (Entin and Serfaty 1999; Serfaty et al. 1998) are transferred to the control room context:

- Preplanning, as in the description by Eccles and Tenenbaum (2004) and Fiore et al. (2001), refers to the preparation phase of a shift, for example during shift handover and in preparation for a non-routine/normal situation such as a scheduled repair task (see Chap. 4).
- Use of idle periods refers, for example, to talking through the "what-if's" and possible complications which might arise in a situation.
- Favouring information transmission over action/task coordination refers, for example, to coordinating critical thinking and exchanging hypotheses in the control room.
- Anticipation of information needs (implicit coordination), refers, for example, to passing on the cues which one sees as well as the collection and restructuring of data to the team members for whom one knows, or anticipates, that they are important for them and to communicate future actions and intentions.
- Dynamic redistribution of workload among team members, for example by the supervisor, refers to the orchestration of actions for example when executing an SOP to avoid becoming over-focused, absorbed or distracted, for example when

Table 5.7 Summary of stage 2 training design

Important training design issues for stage 2
1. Select instances which require collaborative problem-solving that stretch the shooting range of the mind.
2. Provide decision skill training in order to allow decision strategies of experts to be experienced rather than teaching these skills.
3. Provide critical thinking training to train constructive controversy within collaborative problem-solving.
4. Provide stress exposure training to enable operators to cope and maintain performance under stress.
5. Provide guided team self-correction to support teams in reflecting on their teamwork skills.
6. Provide team adaptation and coordination training to train the control room team in recognising and changing situational stress levels, in adapting coordination strategies, and the most appropriate conditions under which to use these strategies.

team members are fixated on a procedure without monitoring the plant (Patrick et al. 2006a, b, Chap. 3).

These adaptation strategies should then, for example, be practised as component practice in addition to and in combination with the instance-based teamwork learning.

The responsibility of the trainer in stage 2

For skill retention and deliberate practice of expert performance, the trainer's important role lies in selecting instances that stretch the "shooting range of the mind" (Bakken 2009) and by enhancing skills and set people thinking by provoking impulses to counteract automaticity through the use of probes and questions. This should foster the critical thinking skills and decision skill acquisition in order to develop increasingly differentiated mental models and teamwork skills for controlling performance. Trainers will therefore try to maintain an attitude of intentionally remaining in the associative phase. Additionally, besides the debriefing content in stage 1, trainers in stage 2 also need the knowledge and skill to debrief the instances with respect to task-related team knowledge, team-related knowledge, process-related team knowledge and goal-related team knowledge (Wildman et al. 2012, see Chap. 3).

As there are no general teamwork skills that fit all control room teams, training designers should elaborate on those teamwork skills that are most relevant for collaborative problem-solving in their own organisations, for example by means of a teamwork context analysis based on a critical incident analysis with the focus on team breakdowns. It is not helpful or constructive to adopt teamwork skills from other contexts without undertaking a critical review and assessment, because teamwork affordances vary greatly (Hagemann et al. 2012).

The effectiveness of stage 2 process readiness training can be assessed by the evaluation possibilities described in Chap. 3 and in studies by Patrick et al. (2006a, b), Sebok (2000) and Waller et al. (2004).

A summary of stage 2 of the SPCRT is listed in Table 5.7.

5.4 Final Remarks

The aim of this book was, and is, to demonstrate from a cognitive and organisational ergonomics perspective how skill and knowledge acquisition for controlling complex technical systems can be fostered in a targeted manner through training. Referring back to the preface, the book aims to

- facilitate the understanding of the task and target job in the context of the organisation (needs assessment) by describing complex technical systems (the process industries), complex tasks and specifying conditions of transfer, meaning conditions under which the later trained knowledge and skills need to be applied in the working context (Chap. 2),
- derive the knowledge and skills required to fulfil the task in order to define training objectives (Chap. 3),
- develop propositions for how to best acquire the knowledge and skills (defining the learning environment, based on learning theories) and the conditions of transfer by providing theoretical propositions for their acquisition based on state-of-the-art research on knowledge and skill acquisition for complex taskwork and teamwork tasks (Chap. 4),
- propose instructional techniques and programs on how to best support skill and knowledge acquisition in High Reliability Organisations which can be transferred to routine, non-routine/normal and non-routine/abnormal situations (Chap. 5).

In this respect, I have undertaken an organisational and task analysis, derived training goals, worked out from the literature propositions about learning in these kinds of environment, and building on this, developed a staged training concept. While writing this book, it became very clear to me that almost every chapter could have a whole book devoted to it. However, for the reader, getting to grips with 1,000 pages instead of 200 would be a laborious undertaking!

It might be noted that the book is very nuclear power and refinery-heavy and only addresses other industries like steel or pharmacy in a few places. This is primarily due to the fact that the areas of nuclear power and refineries are clearly over-represented in the literature, and in other areas, such as speciality chemicals, there are only oral accounts or anecdotal reports. In principle, the propositions and the training design derived from them can also be adapted and transferred to other industries.

The book should represent an introduction for all those who wish to concern themselves with the training of complex skills and wish to use a generic framework, for example when looking at control room tasks in general, but who also desire suggestions for where one specifically and precisely has to look in order to develop training for a particular organisation. Accordingly, the book is oriented towards training designers in organisations as well as researchers who wish to concern themselves with training research and in this respect are called upon to empirically examine the derived propositions and evaluate the training design. It is oriented towards engineers who wish to concern themselves with the cognitive processes of skill and knowledge acquisition, and towards human factors, industrial, organisational and instructional psychologists who wish to become familiar with process control tasks and High Reliability Industries.

I hope that this book contributes to building a bridge between research and practice and to fostering a mutual understanding between engineering science and psychology.

References

Bakken, B. E. (2008). On improving dynamic decision-making: Implications from multiple process cognitive theory. *Systems Research and Behavioral Science, 25*, 493–501.

Baldwin, T. T., & Magjuka, R. J. (1997). Training as an organizational episode: Pretraining influence on trainee motivation. In J. K. Ford, S. W. J. Kozlowski, K. Kraiger, E. Salas, & M. S. Teachout (Eds.), *Improving training effectiveness in work organizations* (pp. 193–221). Mahwah: Lawrence Erlbaum.

Baldwin, T. T., Ford, J. K., & Blume, B. D. (2009). Transfer of training 1988–2008. An updated review and agenda for future research. *International Review of Industrial and Organizational Psychology, 24*, 41–70.

Bjork, R. A., & Bjork, E. L. (1992). A new theory of disuse and an old theory of stimulus fluctuation. In A. Healy, S. Kosslynm, & R. Shiffrin (Eds.), *From learning processes to cognitive processes: Essays in honor of William K. Estes* (pp. 35–67). Hillsdale: Erlbaum.

Bjork, R. A., & Bjork, E. L. (2006). Optimizing treatment and instruction: Implications of the new theory of disuse. In L. G. Nilsson & N. Ohta (Eds.), *Memory and society. Psychological perspectives* (pp. 109–134). Hove: Psychology Press.

Blickensderfer, E., Cannon-Bowers, J. A., & Salas, E. (1997). Theoretical bases for team self correction: Fostering shared mental models. In M. M. Beyerlein, D. A. Jackson, & S. T. Beyerlein (Eds.), *Advances in interdisciplinary studies of work teams* (pp. 249–79). Greenwich: JAI.

Bolstad, C. A., Cuevas, H. M., Costello, A. M., & Babbitt, B. (2008). Predicting cognitive readiness of deploying military medical teams. In *Proceedings of the human factors and Ergonomics Society, 52nd annual meeting* (pp. 970–974). Santa Monica: HFES.

Buckley, R., & Caple, J. (1990). *The theory and practice of training* (Rev. 5th ed., 2007). London: Kogan Page.

Cannon-Bowers, J. A., & Bowers, C. (2010). Synthetic learning environments: On developing a science of simulation, games and virtual worlds for training. In S. W. J. Kozlowski & E. Salas (Eds.), *Learning, training and development in organizations* (pp. 229–262). New York: Routledge.

Carlson, R. A., Khoo, B. H., & Elliott, R. G. (1990). Component practice and exposure to a problem solving context. *Human Factors, 32*, 267–286.

Chappell, S. L. (1994). Using voluntary incident reports for human factors evaluations. In N. Johnston, N. McDonald, & R. Fuller (Eds.), *Aviation psychology in practice* (pp. 149–169). Surrey: Ashgate.

Cohen, M. S., & Thompson, B. B. (2001). Training teams to take initiative: Critical thinking in novel situations. *Advances in Human Performance and Cognitive Engineering, 1*, 251–291.

Cohen, M. S., Freeman, J. T., & Wolf, S. (1996). Meta-recognition in time-stressed decision making: Recognizing, critiquing, and correcting. *Human Factors, 38*, 206–219.

Cohen, M. S., Freeman, J. T., & Thompson, B. (1998/3rd print). critical thinking skills in tactical decision making: A model and a training strategy. In J. A. Cannon-Bowers & E. Salas (Eds.), *Making decisions under stress. Implications for individual and team training* (pp. 155–190). Washington, DC: APA.

Cooke, N. J., & Fiore, S. M. (2010). Cognitive science-based principles for the design and delivery of training. In S. W. J. Kozlowski & E. Sales (Eds.), *Learning, training, and development in organizations* (pp. 169–201). New York: Routledge.

Crandall, B., Klein, G., & Hoffman, R. R. (2006). *Working minds. A practitioner's guide to cognitive task analysis*. Cambridge, MA: MIT Press.

Dennis, D. R., & Meredith, J. R. (2000). An analysis of process industry production and inventory management systems. *Journal of Operations Management, 18*, 683–699.

Dosher, B. A. (2003). Working memory. In L. Nadel (Ed.), *Encyclopedia of cognitive science* (pp. 569–577). London: Nature Publishing Group.

Driskell, J. E., & Johnston, J. H. (1998/2006 reprint). Stress exposure training. In J. A. Cannon-Bowers & E. Salas (Eds.), *Making decisions under stress. Implications for Individual and team training* (pp. 191–217). Washington, DC: APA.

Duncan, K. D., & Shepherd, A. (1975). A simulator and training technique for diagnosing plant failures from control panels. *Ergonomics, 18*, 627–641.

Eccles, D. W., & Tenenbaum, G. (2004). Why an expert team is more than a team of experts: A social-cognitive conceptualization of team coordination and communication in sport. *Journal of Sport & Exercise Psychology, 26*, 542–560.

Elliot, L. T., Dalrymple, M. A., Schiflett, S. G., & Miller, J. (2004). Scaling scenarios: Development and application to C4ISR sustained operations research. In S. G. Schiflett, L. R. Elliot, E. Sales, & M. D. Coovert (Eds.), *Scaled worlds: Development, validations and applications* (pp. 75–99). Aldershot: Ashgate.

Ellis, S. (2012). Learning from errors: The role of after event reviews. In J. Bauer & C. Harteis (Eds.), *Human fallibility. The ambiguity of errors for work and learning* (pp. 215–232). Dordrecht: Springer.

Ellis, S., & Davidi, I. (2005). After-event reviews: Drawing lessons from successful and failed experience. *Journal of Applied Psychology, 90*, 857–71.

Entin, E. E., & Serfaty, D. (1999). Adaptive team coordination. *Human Factors, 41*, 312–325.

Ericsson, K. A. (2006). The influence of experience and deliberate practice on the development of superior expert performance. In K. A. Ericsson, N. Charness, P. J. Feltovich, & R. R. Hoffman (Eds.), *The Cambridge handbook of expertise and expert performance* (pp. 683–703). Cambridge: Cambridge University Press.

Farr, M. J. (1987). *The long-term retention of knowledge and skills. A cognitive and instructional perspective*. New York: Springer.

Flanagan, J. C. (1954). The critical incident technique. *Psychological Bulletin, 51*, 327.

Flin, R., O'Connor, P., & Crichton, M. (2008). *Safety at the sharp end. A guide to non-technical skills*. Aldershot: Ashgate.

Fiore, S. M., Salas, E., & Cannon-Bowers, J. A. (2001). Group dynamics and shared mental model development. In M. London (Ed.), *How people evaluate others in organizations: Person perception and interpersonal judgement in I/O Psychology* (pp. 309–336). Mahwah: Erlbaum.

Fransoo, J. C., & Rutten, W. G. M. M. (1994). A typology of production control situations in process industries. *International Journal of Operations and Production Management, 18*, 47–57.

Frey, D., & Jonas, E. (2002). Die Theorie der kognizierten Kontrolle. In D. Frey & M. Irle (Hrsg.), *Theorien der Sozialpsychologie*. Band III, Motivations-, Selbst- und Informationsverarbeitungstheorien (pp. 13–50). Bern: Verlag Hans Huber.

Goldstein, I. L. (1993). *Training in organisations. Needs assessment, development and evaluation*. Monterey: Brooks/Cole.

Goldstein, I. L., & Ford, J. K. (2002). *Training in organisations. Needs assessment, development, and evaluation* (4th ed.). Wadsworth: Cengage Learning.

Gonzales, C., Lerch, J. F., & Lebiere, C. (2003). Instance-based learning in dynamic decision making. *Cognitive Science, 27*, 591–635.

Gopher, D. (2007). Emphasis change as a training protocol for high-demand tasks. In A. Kramer, D. Wiegmann, & A. Kirlik (Eds.), *Attention: From theory to practice*. Oxford: Oxford University Press.

Greitzer, F. L., Podmore, R., Robinson, M., & Ey, P. (2009). *Naturalistic decision making for power system operators*. Proceedings of the NDM9, the 9th international conference on naturalistic decision making, London, UK. Also available online: http://www.bcs.org/upload/pdf/ewic_ndm09_s1paper2.pdf

Hagemann, V. (2011). *Trainingsentwicklung für high responsibility teams*. Lengerich: Pabst Science Publishers.

Hagemann, V., Kluge, A., & Ritzmann, S. (2011). High responsibility teams – Eine systematische analyse von Teamarbeitskontexten. *Psychologie des Alltaghandelns, 4*, 22–42.

Hagemann, V., Kluge, A., & Ritzmann, S. (2012). Flexibility under complexity: Work contexts, task profiles and team processes of high responsibility teams. *Employee Relations, 34*, 322–338.

Hogg, D. N., Folleso, K., Strand-Volden, F., & Torralba, B. (1995). Development of a situation awareness measure to evaluate advanced alarm systems in nuclear power plant control rooms. *Ergonomics, 38*, 2394–413.

Hollnagel, E. (1998). *Cognitive reliability and error analysis method CREAM*. Oxford: Elsevier.

Hollnagel, E. (2007). Decision about "What" and decisions about "How". In M. Cook, J. Noyes, & Y. Masakowski (Eds.), *Decision making in complex environments* (pp. 3–13). Aldershot: Ashgate.

Hollnagel, E., & Woods, D. D. (2005). *Joint cognitive systems. Foundations of cognitive systems engineering*. Boca Raton: Taylor & Francis.

Johnson, D. W., & Johnson, R. T. (2003). Training for cooperative work. In M. A. West, D. Tjosvold, & K. G. Smith (Eds.), *International handbook of organizational teamwork and cooperative working* (pp. 167–184). Chichester: Wiley.

Johnston, J. H., & Cannon-Bowers, J. A. (1996). Training for stress exposure. In J. E. Driskell & E. Salas (Eds.), *Stress and human performance* (pp. 223–256). Mahwah: Lawrence Erlbaum.

Keinan, G., & Friedland, N. (1996). Training effective performance under stress: Queries, dilemmas, and possible solutions. In J. E. Driskell & E. Salas (Eds.), *Stress and human performance* (pp. 257–278). Mahwah: Lawrence Erlbaum.

Klein, G. A., Calderwood, R., & MacGregor, D. (1989). Critical decision method for eliciting knowledge. *IEEE Transactions on Systems, Man, and Cybernetics, 19*, 462–472.

Klein, G., McCloskey, M., Pliske, R., & Schmitt, J. (1997). Decision skills training. In *Proceedings of the Human Factors and Ergonomics Society 41st annual meeting* (pp. 182–185). Santa Barbara: Sage.

Kluge, A., Badura, B., & Rietz, Ch. (2013a). Framing effects of production outcomes, the risk of an accident, control beliefs and their effects on safety-related violations in a production context. *Journal of Risk Research*. http://dx.doi.org/10.1080/13669877.2013.788059.

Kluge, A., & Burkolter, D. (2012, May 10). Training for cognitive readiness: Research issues and experimental designs. *Journal of Cognitive Engineering and Decision Making*. doi:10.1177/1555343412446483.

Kluge, A., & Burkolter, D. (2013). Training for cognitive readiness: Research issues and experimental designs. *Journal of Cognitive Engineering and Decision Making, 7*, 96–118.

Kluge, A., Burkolter, D., & Frank, B. (2012, October). Being prepared for the infrequent: A comparative study of two refresher training approaches and their effects on temporal and adaptive transfer in a process control task. *Proceedings of the human factors and Ergonomics Society 56th annual conference* (pp. 2437–2441). Boston.

Kluge, A., Grauel, B., & Burkolter, D. (2013b). Job aids: How does the quality of a procedural aid alone and combined with a decision aid affect motivation and performance in process control? *Applied Ergonomics, 44*, 285–296.

Kluge, A., & Schüler, K. (2007). Experience management by means of simulator trainings in high reliability organizations – Re-enacting critical incidents and learning from experience – Examples from nuclear power plants and oil refineries. In N. Gronau (Ed.), *4th conference on professional knowledge management – Experiences and vision* (pp. 77–84). Berlin: Gito.

Kluge, A., Schüler, K., & Burkolter, D. (2008). Simulatortrainings für Prozesskontrolltätigkeiten am Beispiel von Raffinerien: Psychologische Trainingsprinzipien in der Praxis. *Zeitschrift für Arbeitswissenschaft, 62*(2), 97–109.

Kluwe, R. H. (1997). Acquisition of knowledge in the control of a simulated technical system. *Le Travail Humain, 60*, 61–85.

Kolb, D. A. (1984). *Experiential learning. Experience as the source of learning and development.* Englewood Cliffs: Prentice-Hall.

Kolb, D. A., Boyatzis, R. E., & Mainemelis, C. (2000). Experiential learning theory: Previous research and new directions. In R. J. Sternberg & L. F. Zhang (Eds.), *Perspectives on cognition, learning, and thinking styles* (pp. 193–210). Mahwah: Lawrence Erlbaum.

Kolodner, J. L. (1983). Towards an understanding of the role of experience in the evolution from novice to expert. *International Journal of Man-Machine Studies, 19*, 497–518.

Kozlowski, S. W. J., & DeShon, R. P. (2004). A psychological fidelity approach to simulation-based training: Theory, research and principles. In S. G. Schiflett, L. R. Elliot, E. Salas, & M. D. Coovert (Eds.), *Scaled worlds: Development, validation and applications* (pp. 75–100). Aldershot: Ashgate.

Mason, S. (1997). Procedural violations – Causes, costs and cures. In F. Redmill & J. Rajan (Eds.), *Humans factors in safety – Critical systems* (pp. 287–318). London: Butterworth Heinemann.

Merrienboer, J. J. G., Kirschner, P. A., & Kester, L. (2003). Taking the load off a learner's mind: Instructional design for complex learning. *Educational Psychologist, 38*, 5–13.

Miettinen, R. (2000). The concept of experiential learning and John Dewey's theory of reflective thought and action. *International Journal of Lifelong Education, 19*(1), 54–72.

Moore, B. A., Mason, S. T., & Crow, B. E. (2012). Assessment and management of acute combat stress on the battlefield. In C. H. Kennedy & E. A. Zillmer (Eds.), *Military psychology. Clinical and operational applications* (pp. 73–92). New York: The Guilford Press.

Morris, N. M., & Rouse, W. B. (1985). The effects of type of knowledge upon human problem solving in a process control task. *IEEE Transactions on Systems, Man, and Cybernetics, SMC-15*, 698–707.

Morrison, J. E., & Fletcher, J. D. (2002). *Cognitive readiness* (No. IDA-P-3735). Institute for Defense Analyses, Alexandria, VA.

Noe, R. A., Wilk, S. L., Mullen, E. J., & Wanek, J. E. (1997). Employee development: Issues in construct definition and investigation antecedents. In J. K. Ford, S. W. J. Kozlowski, K. Kraiger, E. Salas, & M. S. Teachout (Eds.), *Improving training effectiveness in work organizations* (pp. 153–189). Mahwah: Lawrence Erlbaum.

Norman, D. A. (1983). Some observations on mental models. In D. Gentner & A. L. Stevens (Eds.), *Mental models* (pp. 7–15). Hillsdale: Erlbaum.

O'Hare, D., Wiggins, M., Williams, A., & Wong, W. (1998). Cognitive task analyses for decision centered design and training. *Ergonomics, 41*, 1698–1718.

Orasanu, J. M., & Backer, P. (1996). Stress and military performance. In J. E. Driskell & E. Salas (Eds.), *Stress and human performance* (pp. 89–126). Mahwah: Lawrence Erlbaum.

Ormerod, T. C., & Shepherd, A. (2004). Using task analysis for information requirements specification: The sub-goal template (SGT) method. In D. Diaper & N. A. Stanton (Eds.), *The handbook of task analysis for human-computer interaction* (pp. 347–365). Mahwah: Lawrence Erlbaum.

Ormerod, T. C., Richardson, J., & Shepherd, A. (1998). Enhancing the usability of a task analysis method: A notation and environment for requirements specification. *Ergonomics, 41*, 1642–1663.

Paris, C. R., Salas, E., & Cannon-Bowers, J. A. (2000). Teamwork in multi-person systems: A review and analysis. *Ergonomics, 43*, 1052–1075.

Patrick, J., James, N., & Ahmed, A. (2006a). Human processes of control: Tracing the goals and strategies of control room teams. *Ergonomics, 49*, 1395–1414.

Patrick, J., James, N., Ahmed, A., & Halliday, P. (2006b). Observational assessment of situation awareness, team differences and training implications. *Ergonomics, 49*, 393–417.

Pliske, R. M., McCloskey, M. J., & Klein, G. (2001). Decision skills training: Facilitating learning from experience. In E. Salas & G. Klein (Eds.), *Linking expertise and naturalistic decision making* (pp. 37–53). Mahwah: Lawrence Erlbaum.

Podmore, R., Robinson, M., Sadinsky, M., & Sease, R. (2008, July 20–24). A virtual instructor for simulator training. In *Proceedings, IEEE Power & Energy Society annual meeting*, Pittsburgh, PA.

Reason, J. (1998). Achieving a safe culture: Theory and practice. *Work & Stress, 12*(3), 293–306.

Richardson, A. (1967). Mental practice: A review and discussion (Part II). *Research Quarterly, 38*, 264–273.

Ritzmann, S. (2012). *Entwicklung und evaluation von Crew Resource management training for flight attendants*. Lengerich: Pabst Verlag.

Ross, K. G., Shafer, J. L., & Klein, G. (2006). Professional judgements and "naturalistic decision making". In K. A. Ericsson, N. Charness, P. J. Feltovich, & R. R. Hoffman (Eds.), *The Cambridge handbook of expertise and expert performance* (pp. 403–419). Cambridge: Cambridge University Press.

Roth, E. M. (2008). Uncovering the requirements of cognitive work. *Human Factors, 50*, 475–480.

Rouse, W. R. (1982). A mixed-fidelity approach to technical training. *Journal of Educational Technology Systems, 11*, 103–115.

Salas, E., & Cannon-Bowers, J. A. (1997). Methods, tools, and strategies for team training. In M. Quinones & E. Ehrenstein (Eds.), *Training for a rapidly changing workplace: Application of psychological research* (pp. 291–322). Washington, DC: APA Press.

Salas, E., Driskell, J. E., & Hughes, S. (1996). Introduction: The study of stress and human performance. In J. E. Driskell & E. Salas (Eds.), *Stress and human performance* (pp. 1–46). Mahwah: Lawrence Erlbaum.

Salas, E., Wilson, K. A., Priest, H. A., & Guthrie, J. W. (2006). Design, delivery, and evaluation of training. In G. Salvendy (Ed.), *Handbook of human factors and ergonomics* (pp. 472–512). Hoboken: Wiley.

Schneider, W. (1999). Automaticity. In R. A. Wilson & F. C. Keil (Eds.), *The MIT encyclopedia of the cognitive sciences* (pp. 63–64). Cambridge, MA: MIT Press.

Schraagen, J. M., Chipman, S. F., & Shalin, V. L. (2000). *Cognitive task analysis*. Mahwah: Lawrence Erlbaum.

Sebok, A. (2000). Team performance in process control: Influences of interface design and staffing levels. *Ergonomics, 43*, 1210–36.

Serfaty, D., Entin. E. E., & Johnston, J. H. (1998/3rd print). Team coordination training. In J. A. Cannon-Bowers & E. Salas (Eds.), *Making decisions under stress. Implications for individual and team training* (pp. 221–246). Washington, DC: APA.

Smith-Jentsch, K. A., Cannon-Bowers, J. A., Tannenbaum, S. I., & Salas, E. (2008). Guided team self-correction: Impacts on team mental models, processes, and effectiveness. *Small Group Research, 39*, 303–27.

Smith-Jentsch, K. A., Zeisig, R. L., McPherson, J., & Acton, B. (1998). Team dimensional training: A strategy for guided team self-correction. In J. A. Cannon-Bowers & E. Salas (Eds.), *Decision making under stress: Implications for individual and team training* (pp. 271–297). Washington, DC: American Psychological Association.

Shuffler, M. L., DiazGranados, D., & Salas, E. (2011). There'sa Science for That Team Development Interventions in Organizations. *Current Directions in Psychological Science, 20*(6), 365–372.

Sonnentag, S., Niessen, C., & Ohly, S. (2004). Learning at work: Training and development. *International Review of Industrial and Organizational Psychology, 19*, 249–289.

Stammers, R. B. (1981). Skill retention and control room tasks. In *Proceedings of the Human Factors and Ergonomics Society annual meeting* (pp. 168–172). Thousand Oaks, CA: SAGE Publications.

Steadham, S. V. (1980). Learning to select a needs assessment strategy. *Training and Development Journal, 30*, 56–61.

Sternberg, R. (2009). *Cognitive psychology*. Belmont: Cengage Learning.

Stoffregen, T. A., Bardy, B. G., Smart, L. J., & Pagulayan, R. J. (2003). On the nature and evaluation of fidelity in virtual environments. In L. J. Hettinger & M. Haas (Eds.), *Virtual and adaptive environments: Applications, implications, and human performance issues* (pp. 111–128). Mahwah: Lawrence Erlbaum.

Sun, R. (2002). *Duality of the mind. A bottom-up approach toward cognition*. Mahwah: Erlbaum.

Sun, R., Merrill, E., & Peterson, T. (2001). From implicit skills to explicit knowledge: A bottom-up model of skill learning. *Cognitive Science, 25*, 203–244.

Sun, R., Slusarz, P., & Terry, C. (2005). The interaction of the explicit and the implicit in skill learning: A dual-process approach. *Psychological Review, 112*, 159–192.

Sweller, J. (2006). How the human cognitive system deals with complexity. In J. Elen & R. E. Clark (Eds.), *Handling complexity in learning environments. Theory and research* (pp. 13–27). Amsterdam: Elsevier.

Tannenbaum, S. I., Beard, R. L., McNall, L. A., & Salas, E. (2010). Informal learning and development in organizations. In S. W. J. Kozlowski & E. Salas (Eds.), *Learning, training, and development in organization* (pp. 303–332). New York: Routledge.

Uitdewillingen, S., Waller, M. J., & Zijlstra, F. R. H. (2010). Team cognition and adaptability in dynamic settings: A review of pertinent work. *International Review of Industrial and Organizational Psychology, 25*, 293–353.

van den Bosch, K., & Riemersma, J. B. J. (2004). Reflections on scenario-based training in tactical command. In S. G. Schiflett, L. R. Elliot, E. Salas, & M. D. Coovert (Eds.), *Scaled worlds: Development, validation and applications* (pp. 1–22). Aldershot: Ashgate.

Vicente, K. J., Mumaw, R. J., & Roth, E. M. (2004). Operator monitoring in a complex dynamic work environment: A qualitative cognitive model based on field observations. *Theoretical Issues in Ergonomic Science, 5*, 359–384.

Von der Heyde, A., Presting, P., Kluge, A., & Badura, B. (2012). Social norms and their impact on safety-related rule violations in process control: Does it make a difference if operators are aware that residents will be injured? In *Proceedings of the human factors and Ergonomics Society 56th annual conference, Boston 2012* (pp. 243–247). Thousand Oaks: Sage.

Waller, M. J., Gupta, N., & Giambatista, R. C. (2004). Effects of adaptive behaviors and shared mental models on control crew performance. *Management Science, 50*, 1534–1544.

Wexley, K. N., & Latham, G. P. (2002). *Developing and training human resources in organizations* (3rd ed.). Upper Saddle River: Prentice Hall.

Wickens, C. D., & Hollands, J. G. (2000). *Engineering psychology and human performance* (3rd ed.). Upper Saddle River: Prentice Hall.

Wickens, C., Hutchins, S., Carolan, T., & Cumming, J. D. (2012). Attention and cognitive resources load in training strategies. In A. F. Healy & L. E. Bourne Jr. (Eds.), *Training cognition. Optimizing efficiency, durability, and generalizability* (pp. 67–88). New York: Psychology Press.

Wiegmann, D. A., & Shappell, S. A. (2001). *A human error analysis of commercial aviation accidents using the Human Factors Analysis and Classification System (HFACS)*. Office of

Aviation Medicine/FAA. ADA387808. Retrieved December 8, 2012, from http://www.dtic.mil/dtic/tr/fulltext/u2/a387808.pdf.
Wildman, J. L., Thayer, A. L., Pavlas, D., Steward, J. E., & Howse, W. R. (2012). Team knowledge research: Emerging trends and critical needs. *Human Factors, 54*, 84–111.
Xinwen, B., Erping, W., Ying, Z., Dafei, M., & Jing, R. (2006). Developmental characteristics of two types of shared mental models. *Acta Psychologica Sinica, 38*, 598–606.

Index

A. Kluge, *The Acquisition of Knowledge and Skills for Taskwork and Teamwork to Control Complex Technical Systems*, DOI 10.1007/978-94-007-5049-4,

The manufacturer's authorised representative in the EU is Springer Nature Customer Service Centre GmbH, Europaplatz 3, 69115 Heidelberg, Germany. If you have any concerns regarding our products, please contact ProductSafety@springernature.com

Printed and bound by CPI Group (UK) Ltd, Croydon, CR0 4YY
30/09/2026
02225444-0004